WHERE THE RIVER BENDS

AN INSPIRATIONAL CREATION

OF

RAYMOND ARNOLD WILLS

A Gypsy Poet production

Contents

My mother said

I never should

Play with the gypsies

In the wood

If I did

She would say

Naughty boy to disobey

Disobey one,

Disobey two,

Disobey over Waterloo.

Anon

Billy Cole, a thirty-year-old Hampshire Traveller "Real legends is our history, like. Take 'em away and what we got? We got nothing!"

The Gipsy's Camp

How oft on Sundays, when I'd time to tramp,

My rambles led me to a gipsy's camp,

Where the real effigy of midnight hags,

With tawny smoked flesh and tattered rags,

Uncouth-brimmed hat, and weather-beaten cloak,

Neath the wild shelter of a knotty oak,

Along the greensward uniformly pricks

Her pliant bending hazel's arching sticks:

While round-topt bush, or briar-entangled hedge,

Where flag-leaves spring beneath, or ramping sedge,

Keeps off the bothering bustle of the wind,

And give the best retreat she hopes to find.

How oft I've bent me oer her fire and smoke,

To hear her gibberish tale so quaintly spoke,

While the old Sybil forged her boding clack,

Twin imps the meanwhile bawling at her back;

Oft on my hand her magic coin's been struck,

And hoping chink, she talked of morts of luck:

And still, as boyish hopes did first agree,

Mingled with fears to drop the fortune's fee,

I never failed to gain the honours sought,

And Squire and Lord were purchased with a groat.

But as man's unbelieving taste came round,

She furious stampt her shoeless foot aground,

Wiped bye her soot-black hair with clenching fist,

While through her yellow teeth the spittle hist,

Swearing by all her lucky powers of fate,

Which like as footboys on her actions wait,

That fortune's scale should to my sorrow turn,

And I one day the rash neglect should mourn;

That good to bad should change, and I should be

Lost to this world and all eternity;

That poor as Job I should remain unblest:--

(Alas, for fourpence how my die is cast!)

Of not a hoarded farthing be possesst,

And when all's done, be shoved to hell at last!

John Clare

FOREWORD

Betty Smith Billington- Director of Kushti Bok.

Kushti Bok represents Traveller and Gypsy families and works closely with the local Racial Equality Council, Dorset County Council, South West Dorset Multicultural Society and Dorset Police.

"I was born in Christchurch, Dorset in 1947 and come from a very old Romany family (Mainly Whites)whose roots have been in Christchurch/New Forest/Southampton/Poole Dorset for at least 300 years.My family is constantly mentioned in the local Red House museum's records. They have an oil painting of my Great granny's sister Eliza White who was a well known flower seller from Purewell in Christchurch".

"Ray Wills author of "Where the river bends" apart from being such a talented story teller and poet is one of those rare people who want the world to be a better place for the human race to exist and better facilities for raising families". "I first came across Ray on Facebook. We happened to be on several of the same Romany sites and I noted that he along with many others of his cam padres were sympathetic to the plight of Gypsy/Romany/Travellers regarding places to live or park up their caravans. He was especially concerned with the welfare of people at Dale Farm who were at that time facing eviction. I was also sympathetic to this cause and so whenever Ray commented or posted statuses I usually made comments"." It was through these comments that I discovered Ray and others (One being David Essex O.B.E.) had compiled a book of stories and poems. Namely "GYPSY

STORY TELLERS". "Ray and I shared similar views and we soon became firm FB friends. We also discovered that we were in fact related". "Ray knew many of my Paternal Grandmothers sisters who we had lost contact with. He helped to bring many of my long lost cousins back into my life".

"This new book "Where The River Bends" is mainly focused around the area in which he and his ancestors grew up and he has included many little snippets supplied by myself and others. Mine was all about my Grandmother Betsy Smith(nee White)the original Bournemouth Flower girl". "Ray became aware of my involvement with Kushti Bok and the good work that we do for Gypsies/Travellers/Roma and I invited him to attend one of our monthly meetings in Kingston Maurward College, Dorchester. The Result of which was that Ray donated the proceeds of his last book "Gypsy Story tellers " to Kushti Bok. To enable the group to carry out further educational work for the benefit of Gypsy and Travelling families". "After consultation with Ray, Kushti Bok decided to hold meetings in the Dorset area. To get a better count of the local Gypsy/Traveller/Romany needs for permanent and transit sites. In readiness for the next needs assessment of 2016/2017".

"Our aim is to get as many local Romany/Gypsy/Travellers and local community members together at these meetings. to educate the general public (ie: Site objectors) and make them more aware of the positive side of having GTR sites in their area".

"We are the Lords of the Universe, of fields, fruits, crops, forests, mountains, of the rivers and springs, of the stars and all the elements. Having learned early to suffer, we suffer not at all". "We sleep as calmly and easily on the ground as on the softest bed, and our hard skin is an impregnable armor against the assaults of the air. Fame, honor, and ambition have no power over us, we're therefore free from that base servitude in which most of the great are illustrious and unhappy, nay rather, very slaves". "But our places are the tents we carry with us....we dwell in these tents, busied in the present, and without overmuch care for the future". CERVANTES

Where the river bends

I was born amongst the Gypsies

not far from Canford Heath

I grew up on the heather

where the paths did wind and the tree's did weep

Where the lizards danced in sunshine

and the sand tickled my feet

where the birch grew on the commons

where John Augustus of times would sleep

Oh the river it did bend there

and the furze did smell so sweet

not far from the Canford arms

where the willows leaves did weep

Oh the Canford Magna highway

with its school for toffs and kings

the manor house stood proudly

where the Stour river we did swim

Oh the vardo wheels did turn there

where the benders bedded down

high up on the heathers

not far from old Newtown

Oh the brickyards and the viaducts

the steam laundry down the lane

the Turbary common wastelands

where Knobby Wotton made the daisy chains

The folks they danced there daily

and the chimneys were stacked high

high upon the skyline

where you could watch Poole trains steam bye.

Ray Wills

ABOUT THE AUTHOR

Ray Wills is an accomplished social activist, author and poet. Ray spent many decades working in the UK.Promoting, establishing and operating a vast variety of community projects, adventure playgrounds, play centres and town wide play schemes. His previous publications have included editing of an anthology of stories and poetry entitled 1)GYPSY STORYTELLERS published by Francis Boutle Publishers and 2)ROMANCE IN THE EVERGLADES a book of Rays contemporary poems.He also contributes regular articles relating to Gypsy history and culture to the monthly publication Travellers Times.He was a founder member of Poole writers group and a member of Kinson writers and gives speeches on local history and Gypsies to local schools and community groups.Ray has years of experience in all areas of community work including the formation of action groups, tenant/resident bodies and pressure groups.He was involved in the early development of Adventure Playgrounds, formation of numerous play forums, councils and play steering committees. He is A former Fellow member of the Institute of Play and The National Association of Recreation Leaders. With qualifications in both Youth Work -(City and Guilds) and Community Project management- Dip Management -(Royal Society of Arts).

Acknowledgements

The Author is indebted to the Director of Kushti Bok Betty Smith Billington- for her Foreword and to both Bryan Keets and Robert Matthews for their contributions on the New England campsite at Kinson in Bournemouth.

INTRODUCTION

"They hung the man and flog the woman
Who steal the goose from off the common
But leave the greater villain loose
Who steal the common from the goose"
- Poem of protest 1764.

"Pack, and be out of this forthwith,
D'you know you have no business here?
'No, we hain't got,' said Samuel Smith,
'No business to be anywhere.'
So wearily they went away,
Yet soon were camped in t'other lane,
And soon they laughed as wild and gay,
And soon the kettle boiled again."
Anon

The Gorse And The Brier
As a child I did play in the gorse and the Brier
I lit up the heath with a match made a fire
the fire engines came from Poole town that day

some came from Ferndown and a longs way away

Oh I collected the Coney's from top of Lodge hills

with sacks and my go cart of rusty of wheels

I chased on the heath the Rabbits and hares

before I went in the nights to visit Poole fair

I knew all the Gypsies that ran on the sands

with lizards and adders and their diddy coy bands

there was birdsong and laughter and fern that went out to Poole

where the bog stretched across to meet Waterloo

The Gypsy queen told me that if I was real good

she would tell me my fortune with the clans brotherhood

I was raised on the Manning's where the goldfinch were in tune

where the gaffer was Roger's and the sun shone each noon

Though the pathways have gone now and its industrial land

where the tower park stretches with houses so grand

though I can still hear the warblers as they sing in the briar's

whilst the pony's are staked out on the grasslands a while

Gone are the travellers and the noble Lord Guest

with the house and the lodge where the Freemasons met

only our memories all haunt us today

as we ponder and gaze at the hills far away.

Ray Wills

Arthur Symonds "Why are we setting ourselves the impossible task of spoiling the Gypsies?. They stand for the will of freedom, for friendship with nature, for the open air, for change and the sight of many lands; for all of us that are in protest against progress. The Gypsies represent nature before civilization, the last romance left in the world. No race is more widely scattered over the earth's surface than the Gypsies; Go where one will in Europe, one comes upon Gypsies everywhere".

Rosie Smith "It gets me so upset when I hear all the bad things Gypsies are meant to do but never is it said what we have had done to us, over the years being bullied by gavvers, government council, teachers and just gorgers in general. And although things are getting better, still we get discriminated against in a time and age when people should know better".

John Clare (1793-1864).

"I cannot help but love the Gypsies, for like the wild flower's they are beautiful" ." I chose to live with the Gypsies for awhile and during that time they taught me to play the fiddle". Clare became involved with a Gypsy girl, and as a result wrote a love poem to his nut-brown Gypsy maid.

Robbie Burns'.

One of Burns beloved sweethearts Jeanie was a half-tinker, half-Gypsy woman, who when the tree buds commenced to swell in the spring, yearned for the sweet green places, and unable to stay her hunger, not even for the love of Burns, would leave the two.

Travelling on

I studied their cultures their rhythm and rhymes

I wrote it all down so sweet on the vine

the hard times and good days all travelling free

with the pony and trap and the verdos to see

Oh the journey were long and the folki were rare

with tackle and bridles and work at the fairs

there was mud on the ground and mud in your eyes

but the travellers and Gypsies were true to the sky

The roads that they took there and the twisting of yarn

the flowers they made there and the speeches were long

the stories were told around campfires so bright

*where the old one's told yarns and the zunners would sit late into the
night*

The travelling ways have all gone its true

but the people are rich in histories blue

where the lights twinkled nightly and the moon cast its spell

by the water that ran and the furze it did smell

Oh the travellers were housed and the way they have gone

like the light of the vardos in the darkness of man

where the tales that they told were passed down the lines

of the family names like good port and wine

So heres to the ways and the goodness of days

when they rode on the tracks where the cuckoo once strayed

where the families bred and the lifes that they led

were special and true like the old roads of Poole.

Ray Wills

WHY I WROTE THIS BOOK

Famous poets and artists through the ages have always been inspired by the freedom life of the Gypsies and have written numerous poems dedicated to them or painted pictures of them depicting their Gypsy lifestyle.This book contains an assortment of my poetry and tales as a tribute to their Romany ways and the travelling folk who roamed these lands. In a period of history when although times were hard there was much to be said for the way of life as depicted in the following poems and illustrations. I wrote this book to find answers to my many questions and concerns. To find answers to such questions as, "Why was there and still is so much prejudice and antagonism towards these people known as Gypsies, travellers and Romani"?. "Why was there so much feuding and bitterness even amongst and between these people as well as against them"?. "Why are so many ashamed to say that they have Gypsy origins"?. "What was the real reason many travelling folk are called Diddycoys" and where did the term originate from"?. "Where did this all come from and just where did they themselves actually really come from"?.

Such questions led me on a long search and fresh insights, knowledge and understanding into these fundamental questions and others like.Was there really a place which they often referred to throughout their tales of a homeland which they called "Little Egypt"?Were they from the lost tribes of Israel and do they have royal blood as many of them believe.

So many Gypsyologists, writers, historians, poets and artists studied their lives over past times and recent decades and all came up with varying conclusions. I needed to find answers to these questions and others. This book is my attempt to do so and with it provide an insight into the Gypsy travelling fraternity. Following my involvement as Editor and coordinator of the book "Gypsy Storytellers" Anthology published by Francis Boutle. A book which occurred directly as a result of the contentious events at Dale Farm in Basildon Essex England in 2011. When Gypsy travellers were forcibly evicted from their homes on the Dale Farm travellers site under much media coverage and worldwide human rights concerns. This evoked a campaign to raise money for the welfare of Gypsy and travelling families. Throughout my time editing the "Gypsy Storytellers I met up with numerous contributors worldwide as well as interacting with hundreds of individuals and webpage organisers. Many of whom were Gypsy travelers or their supporters. As a result of which I discovered my own family lineage which confirmed my Gypsy roots. Through my involvement with Gypsy Storytellers I have made many friends from the Gypsy travelling community worldwide and have been asked to and enjoyed talking to many organisations and schools about Gypsies. This book for me is in many ways the result of that journey of discovery and of those friendships.

So who were these strange mysterious Gypsy Travellers' and where did they come from with their course and strange dialect. Their rich flamboyant clothes and lifestyles and freedom loving ways?. What and where were their origins?. How true were the stories they told, all their myth's and their fanciful legend's?. Some said they were descendant's of the Egyptian pharaoh's with royal blood lineage and many had grandiose title's before their names. How much of these stories were really true and how much of this was just invented, made up from peoples own ignorance, suspicions imaginations and misunderstandings.With their nomadic lifestyles, vardos,caravans, benders and tented homes and their love of nature the Gypsies left an indelible mark on the English countryside's, what's the truth behind their mystique?.

Gypsy is a carefree word to some, but it is not a carefree word to this race of peoples who were branded with it. Hundreds of thousands of Gypsies were taken as slaves in Europe for very many centuries and then when slavery ended they were treated as second class citizens wherever they went. This eventually culminated in more recent history in over a million of them being murdered in the Nazi Holocaust and in recent times again being discriminated against wherever they go throughout the world.

There are two distinct and contrasting views of Gypsies. One being the romantic mystique freedom loving nomads of the road travelling with their Vardo and Cob and Vanner horses. The other tells of a hard life on the roads out in all weathers in severe circumstances, poverty stricken and amidst great persecution and community stigma. There is also the commonly used slanderous and derogatory phrases often thrown around today by the ignorant folks. Derogatory sayings associated with and referring to Gypsies such as diddycoys or pikeys and with the common remark thrown around "Of course these are not real Gypsies", ("whatever a real Gypsy is").

Gypsy travelling folk are much the same as any other group of people in society with similar characteristics and attributes, they are all each one an individual. So many words have been written about them over the years often falsely depicting them as tyrants, thieves, vagabonds, wasters. But it must be remembered that each one of them is an individual, no group of folk is the true Gypsy traveller.

Through centuries they have been poorly misrepresented, depicted and despised. Often false tales and descriptions have been copied down word for word from old transcripts, recording them as wandering parasites, child stealers, no more than thieves and scoundrels. So many writers have used these biennial descriptions copied down into realms of chapters, books and readings. As if these descriptions represented each one individual or group or race. As if they all are one group of peoples. Often these descriptions were copied from extremely biased sources, centuries ago so often presented again and again as fresh new true accounts in fresh documents. Gypsies are depicted as a unique race with no homeland of such, a combination of peoples of Romani, Travellers from all areas of the British isles. Consisting of show and fairground people, skilled artisans, horse traders, storytellers, entertainers and lovers of the open road.

The reader will note that throughout this book I use the terms Gypsies or Travellers, preferring not to get tied down into any heavy or lengthily debate over the preferred chosen name of such nomadic peoples. Or any deep philosophical discussion over which or who, whether Roma, Sinti, Dom, Nomad, Traveller, Gypsy, showman etc. I purposely choose unity preferring to use the common public terms of Gypsy or Traveler throughout. For there is far too much badmouthed friction against any of these nomadic people in the world as it is.Without encouraging any within and between the nomadic peoples of the world. As a result and as a poet and lover of freedom I write here not just of one particular grouping, but of all travelling folk with their stories and their rich cultures and traditions and all with their strong emphasis on family life. This book is not an attempt to be an academic study of the Gypsy and travelling folk. Though many areas are covered in some depth. It's more of a laid back imaginative jaunt and poetic ramble and insight into a local history in southern England of the Gypsy and Travellers' community and of their way of life. This is also a tale of the character's and folk's from the literary and art world who once frequented or lived in this terrain at a particular time in history. Building close friendships with the Gypsy community and leaving behind their indelible mark both on the local landscape and its rich southern heritage.

Roma Therapy

I'm off for a little Roma Therapy today
got my vardo packed with goodies and I must be on my way
I'm taking all those little roads which these days no one knows
I'm blessed with tales and stories and with trinkets to be sold
I'm travelling through the old ways that the farmers once recalled
where fairs and shows were plentiful and the ways that all did know
I'm taking all my songs and im heading for the hills
where the good lord fills my dreams at night
and the stars frequent my reels
I'm turning these old wheels again and my horses are good stead
I'm rambling through the country got no reason for to speed
I'm following the old ways the tracks and trails I know
where our ancestors rode afore and took them fairground shows
I've got wisdom up my sleeve and a ton of words to sing
I'm taking all my therapy of which the good lord springs.

Ray Wills

CHAPTER ONE

Wanderers All Their Days

And Jesus saith unto him," The foxes have holes, and the irds of the air have nests; but the Son of man hath no where to lay his head". (Matthew 8.20)

Among the Travelers, old age is not penalized. The old man or woman is an honored and still-useful member of the community. Their songs and stories are regarded as important contributions to the group and the possession of them benefits each individual within the group.

-Travelers' Songs from England and Scotland, by Ewan McColl and Peggy Seeger.

Intuitive Gypsy Roma

The third eye intuition dictates

the fortune tellers contemplates

insightful, precise and origins of the East

like cards of wisdoms readings and bells on feet

Tents of drapes and occult themes

wisdoms, stories, myths and mankinds dreams

the oracle and the eyes of themes

the gaze of the look into the stars and the dark mysterious worlds of
wonders and faith

tattoos and songs rich in tone

nomadic life of Indian homes

Past and future in one look

wise and rich in history and traditions past

insightful wisdoms and love of the craft.

Ray Wills

"And a mixed multitude went up also with the Children of Israel". (Exodus xii.38)"And he (the king of Babylon) exiled all Jerusalem, and all the officers and all the mighty warriors ten thousand people and all the craftsmen and smiths". "None remained except the poorest people of the land. And he exiled Yehoyakin to Babylon, and the king's mother, and his wives, and his notables, and the leaders of the land, from Jerusalem to Babylon, and all the warriors, and craftsmen and smiths." (2 Kings 24:14-16); "But the commander of the army left some of the poor of the land as vinedressers and farmers."

(2.Kings 25:12)."From Europe I follow the roads of the Roma into the orient: to Armenia and Iran where the Sassanid's once ruled, and before them the Achaemenids. From here the road leads to another land where the Indus-river flows to the land where the Kushans once held sway".- Leksa Manus's- The Roads of the Roma.

"Lamech took unto him two wives and the name of the one was Adah and the name of the other Zillah. And Adah bore Jubal. He was the father of all such as handle the harp and organ. And Zillah she also bore Tubal Cain, a instructor of every artificer in brass and iron". -Genesis chapter iv verses 19-22.

24

Exodus

In the Indian continent where Hindi was brave

they danced and they sang like Sultan's enslaved

amidst armies advancing and treason's and plots

they humbled themselves for all that they got

They played to the Kings and they fought in the wars

they were slave's to the rich and they danced for both the rich and the
poor they fled from the terrors of mens arms and wars

in the battles that raged there and the might of the swords

They were shackled and burdened, tortured and maimed

they scattered their brethren through valley's of flame's

the music they played there and the folks all did dance

whilst their lives were in torment, imprisoned and chanced

They fled to Europe through Egyptian great plains

their tale's they all told and they played all their games

from tyrannical doctrines of torment and pain, then they all gathered
their brothers and rode on again.

Ray Wills

ORIGINS

For many years it was believed that Gypsies originated from Egypt for they were called "Egyptians" or "Babylonians" and it was believed that they had a homeland called "little Egypt" and were descendants of the biblical lost tribe of Israel. The Gypsies themselves told stories of those days in tales or "Says". They also were great readers of fortunes and had uncanny intuitive ways, as well as knowledge of the Hebrew bible, despite having had no education or access to such books. Although in recent years this link with Egypt has been questioned by some so called modern experts who claim that these people actually originated from India. The historical accounts from numerous sources appear on the surface to support this modern theory. For a study by A.F.Pottl and Fr.Miklosich, established the Gypsies 'Indian origin and connection and thus the routes of their migration to Europe. This was supported by another study published in Nature, which examined Y chromosomes in DNA samples comparing the genetic signatures of European Roma men with those of thousands of Indian's from throughout the sub-continent. These two studies went some ways to confirm the majority view that both the British and the European Roma Gypsies were connected with India.

Early records state that Gypsies first fled from Alexandria the Great's invasion around 330 BC who was known to them as "Alexandra the Evil One". They were thought to have been driven from northern India close to the River Beas in the Punjab. Alexandria armies had waged war on this continent for over a decade. It was said that it was from this experience that the Romanies were said to have developed their wandering ways or "wanderlust".

These Gypsies are often referred to as Roma, Sinti or Sindhi,Kale, or Romani.Thus it is commonly believed by many today that they have their origins in northwestern India which is referred to today as Pakistan. As opposed to the original story of their origin that they came from Egypt hence their name Gypsies. There are numerous accounts of when it was that they actually left India. These waves range from as early as the 4th century the 6th and others the 10th, but no one really knows for sure.

One of these theories was that a small number of Indians were forced to become nomadic craftsmen and performers. These grew in numbers though were permitted to live close to the Persian river from 440 to 443. At that time the word Gypsy was not in use and names for these nomadic peoples included Zott, jat, Luri, Nuri, Dom, Sinti, Domarai and Athergani. Around 820 the Zott settled on the banks of the River Tigris until 855.Then the Byzamtas attacked and took them as slave prisoners for they were skilled workers in all types of craft with metal,wood and engineering. Along with their performing and fortune telling skills.

From 1001 to 1026 King Muhmud of Ghazni attempted to destroy all the Sindh and Punjab peoples in India and used these Luri who were said to be good warriors.

It is believed that Gypsies left in large numbers/waves throughout these centuries and that many of them were also brought then by Muslims to Europe as slaves. With great numbers of them settling in Turkey and North Africa via

Persia which is the present day Iran.

Today's Gypsies call themselves 'Rom' and their language is known as 'Romani', thought to be closely related to groups of languages and dialects (such as Hindi, Gujarati, Marathi and Cashmiri) and which are still spoken in India and of the same origin as Sanskrit.

John Sampson's theory of the arrival of Romania Gypsies in Europe are based on a comparison of the phonetics of Romani and Indian languages. For according to John Sampson the caste known as Dom left India, and spent some time in Persia and the borders of the Mediterranean. They settled there and are known as Dom to this day and they then moved in to Armenia and some settled there and these are known as Lom (or Bosha)and the rest moved into Europe these are the Rom or Romanies of Europe.There was great debates amongst John Sampson and others in the Gypsy Lore Society on which part of the Indian sub-continent the Romani's had occupied before leaving for the west, but at these times there was little opposition to the "Dom theory" itself. Based mainly on their use of the words they borrowed from Persia, Armenia, and Greece.

Romani People

Exodus freedoms from invading lands
conscripting soldiers with weapons on hand
fleeing the countries and fleeing the lands
Romani peoples of pure Gypsy bands

Through hillsides and palaces all set for a King

entertaining the people, soldiers and Queens

the torture and hangings and prejudice flies

all in the face of another mans eyes

Through countries and battles and many lives lost

all for the whim or a coin that was tossed

herded and branded, suffering loss

through the eyes of the victor and the talk of the cross

Poverty stricken and travelling free

over the countries to seek liberties

caste' of the brethren and skin of their race

only the sorrows are seen in the face.

Ray Wills

These Gypsies were often described by onlookers as dark-skinned magicians, entertainers, smiths, horse breakers and other skilled trade workers and at that time lived in tents. An Arab historian relates that 10,000 of these Indian dancers and musicians were brought to the court of the Sha of Persia (Iran) in 420 AD.

Just a decade later in 430 12,000 Gypsy dancers, musician's, from a tribe of India were given as a gift to the court of the Shah of Persian King Bahram V. These were described as being of "baptised heathen's" due to their being of dark skin and wearing Saracen-style clothing and carrying weapon's and were said to be workers with animal's, silversmith's and entertainers.

Amongst them were broom makers, chimney sweeps, brick makers, musicians, dancers and bear leaders. Though the smiths working with metals remained the paramount group. Very little has changed in their particular main skills and trades since then for over hundreds of years though with smith-craft being the Gypsies main occupation in the Balkan peninsula. On a particular day there were not less than sixty smiths who pulled along a carriage in which sat three workers at their forges. Whilst on another day 400 of them were said to be sat under the Sultan's window and worked there,he was so pleased that he gave orders for thousands of aspires to be distributed among them.In the kingdom of Hanigalbat-Mitanni, in the upper Mesopotamia a language similar to Romany was spoken and the people living there were known as Hurrians. In AD 800,it was reported that Saint Athanasia gave food to these "foreigners called the Atsingani" near Thrace.

Later in AD 803,Theophanes the Confessor wrote that "Emperor Nikephros 1 had the help of the "Atsingani" to deal with a riot with their "knowledge of magic". Was it really true that these Athingani performed magic?, Or was it more likely as Avraham Sandor suggests in his "Myths, Hypotheses and Facts Concerning the Origin of Peoples" - The True Origin of Roma and Sinti. That they were acquainted with the strengths and properties in herbs, water, the earth and animals, or even in poisonous snakes. Perhaps the Athingani were not merely magicians but had discovered and understood what nature had in fact taught them. Perhaps the observers who said that they performed magic were themselves ignorant and did not fully understand nature that well.In 855 a vast number of these were captured in Syria by the Byzantines these were said to be great acrobat's and juggler's they were also referred to by many as being itinerant fortune tellers, ventriloquists and wizards.

The Desert of the Gypsies

It was first recorded that some 27,000 or so Zotts, were taken prisoner by the Byzantine when they conquered Ainzarba from the valley of the lower Tigris and moved to northern Syria. All of these people were taken as slaves along with their cattle,to carry the stolen treasures and spoils of war to Afghanistan. This was known as "The Desert of the Gypsies". Indian society then was organised by a caste system and into numerous tribes defined by particular trades such as (jatis) brick-makers, musicians, basket makers, rat catchers, acrobats, fortune tellers and animal trainers.

 Those who arrived in Romania were divided into groups, 1) state owned- being mainly metal workers, 2) privately owned by the landowners 3) or owned by the monasteries 4) Another group of these slaves were given as "gifts" to the aristocracy, or 5) Those auctioned off on the many slave auction blocks which were around at that time. For now they're were very many new slaves with new fresh skills for the wealthy landowner masters. A visitor to one of these estates wrote "The landowner had all that he needed on his estate: cooks, bakers, gardeners, masons, shoemakers, blacksmiths, musicians, labourers, other classes of workers – and all of them Tziganes".With so many of the male population at war or dead, the state was grateful for this fresh slave supply of labour, for to harvest or collect minerals for their wars. Those slaves who were left behind worked in the monasteries,whilst others worked in the mines, the rivers and out in the countryside.

These changes created great social movements between them and others as never before, for they now shared many different customs and cultures with those of the outside world, with many of them intermarrying. In the mining camps Gypsy slaves worked alongside the Tatar and Ottoman prisoners of war, the Romanian criminals and the peasants.

Following a great battle (1192 AD)it is believed that all of these Gypsy slaves were finally freed, with the bulk of them begining their long migration,travelling towards Asia then onto North Africa, into Spain and then the European continent. Though some of them had stayed behind.

 The Greeks had been warned by Balsamon to avoid these Gypsy "ventriloquist's and wizard's" who he said were in league with the Turks, or "in league with the Devil".

Throughout the next three centuries they were invaded by many armies including Genghis Khan who had driven the

Sinti Gypsy metal workers from their homeland in the Sind.

In 1322 two Friars Minor, Simon Simeonis an Irish Franciscan and Hugh the Enlightened, noted the gypsy presence in Crete. Outside the town of Heraklion and observing Greek Orthodox rites and living in low black tents like the Arabs or in caves. They described them as "asserting themselves to be of the family of Ham" or that of "The descendants of Cain"', "they rarely or never stop in one place beyond thirty days, but always wandering and fugitive, as though accursed by God", "going from field to field with their oblong tent's, back and low".

Having studied and researched this in some depth; I am not of the same opinion as some recent day commentators. In fact these Gypsies I feel may well have been of actual "royal blood" which accounts for their acceptance by all the other royal households at that time along with the Roman Catholic church and state authorities. For they had actually journeyed to the Holy lands, to many of the European holy places and to have had ordinance with the Pope himself in Rome during these years. The Pope in earlier times had after meeting them demanded that they should be given safe conduct and passage throughout all of Europe. As a result, for a while many of them were thus able to travel in relative safety, and could expect food and lodging from the churches. Much protection was offered to them during these times by the Christian church and the state, which they obviously enjoyed and took full advantage of.

Gypsies were also given safe passage by Sigismund of the Holy Roman Empire, then after his death, they moved around Europe with similar letter's from the Pope. As a result of these stories and with the support they received, Gypsies were soon under the protection of many King's and leader's throughout Europe.Their journey's taking them into countries where they were either welcomed or else later to be persecuted.They were known by a variety of names including Saracens, heathens, bohemians, Egyptians and Albanians.(The letters from Sigismund were said to be legitimate, but those papal letter's were later thought by many to be forgeries).

The present day popular theory of the Gypsies origins in India strongly based on DNA, is however strongly disputed by many others, including Sándor Avraham in his article entitled "Myths, Hypotheses and Facts Concerning the Origin of Peoples" -The True Origin of Roma and Sinti. Sandor provides many reasons why he believes the Roma actually had Egyptian or Hebrew roots or origins.

It is also known that there is no longer one people in India clearly related to the Roma. Sandor Avraham believed that Roma's "prehistory" began in Mesopotamia, in the lower Euphrates Valley; and their "proto-history", in the lower Nile Valley and Canaan. He strongly believed that their origins were closely linked with the Hebrew Jews as all the practices of cleanliness and family, courtships, marriage and death. For Roma's destiny after death is Paradise, while Gadje non gypsies are redeemed and deserve Paradise only if they have been good towards Roma. This is so similar to the Jewish concept of "righteousness". Sandor also believes that their close family reliance has strong similarities to those of the Jewish faith, rather than any Indian culture and common links.

34

Another commentator Judith Okey also observed that "The Gypsies make a clear distinction between the inner body the secret ethnic self and inner retreat and the outer body, which is potentially a source of pollution and must be kept separate. This cleanliness purity closely ties in with the biblical Hebrew customs".

My Gypsy poetry friend Melissa Townsley a commentator of today writes " In the historical record it is written that 'Right across Europe, when groups of Gypsies arrived in a new city, they were initially welcomed by the local gentry and royalty. They were paid for playing music or telling fortunes and were given permission to camp, often on the outskirts of towns or just outside city walls. In the Scottish court in April 1505 there Is a record of Gypsies being paid £7 at the request of the King, possibly either for providing entertainment to the court, or because they were thought to be pilgrims. Reports suggest that these early groups of Romani Gypsies carried papers with them certifying that they were pilgrims carrying out penance and asking for a guarantee of safe passage across the realm.' Why would that be anything but the truth if you look at history. Why would people from Egypt be on a pilgrimage to Scotland? To visit their dead Queen of course. But lets not look at history. Lets just eat any bits they feed us. I will not accept the added insult on my ancestors, that they arrived here as liars. There is no proof that would call the King of Scotland a liar.(other than the most likely racist opinion of a modern scholar) The King was an educated man and had knowledge of the people he was dealing with. Because the man got up out of his throne to give them a personal greeting. And he accepted the papers and documents as real.

In India they were known as "The Untouchables"

Most of the "out of India theory" is based on work done by a linguist Franz Miklosich's studies. Which was long ago in 1880. Modern scholars often just refer to his work. And I don't think doing some DNA tests on a small number of Roma over in the east of Europe is the answer, for what their own historians describe as wave after wave, after wave, of migrations. Even looking at Gypsy treatment in India suggest they are outsiders, that are not from there. Indians were so scared of even touching a Gypsy that they were caste as 'untouchables' Yet the historian's won't talk about that.

The Roma themselves also relate their wandering to the Pharaoh, something that is exclusive of the Hebrew people. The oldest recording of the arrival of Roma in Europe report their own declaration as having been slaves of the Egyptian Pharaoh. This could be part of their historic memory or else it was something that they invented in order to find acceptance by the wider community.

 If Roma as it is claimed and they have stayed always in India until the 11th century c.e. it is believed that they would have practiced the most widespread Hindu religion in that area long before the rise of Islam, when the fire-worship was still the dominant religion. No doubt they would have taken many cultural elements of its Brahmanism,along with the fortune tellers "intuition" which is in many ways similar to the Hindi faith and third eye.

Gypsy and their roots link with Persia

Most commentators however suggest that they the Gypsies actually were living in Persia (the modern day Iran)in those years. Which would account for some of their fire worship rituals. There are also other complementary elements or of a rather superstitious nature, all of them linked with the fire-worship of ancient Persia. Their other customs only practiced outwardly, like fortune-telling, palmistry, tarot, etc.

Which they no doubt learnt from the ancient Persian Magi and alchemists. Although some commentators believe that it was during their captivity in Egypt, the lost tribes of Israel were educated in Astrology and supernatural psychic arts, which today is inherent in many Romany, also as fortune-tellers. It is apparent that Indian Immigrants don't have this ability.

DIDACHE - THE WAY and the Gypsy

The term Didicoy has been widely used constantly over decades as an insulting slang expression, particularly by and amongst non Gypsies as an insult term for all Romani people.(Gypsy outside the Romany tribes and of mixed blood). Didikai, didikoi, DIDIKAI', "Didicoy" being a Romani term for a child of mixed Romani and non-Romani parentage; as applied to the Travellers. It refers to these peoples as not real "Gypsy" by ethnicity or blood or true blood Roma' and lead a similar yet distinct lifestyle". So someone would call one of these traveller as a 'Didicoy' as a means of identifying them ethnically from a true 'blood' Roma.It is also somewhat ironic that The Didache, is also an early handbook of an anonymous Christian community, which spells out a Way of life for Christians and how to take in wandering prophets. The Didache "The Teaching of the Twelve Apostles,"(pronounced did-uh-kay) is a book manual of early travellers teachings of the word of Christ.

The Roman Catholic Church and Gypsy predjudice

Over time I am of the belief that the term did- uh- kay came to be used in a derogatory way about these Gypsies who followed "The way". Particulaly after the Roman Catholic church in later years were to denounce and ban the Gypsies from the faith in the 16th century.Which was the start of the predjudice against them throughout the world. It is the earliest Christian writing outside of the New Testament and it provides a window into the life of the earliest Christians as they applied the teachings of Jesus to their community of faith.

For the idea of community was integral to the early Christians who saw their faith not as an individual endeavour, but as becoming part of a community "where two or more are gathered in my name". The Didache was actually used by early Christians then as a "training manual" to prepare an individual before joining the Christian community.Those early Christians were less interested in the orthodox Christian philosophy of Catholicism than in their experience of "The Way " the life the Christian community lived. The Didache is mentioned in many early Christian writings, and historians knew that it had existed, however over time the text of the Didache had been lost.

The content of this important early Christian writing remained a mystery until 1873 when Philotheos Bryennios, a presbyter in the Orthodox Church, discovered a copy of the text hiding in plain sight. Bryennios was trained as a church historian in Germany and while working on an 11th-century manuscript in the Library of the Holy Sepulchre in Istanbul, Bryennios found a copy of the Didache among its pages and published a copy of the Didache in 1883.

 The Didache came to be seen as one of the most important early Christian writings outside of the New Testament. As followers of "the Way", the Didache community lived their lives of faith in a religiously diverse and often hostile society. The Didache teachings helped the community shape the ways they were distinct from the common culture. The early Christians believed that its teachings had the way of Jesus, the way of love. It was for them the way of abundant life.

I also believe that the Didache "The Way of Life" of the Ist century may well have become accepted in the Gypsy travelling community at sometime in their early history.No doubt if this was a fact they would have I believe quite possibly taken up "The Way" of the Didache with its Hebrew links as opposed to following the Roman Catholic church with its theological customs.This Christian way of living could well have been adopted by the Gypsy travelling community and caused them to be associated with this christian cult as opposed to the accepted Roman Catholic church at that time with all its rituals .

The Didache -:"The Way"- community customs and practices are common amongst the Gypsy community and has a great bearing on their culture and family social life. No doubt this may well account for a great deal of their victimisation by society ever since. As they were no doubt seen as being a very secretive peoples and different from the socially accepted Roman catholic church or with their possible earlier Indian connections. With the term Didache becoming   · associated with the Gypsy community by the non gypsy as being not acceptable and therefore came to be used as a derogatory term. They the Gypsies were seen as outcasts with the common use of the term Didicoy insult being associated with the followers of the Didache. Hence we have the modern saying that "these are not real Gypsies, but didicoys" infering to them as being that of an inferior race of nomads.Thus this no doubt led to the problem of the settled faith communities who were mainly Catholics being in conflict with travelling, itinerant preachers and prophets of the Christian The Way of Christ.With these early Gypsies being followers of the Christian Didache (THE WAY) the earliest known document outside of the New Testament and not the accepted Roman Catholicsm. It may well be that the Catholic church frowned upon their Hebrew ritual cleansing practices. As it did with the orthodox Jews themselves and that this may well account over time for this change in attitude by the catholic church against the Gypsies. For by 1564 Pope Pius V had expelled all Gypsies from the Roman Catholic church this was undoubtebly a major event and a means of branding them as non christian.So turning the general public across the world against them as depicting them the gypsies as being a wicked God forsaking peoples or race.

Followers of "The Way"

It would have been very evident that these travelling Gypsies were followers of the Hebrew/Christian "Way of life" with all its customs rituals and beliefs associated with the Christian faith. Such as baptisms, communion etc. They were also seen as being very clean in their homes and in their morals. For they did not permit sex before marriage with strong similarities to those of the Jewish faith, with customs such as to circumcise all male infants.Along with their associated practices of cleanliness, courtships, marriage and death and were extremely family orientated.

This may well account initially up to the 16th century for their acceptance by each kingdom they travelled through as being Christian travellers. Thus they were initially well accepted by the church and leaders who provided them with alms and shelter as advocated within the words of the Didache. This was common until they were denounced by the Roman Catholic church. For the way of life for their culture was seen to be rich and strong when they got to their destinations. "If he who comes is a traveler, help him as much as you can, but he shall not remain with you more than two days, or, if need be, three". "And if he wishes to settle among you and has a craft, let him work for his bread. But if he has no craft provide for him according to your understanding, so that no man shall live among you in idleness because he is a Christian".There are many interesting details among Gypsies that suggest their origin in some Israelite Tribes: For instance, among Sinti groups and many Rom, a respectful way to address a person is the word "Manush", that suggests "Manassheh" (French Sinti call themselves with this term). The Roma also relate their wandering to the Pharaoh, something that is in itself exclusive of the Hebrew people.Those from Madras are only the Lambadi tribe of Gypsies. The ones that emigrated to the West were settled in Rajasthan (Rom) and Sindh (Sinti), the same area of the B'ney Yisrael of India. Lambadis may belong to the same migration as Jews of Cochin, who came from Yemen, as well as Lemba in Southern Africa came from Yemen. So, we have the same areas for both Israelites and Gypsies in India.

It is supposed that the Roma had converted to Islam in the Seljuq Empire (a vast area stretching from the Hindu Kush to eastern Anatolia and from Central Asia to the Persian gulf). There conversions for many were no doubt as a means of gaining citizenship and thus as a means to escape from slavery. Though the Sinti allegedly refused to convert and remain enslaved. Both the Sinti & Roma eventually migrated to Germany in the 15th Century and were then converting to Christianity.

Their "Says" and stories

Although the Bible itself was not freely available at that time it may well be that these biblical stories were handed down from one generation to the next generation within these Gypsy storytelling or "Says" sessions or through "The Way".Therefore the Romany religious connections with the Hebrew and Christianity was paramount and may go some way to explain why they have retained their religious values, traditions and cultures up to the present day. The Roma knew the Bible, maybe because that very biblical history was deeply engraved in their collective memories so rooted in their life throughout their long exile in the East. They did not follow any of the Hinduism cultural ways to any great extent or any other which was prominent there. Roma knew Christian bible teachings whilst in the Muslim and Hindu territories in India, Persia and the Arab lands, Byzantium. There are many reasons to presume that Roma were Christians since the first century c.e, When the Didache book writings were first acessable.There are historical accounts reports that during this time massive conversions took place in Assyria, where the Christian Apostles travelled to India to seek out and rescue the "lost sheep" of the House of Israel.So that this maybe explain why they did not adopt any Hinduism element in their religious conception. It's amazing that despite the modern day views about their Indian origins there is a complete absence of any Hindu, Brahmin or reincarnation elements in the Gypsy Romany spirituality beliefs.

Gypsies and Hebrew Jews - similarities

This biblical Hebrew link is also apparent in recent years asthe great evangelist Rodney Smith wrote in the 1800s that-"Eighty out of every hundred Gypsies have Biblical names. Yet they have no bibles and if they had could not read them. Whence then these scripture names?."Do they not come down to us from tradition?.

All of the Gypsy women in the Balkans had christian names as recorded in tax returns of 1522-23. Gypsies have often used standard common forenames such as Samuel, William, or Mary, but they were also fond of unusual or biblical names. Such examples of male names include Elijah, Amos,Goliath, Hezekiah, Nehemiah, Noah, Sampson, Shad rack, Noah,Solomon Amber line, Belcher, Dangerfield, Gilderoy, Liberty, Major, Nelson, Neptune, Silvanus, Vandlo. Whilst female names in common use included those of Anselina, Athalia, Britannia, Cinderella, Clementina, Dotia, Gentile, Sabina, Tryphena, Urania, Fairnette, Freedom, Mizelli, Ocean, Reservoir, Sinfai, Unity, and Vancy. The recently discovered Israelites of India were in the majority all Christian, not Hindu or other castes. There is no race in the world who experimented with such a large array of conversions in such a short time. For Roma experienced many tongues from different countries in roughly the same time. Many Roma tell the story that, long time ago, their leader was called "Faraó" which is Pharaoh. In Hungary, for many years Roma were even called "Faraó népe", the Pharaoh's people.

Gypsies are very similar to Hebrew Jews in many ways with their customs,culture and ways with no obvious links with the India culture and Hindu complex ideologys. Thus contradicting the view that they have Indian roots.

This includes that of-

1)Keeping the seventh day holy. 2) Lighting candles on the evening of Parashat (Friday).3) Blasphemy is a sin, as is cursing an elder. They have a strict code of Law. Claiming to be Egyptian in origin and make pilgrimages to the burial place's of their ancestors. Its extremelly doubtful that they could have heard any biblical text before reaching Europe. Or even in certain European areas where the Scriptures were not in the hands of the common people at that time and were not written in their language. Though it is very apparent that they were very familiar with Christianity when they first arrived in Europe and it may well go some way to explain why they sought out the western Christian Europeans nations following their exodus from India. Most Roma are able to have access to read the Bible now and claim that "All our laws and rules are written in the Bible!".No other peoples except for the Hebrew Jews may say such a thing.

STORYTELLING

"The Gypsies are an imaginative folk, delighting, like children, in romances and romancing ; and if one may judge from the array of folk-tales I already collected from them, these wanderers appear to possess the gift of story-telling in generous measure". Revd George Hall.

Traveller's stories

At the edge of civilization in a world of basic gain

the early man was sanctioned to tell stories around the flames

where the wood it kindled memories and the nomad wrote his lore

the early civilizations first wandered across these shores

Where the buffalo and bison rode across the plains

where the bush was wild and fertile and the aborigine grew to fame

where the Africans jungle hid the reptiles and the game

where the Eskimo,s were warm around each naked flame

The Indian continent was hidden from mankinds future greed

where the Rajahs built their future wealth and the poet Tennyson sneezed

all across the valleys and the hills of reckless gain

the wandering nomadic tribes whispered loud their names

The Indians and the nomads of every cause the same

have sat around the campfire and blessed the divine flames the showmen came to prosper and the fairground stories told

where the Hurdy gurdy player tells stories oh so old

The story tellers gathered and the fortune lady spelled

the stars at night were awesome and the coins fell in wishing wells

the circus entertainers and the horseman rode so free

from the foothills of Kentucky to the rose of Tennessee

the Gypsies and the travelers with the tinkers on a spree

were sitting around those campfires quoting histories

The darkies on the bush land and the Zulu tribe's of war

one hand on the book of life and the other wild and raw

the churchy congregations and the super human crew

were stranded on the worldly themes and lost their roots to fools

the storytelling legends were written in the sand

amongst the chosen peoples and their loyal traveling band

Ray Wills

For thousands of years and for generations of people, storytelling was the most common entertainment and most practical way of teaching. This activity took place in their gatherings and communal places, such as around their campfire yog. The focal point of the yogs, the flame, the sounds of the night. All provided atmosphere to these storytellers who shared their wisdom with students who, in their turn, become storytellers themselves, to the next generations.

Those early Gypsy ancestors created myths to explain everything and natural Communities were strengthened and maintained through these stories or "Says" were pased down from generation to eneration which connected the present, the past and the future. Often they assigned superhuman qualities to ordinary people in these stories, hence the origins of the hero tale. This early storytelling often would combine stories, poetry, music, and dance. Storytelling was natural for everyone but those who excelled at it became entertainers, educators, cultural advisors and historians for the community.

To this day, in Eastern Europe, the Gypsies still pursue their ancient role of storytelling, mystifying their hearers with stories which perhaps they originally took with them out of India many centuries ago. Gypsies called this passing of history or stories "Says". So that today as a result of their faith and culture we have the legends, myth's and belief's surrounding the origins of the race of these nomadic, freedom loving people,those whom we refer to here as Gypsies or traveler's.

When the Gypsies first arrived in Europe, they were full of these stories and legends and they would no doubt tell them to everybody they'd meet and who would listen. Just as they had previously told such stories, when they sat around their campfire yog's. For these were the source whence other stories grew, just like the tales of the wandering Jew's which typifies the Hebrew, so does the story of the Romany nomadic Gypsies.

The following are a variety of these many Gypsy Tales, Myths and Legends.

1) At the beginning of the world "God made the 'Busno'the non-Gypsy out of slime, then he made a woman out of the Busno's spare rib. Later on he found that the world was so dull with these two Busnos and their children, that he said to himself, 'I must liven things up. 'So one night, when the man was sleeping in his cave, God goes and takes a bit of his jawbone and in a twinkling of an eye he makes out of it a stiff and sturdy Gypsy alive and kicking.

2) According to Shahameh, king Bahram V Gor learned that the poor could not afford to enjoy music. So he asked the king of India if he would send him ten thousand luris,men and women, who were expert lute players. When the lures arrived, the king gave each one of them an ox and a donkey along with a donkey load of wheat. With the intention that they could live on their labor, agriculture and play music constantly to entertain the poor. However the luris ate the oxen and wheat and returned a year later with their bodies suffering from the effects of hunger and starvation. As a result King Bahram was extremely angry with them for wasting all that he had given them. He told them to pack their belongings and he banished them for good from his kingdom so that they and all their offspring became nomad's and wanderer's of the world forever. Many of these are said to be the forefathers of the present day Gypsies.

3) It is also said that God fashioned the first man from a sour lime and baked him in an oven, but he misjudged the baking-time and burned the man quite black. Thus it was this man that became the ancestor of the Negroes,and then

49

God made another man and though he took care with his cooking he failed to calculate the ingredient's successfully and this became the first white man in the world. But it was third time lucky, and the Lord baked a perfectly brown man that became the ancestor of today's Gypsies.

4)When the Gypsy people were driven from their home country and they arrived in Mekran, they constructed a machine that they attached a wheel to. But nobody was able to move that wheel, until, in the midst of their efforts, an evil spirit approached the chief, whose name was Chen, and told him that the wheel would turn only when Chen had married his own sister, Guin. The chief accepted this advice, and after having married his sister, the wheel finally turned. The name of the tribe then became the combined form of these two siblings' names, Chenguin, which is still the term used for these people in some other languages, such as Turkish. The legend concludes that the consequence of this unnatural marriage was a curse over the Gypsies. They were condemned, from then on, to wander the earth forever.5) In the Turkish-occupied Balkans the story was told that the first Gypsy was born from a union between a brother Chen and his sister Guin, hence the Turkish name for the Romani's, Cingene.6) In a Gypsy empire of long ago, headed by the mighty czar Firaun. After challenging God he was severely punished, and was drowned at sea together with his army. The few survivors are the ancestors of the present day Gypsies. 7) Further tales include those stories of the Sun and Moon and that of the Romani's being descendants of a prehistoric people, or a race of Jews who later became mixed with Christian vagabonds.

Tales relating to the Christian and Hebrew scriptures.

1) In the Hebrew old testament the bible tells that of Cain being sent into the desert and his offspring are destined to be nomadic people's all the days of their lives. As the punishment for Cain's sin of killing his brother Abel.They are thus outlawed by God to be a 'wanderer, a fugitive. One story saw the first Gypsy as the son of Eve, from her mating with Adam after his death. The fact that such a person's offspring would not have survived the flood was conveniently gnored.Yet others have seen in Tubal Cain and his half-brother the ancestors of the Gypsies. As the Book of Genesis puts it (chapter iv verses 19-22): Lamech took unto him two wives and the name of the one was Adah and the name of the other Zlllah. And Adah borc Jubal. He was the father of all such as handle the harp and organ. And Zillah she also bore Tubal Cain, a instructor of every artificer in brass and iron.

2) Another story is that the Romanies are descended from Abraham's children by his second wife, Keturah. She bore him six children Zimran, Jokshan, Medan, Midian, Ishbah and Shuah (Gen xxv 1,2). Their descendants later accompanied the Israelites when they left Egypt for the Old Testament says:"and a mixed multitude went up also with the Children of Israel'. (Exodus xii.38.

3) Another story told is that the Gypsy bodyguard's of Christ, drank far too much wine and were thus too drunk and unable to defend him.

4) Gypsies were also accused of not giving shelter to the Virgin Mary and Her Child as they fled out of Egypt.

5) Gypsies were expelled from Egypt for trying to hide Jesus.

6)Following the crucifixion of Christ the Virgin Mary was consoled by a frog. The creature begged her not to cry and told her she must accept Her destiny. Mary found comfort in this and blessed the frog forever saying that wherever it lived the water would be pure and clean.!

7)The most familiar story is The legend of the 4th Nail is a story known by all Gypsies throughout the world. Many years ago a blacksmith was travelling through the holy land. Then one night, a Roman soldier came to his door and asked him for four long nails. The blacksmith agreed, and went to sleep and had a dream he dreamt of an old man, who warned him in his dream. The old man told him "Do not give the soldier four nails but make four nails and keep the fourth. Wrap them all in cloth, and only give him three."The next morning when the soldier arrived, the blacksmith did as the old man in his dream had suggested, he gave the soldier just three nails and he kept the fourth nail in his pocket. The fourth nail was destined to pierce Christ's heart and in exchange for sparing Jesus that horrific pain, God granted the blacksmith and all his descendants the right to roam all of the earth. The four nails in the dream represented those intended for Jesus crucifixion. The old man in the blacksmith's dream was God Almighty and the blacksmith was of course the Gypsy.

8) Another story relates to two Jewish brothers, Schmul and Rom-Schmul. The first of them exulted at the Crucifixion; the other would gladly have saved Our Lord from death, and, finding that impossible, did what he could stole one of

the four nails. So it came about that Christ's feet must be placed one over the other, and fastened with a single nail. And Schmul remained a Jew, but Rom-Schmul turned Christian, and was the founder of the Romani race. When they were just going to crucify Jesus, one of our women passed by, and she whipped up one of the nails they were going to use. She would have liked to steal all four nails, but couldn't. So it was always one. This explains the how's and whys of Jesus crucifixion with only three nails, a single one for the two feet. It explains why Jesus gave the Manousch leave to steal once every seven years."'

8) The Lithuanian Gypsies say that 'stealing has been permitted in their favour by the crucified Jesus, because the Gypsies, being present at the Crucifixion, stole one of the four nails. Hence when the hands had been nailed, there was but one nail left for the feet; and therefore this allowed them to steal, and is therefore not counted as being a sinful act.' They said that they were Egyptian penitents on a seven years' pilgrimage. That the Saracens had attacked them in Egypt, and, having surrendered to their enemies, they became Saracens themselves and denied Christ. Now, as a penance, they were ordered to travel for seven years without sleeping in a bed.

 9) Other Gypsies said that their exile was a punishment for the sin of having refused hospitality to Joseph and the Virgin Mary when they fled into Egypt with the newborn Christ-child to escape the anger of Herod. According to Aventinus they were condemned to travel about for seven years because their ancestors had refused to receive the Virgin and the Christ-child, the same is stated in Trausch's

Manuscript Strasburg Chronicle of the 16th century.

10) An old tradition asserts that Caspar, one of the three Magi, was himself a Gypsy, and that it was he who (as their ruler)first converted them to the Christian religion.

11) The Romani's also at one tine believed that they possessed a God-given right to beg, especially for clothing. For when the two Mary Saints, Mary Salome and Mary Jacoby, fled Palestine after the crucifixion of Christ, Sara, the dark Gypsy servant of Mary Jacoby, when the party arrived at a Provence fishing village in the wild Rhone delta, begged clothing and food from the fishermen and their wives, for the two saints. The boat left the shores of Palestine without Sara the Gypsy, but that Mary Jacoby hearing the lamentations of her loyal servant, cast her cloak upon the sea, and the Gypsy rode upon it to the boat.

12) Another tale is that of St. Peter travels with Christ as his servant, and they are often hard put to it for a livelihood. Christ sends St. Peter to find a sheep, and, bidding him cook it, goes to heal a sick person, who rewards him richly. Peter eats the sheep's liver and kidneys, and Christ, when he comes back, asks where the liver and kidneys are, 'for Jesus, who is God, knows everything.' Peter replying that the sheep had none, at the end of their meal Christ divides into three heaps the large sum received from the farmer whom he has healed. 'For whom are these three heaps?' asks Peter. 'The two first for each of us,' Christ answers, 'and the third for him who ate the liver and kidneys.' 'That was me,' says Peter. 'Very well,' Christ answers, 'take my share as well. I return to my own.' And then it is that Christ takes the cross, etc. 'You see,' the narrator ended, 'that it

was God Jesus who at the beginning of the world founded all the estates of men--first doctors, for he healed for money-- and who taught the Gypsies to beg and to go barefoot, whilst St. Peter instructed them how to deceive their like.'

13)Before Jesus was captured by the Roman soldiers he was being pursued, and the soldiers were asking everybody if they had seen Jesus. Everyone said no, except the beetle, who told the soldiers where Jesus had gone. As a result of this Jesus was captured and, as a punishment, he turned the beetle blind, so that he would not be able to help the Romans any further.

14) The Legend of Saint Barbarus, the Roma saint

A Bulgarian version of a 14th century legend tells of a well-known and popular saint in the Balkans which relates that Barbarus was from an Egyptian family. When he was 25 he joined pirates and with them participated in a raid on the Albanian coast in the region of Durazz. Only he lived he was also a secret Christian. Following his escape from the ships wreckage , he made his way to a forsaken place and did penance. The following year he was seen by a hunter who was captivated by his dark looks. He did not understand him, but he realised that he was a Christian. The hunter spoke of Barbarus to the large local group of Egyptians and they visited the Saint and spoke with him in their language.

Gypsy Storytellers were honoured by royal courts

During the Middle Ages the storytellers of these and the other various myths, legends tales and stories became honoured members of royal courts, or were seen in the market places. A storyteller, troubadour or minstrel was expected to know all the current tales, to be well informed on court scandal, or to know the healing power of herbs and medicines. He could quickly make up tales at a moment's notice ,recite or sing verses to a lord or lady, or to play two instruments at court.' Storyteller's journeyed across many lands, they would gather news and learn all the most popular tales swopping or exchanging these many stories. They often changed these tales too, which made it difficult to trace their actual origins.

Roma acknowledge themselves that they came from Egypt at sometime in their distant past. This story also played on legends of a common heritage of Gypsies and Jews, which were partly based on actual overlap of these two ethnic cultures in marginal trades and ghettos.This Egypt link with the Gypsies was very strong then too for Egypt itself being linked with the Hebrew bible stories. Such as Moses the Magician, Joseph dreams and interpretations, Daniel in the lion's den and the great strength of Samson. Not to mention the David and Goliath and David's music. There was also the wise Magi's who visited Jesus at his birth.Which gave many of them safe passage in a hostile Europe. The story claimed that they had been oppressed and forced into idol-worship in Egypt, and that the Pope had ordered them to roam, as penitence for their former lack of faith.

No doubt at the times of these Christian crusades to the

Holy lands and the prominence of the catholic faith in the world at this time in Methoni "Little Egypt" all played its part. Along with the importance of the Pope in the world. All of this no doubt went some ways to give the Gypsies a certain mystique and credibility in the world during these times.

It's said by some that the Gypsies too had themselves spread many of these myths and legends about themselves throughout Europe. That the greatest of these myth's or stories was presented in the so called forged papal letter, which stated that the Gypsies had been sentenced by the Pope for all their many sins to live as nomads, never to sleep in a bed. As well as such a story, the letter gave Instructions to those reading it to give the Gypsies food, money, and beer and to let them all off from paying any toll's and taxes.

The story is that when they arrived in Europe that they had asked to see the Pope and as a result of that meeting he gave them the freedom to travel throughout Europe after they had become catholic's. This was on the understanding that they would spend seven years as wanderers and they also told Emperor Sigismund and all of Europe, that they were destined to be wanderers for their sins. This acceptance of their ability to travel throughout the lands with approval of the Roman Catholic church was to be their greatest honour until in the early sixtenth century when the Pope took this right from them and denounced them from the church.

Gypsies had travelled a great deal throughout all of the countries of the middle east with many settling within them.

The Byzantines knew very well who the Athinganoi were, and they identified Roma with them. This fits well with the information we have about that particular group and with the description of the present-day Roma. There's not enough factual evidence however to prove that the Athingano were Roma, but in the same way there's none to say that they were not.

The Athinganoi were given such a name because of their ritual purity laws, which regarded impure any contact with other people, these resembled greatly the Romany Gypsies strict hygiene laws and practices. They practiced magic, soothsaying, snake-charming, etc, and their belief was a kind of "reformed" Judaism mixed with Christianity as they kept various Torah rules, believed in the Oneness of God, however they no longer practice circumcision but still perform baptism up to the present day.

*   *   *   *

CHAPTER TWO

Gypsies in Europe

"When Roma decided to leave the land in which they had dwelled for centuries, they had a defined goal to get to the Christian realm in the West. They departed hastily and hurried to reach the lands they were directed to, without staying for long time in the countries they found on their way". Sándor Avraham.

Europeans were aware of the presence of the Romanies and viewed them as a foreign, undesirable population.

"Full of riddles and confusion and surrounded by an aura of secrecy"-Shcherbakova-(1984).

Gypsy chronicles

I read those Gypsy chronicles when I was travelling down the line

the words were full of sorrow yet the writings were divine

when the world was full of freedom songs

when the water it flowed free

on the hill's across the common's in the land's of liberties

I chanced upon a wise man he wore a golden chain

he had the cross of Jesus and he sang that old refrain

his guitar it did hum then and his melodies were free

he sang of peace and faith there in the seasons neath the tree

Oh the stories that he told me of good and bad and more

with diction made of harmonies stolen from lifes shores

the trees did stand forever and their boughs were full of bloom

to where the heather blessed the valleys and the young gals once did swoon

For lover's they were courted there and the grass was tall and green

where the honey flowed daily in the bosom's of the moon

the stars came out each evening and the peddler sold his wares

Johnny onion rode his bicycle with that old string chain on the frame

The wine did flow there freely and the gals did dance and sway

where the river's bent their journeys and the troubadour did play

where we boys spent many happy hours singing in the hay.

Ray Wills

The first Gypsies to arrive in Europe claimed to be the Christian nobility of Egypt, who had abandoned all of their possessions in order to keep their faith when the Muslims gained power. "Egyptians" as a name was possibly brought to Dubrovnik by Italians where together with the former name Jedupi for Gypsies the name "Egyptians" started to be used.Usually Roma were called by different names according to their immediate provenance in Western Europe the first Roma were known as "Bohemians", "Hungarians", while

Arabs called them "Zott", meaning "Jat", because they came from the Indus Valley.

In their appearance and in their lifestyles the Roma were genetically similar to other European's and their arrival from northern India no doubt happened a great deal earlier than was originally thought, David Comas stated "Now we can see that they arrived in one single wave from the north-west of India around1,500 years ago".

The first and to date only reliable account of the origin of word Gypsy for the members of "specific" group, dates back to 1068. For it was then that the Georgian monah St George Antonski, from the monastery of Iviron(Greece)reports to his people that on the mountain of Athos in the time between 1001 and 1026 a group of "Athiganos" arrived.It's interesting that these very first accounts of "Gypsy royalty" in the 11th century continued with such accounts of Gypsy kings and nobility travelling the world right up until the late 16th and early 17th century.

In 1332, a Franciscan monk from Ireland visited the island of Crete. While there, he wrote this description of what he called "the descendants of Cain," whom he met outside the town of Heraklion: "They rarely, or ever remain in one place more than thirty days; but ever, as though bearing God's curse with them, after the thirtieth day, go like vagabonds and fugitives from one locality to another, in the manner of the Arabs, with small, oblong, black, low tents, and run from cavern to cavern, because the place where they establish themselves becomes in that space of time so full of vermin and filth that it is no longer habitable." This was the first written account in Western Europe of the people who would come to be known as Gypsies, or Romani.

This nobility and story of an Egyptian origin had apparently appeared to convince Europeans for numerous decades until the early sixteenth century by which time the church were also persuaded and convinced these papers and stories were actually somehow fraudulent. In 1564 Pope Pius V expelled all Gypsies from the Roman Catholic church this was undoubtebly a major event and a means of branding them as non christian.So turning the general public against them as a wicked peoples.It was then that the mainly roman catholic church isolated its followers from having anything to do with these so called Gypsies. It's also evident that masses of them were used as slave labour and false stories about them were prevalent as declaring them an underclass.

THE "LITTLE EGYPT" CONNECTION

Gypsies have always claimed that they came from a homeland which they referred to or called "Little Egypt". There have been lengthily debates throughout recent time as to whether or not such a place actually existed.There are many who are of the opinion that these early Gypsies reference to "Little Egypt" was to their last main settlement place or campsite. In England such places were in the forests.

Little Egypt Race

In times of Knights Templar, Richard Lionheart and the Turks

In our community shanty town by the little remote seaport

We lived a life simple with families and kin

we entertained the Holy pilgrims and allotted for our sins

We danced sang and entertained

with our fancy clothes and trinkets we held the reins

we entertained the pilgrims from the Holy lands again

we were a Gypsy race and we worked in sun and rain

so proud of our skills in smithery and games

In our Little Egypt on the Greek highway

where Christian pilgrims stopped to rest and pray

we were a race of Gypsy grace

afore we left our homeland space

to seek our freedoms on the distant plains.

Ray Wills

In those early days leading up to the 15th Century there were many regions frequented by Gypsies which were christened "Little Egypt" this could well have been because of the Gypsies fertility. This too may well have been the case for Methoni, Mythoi,Epirus in Greece.The term "Little Egypt" may well also have been another name or reference for the land of Palestine.

By the 15th century these same Gypsies tribes made regular pilgrimages to Rome, various holy places in Europe and even to Jerusalem too.To be able to travel such distances with thousands of members in their caravan entourage and to survive it's obvious that they no doubt were not poor. Despite some of the many accounts depicted of them over the centuries by numerous scholars and commentators as vagabonds, thieves and being shabbily dressed. However very many of their leaders, Kings, Queens, Princes, Dukes, Counts, Earls and noblemen were said to be richly dressed in fine clothes with plenty of gold as had been told in numerous accounts over the centuries.

Royal Blood

Royalty blood riding through the plains

misplaced forgotten people there they go again

gold and silver pots and pans donkeys mules misplaced man

trinkets prophecies in biblical sets

Casanova lovers' violas, accordions and castanets

kings and Queens, Counts and Dames

caravan people, black and free biblical names

Solomon Levi histories

Persian cloth and silk from the east

Christian teachings and Roma speech

place those cards and roll that dice

fortune tellers and storytellers in the night

crowns and paupers, entourage free

papal letters, sanctuary

In Rome with the Pope, holy lands pilgrims eloped

Turkish warriors swords and shame

Gypsy brethren know their name

penances and Christian oaths

noblemen escorts in bridal betroth's

seeking truth and liberties

brother band across the seas.- Ray Wills

In 1350 Ludoliphus of Sachem also told of a people with a unique language whom he called Mandapolos (meaning prophet fortune teller). In those times Gypsies were in Thrace, Macedonia, Greece, Yugoslavia and Rumania.

In 1384 Leonardo di Niccolo Frescobaldi writes that beyond the city walls he caught sight of a number of "Romnites" who he imagined were sinners repenting their deeds.

Grippe wrote in two centuries later in 1530:"Those people (the Gypsies) coming from a region lying between Egypt and Ethiopia".

The main reason for the general public at that time verbally attacking and taking it out on Roma Gypsies, was to punish them for the various kinds of entertainment which some Romajati (castes) or families provided. Entertainments which were frowned on, such as snake charming; performing bears and palm reading, or fortune telling. Such practices and entertainments though popular at the time amongst many was condemned by the orthodox catholic church; being connected with heretic deviation from true Christian orthodoxy, however the results of these policies were contradictory.Descendants of Chus, son of Ham, son of Noah, still bear the mark of the curse of their progenitor".

LITTLE EGYPT – Gyppe near Methoni

Gyppe or "Little Egypt" was a large Roma settlement which was situated close to the city of Methoni on the western coast of Peloponnesus. The city of Methoni with its natural port was situated halfway between Venice and Jaffa, and therefore it was a welcome ideal place for pilgrims to rest on their way to and from the Holy Land.

A Byzantine author Mazarus in 1416 said that the Peloponnas was inhabitated by seven principle nations and that one of these was that of the "Egyptians".

It was first recorded that there was a large population of these people at the seaport of Modon on the most popular route to the Holy Land. They had settled in the so called Gypsy Quarter, which was a tent city just outside the city walls itself and which was often referred to as being "Little Egypt". There are numerous particular accounts of this so called Gypsy homeland.This "Little Egypt" (as recorded in 1483)consisted of some 300 families probably around 2000 people in total. Konrád Grunenberg in 1486 also mentions three hundred Roma dwellings in Methoni.

Bernard von Breydenbach wrote that "In the surroundings of the city there are many hovels numbering about three hundred which are inhabited by poor people resembling Ethiopians, black and unattractive." He adds that in Germany there were people called Saracens who claimed they came from Egypt. However he said that in reality they actually came from "Gyppe", not far from Methoni and were spies and traitors. With him travelled the painter Eberhard Reuwich who, in 1468, had originally drawn the Greek city of

Methoni with a Roma settlement.

In 1491 Dietrich von Schachten describes their gypsy homes "Beyond the city walls of Methoni, on a hill near the walls, there are many poor small hovels, homes of Zigeuner, as they're called in Germany. They are very poor people, predominantly blacksmiths. They work in a sitting position. In front of them they have a hollow in which they maintain a fire, and when these men or women have bellows in their hands, they are quite satisfied. They fan the fire with bellows that are so wretched that it is indescribable, and they produce nails of very good quality". In 1497 Arnold von Harf writes "These people came from a land called Gyppe, lying about sixty kilometres from Methoni". "The Turkish ruler occupied it sixty years ago, but many noblemen and lords refused to submit to his will and escaped to our country, to Rome, to the Holy Father, looking to him for safety and support"."Upon their request he dispatched letters to the Roman emperor and all the princes of the empire with a recommendation that they guarantee the safety of movement and support of these people because they were expelled from their land for their Christian faith".The population falling to roughly half by two decades later. During the battles with the Turks, many Christians migrated from threatened areas to Europe along with the Roma and the inhabitants of Methoni, which culminated with the conquest of Methoni in 1500.And by 1519 there were just some thirty huts still remaining there.Jacques le Saige recorded that "On the island of Zakynthos, there are Roma blacksmiths who work in the manner of those in Methoni".

In Byzantium the word "great" meant a land lying

outside of its sphere of power, while areas lying on the land or close to the border of the empire were given the adjective, "little"."Great Moravia", in use by the Byzantine emperor Porfyrogennetos therefore was not great itself in area, but it lay beyond the Byzantine border.The name "Little Egypt" arose similarly, for example, to the name "Little Armenia" (a land in Byzantium where Armenians lived). Therefore "Little Egypt" was a place in Byzantium where "Egyptians" or people thought to be Egyptians, most probably Roma lived. Although it's still not too clear why that locality itself was called "Little Egypt". Whether because to the district of Gyppe or just because these "Egyptians" lived there. Or could it be due to it being before the Roma settlement, real Egyptians lived there? Or did the place (places) get the name from Roma who were also called, among other names, Egyptians?. "Little Egypt"was also the name used for the part of Pelopennesos Imarin Asia Minor or an area around Antioch Antalia, Persia.I recently had a discussion on the subject of the origin of the Gypsies and the "Little Egypt" location with Roy Mc Donald who has traveller roots he had spent some time in India as a British service man during WW11. He said that he recalls that at that time 1939-45 there was also actually a district of that name in India where the Gypsy community lived.

A very recent political movement, "Egyptians of the Balkans", claim that four centuries before Christ, their ancestors had emigrated from Egypt to Greece and founded a region called "Little Egypt "and that from there they migrated to Macedonia and Kosovo. These people do not speak Romani and also saw themselves as a different group from the Romani's who live in the same regions.

Gypsy Pilgrims and Royal Caravans

The Gypsies came to Europe with tales that they were fleeing from the Holy wars and Holy land's and that they were the wanderers similar to those of the Cananites in the bible.They said that they came from "Little Egypt" and that they were of "Royal blood". These stories gave them a certain amount of respectability in the eyes of the law, the church and the state at that time and gave them safe passage through the lands. This was particularly so after enduring so many years of ill treatment throughout their journeys. Just as there had earlier been in the early ages of Saxon and Norman England with its people of royal birth, Kings, and Queens, lords and ladies, dukes, barons, etc. So it was with the Gypsies when they arrived, where each clan had their own royalty of Kings, Queens, lords, dukes,barons, counts, etc. Which gave them some authority and an air of respectability and importance, both in their clan and particularly so in the wider community.

In many areas where they presented themselves as pilgrims, Gypsies were said to be protected by a letter from the Emperor Sigismund and King of Hungary and Bohemia, the son of the Emperor Charles 1V. Similiar to the modern day passport.Sigismund was known as being the great leader who had taken all the numerous armies of Christendom on a Crusade against the Turks in 1396.These Gypsies began their westward journeys, travels or pilgrimages throughout the next centuries.

Gypsies and accounts of their journeys in the 15th and 16th centuries.

There were very many accounts of the gypsies journeys from 1417 to 1422 led by one Dukes Andreas and Michael of "Little Egypt" presumably his brother along with Counts and numerous royal leaders.The following are some of these...

At Luneburg; in 1417 and 1418 the monks Cornerius and Rufus of Lubeck, tells of Gypsies they saw, a band of 'Secani' or Tsigans, "there was said to be some 300 to 400 in number, besides children and infants in Germany 'from Eastern parts' or 'from Tartary". Refering to their "most ugly faces, black like those of Tartars." "Then they went onto Hamburg, Lübeck, Wismar, Rostock, Stralsund, and Greifswald.

At their head rode the Dukes Andrew and Michael along with many Counts, all of whom were richly dressed, giving the impression of wealth and respectability with silver belts, and leading like nobles dogs of chase". Although their followers were far from well dressed being a shabbily and a motley crew with their women and children following behind them in wagons.The gypsy 'nobles' stayed in the local hostelry, whilst the others camped or dossed wherever they could find shelter. Their routes took them through Hungary and Germany, Westphalia, in the free cities of the north, and onto the shores of the Baltic. They then turned south to Leipzig and Frankfurt-am-Main and then entered Switzerland.(Kenrick 1972:19).

In 1538 the Swiss chronicler Stumpf described their arrival in Zurich in 1418. Being some 14,000 Gypsies who supposedly had been driven out of Egypt as Christians and were completing a seven year pilgrimage. These people apparently carried a lot of gold and silver with them and it was said that they did not behave as thieves.On August 22, 1419,"Saracens", led by "Duke André of Little Egypt" appeared in Chatillon-en-Dombes.Then in January 1420, "Duke Andreas" and 100 companions arrived in Brussels."

Then they went onto Hamburg, Lübeck, Wismar, Rostock, Stralsund, and Greifswald. At their head rode the Dukes Andrew and Michael along with many Counts, all of whom were richly dressed, giving the impression of wealth and respectability with silver belts, and leading like nobles dogs of chase". "Although their followers were far from well dressed being a shabbily and a motley crew with their women and children following behind them in wagons.The gypsy 'nobles' stayed in the local hostelry, whilst the others camped or dossed wherever they could find shelter".

Their routes took them through Hungary and Germany, Westphalia, in the free cities of the north, and onto the shores of the Baltic. They then turned south to Leipzig and Frankfurt-am-Main and then entered Switzerland. In March of the same year, their arrival is reported in Deventer (the Netherlands). These people were said to have practiced palmistry and necromancy and at Sisteron in Provence as 'Saracens' they got large rations from the terrified townsfolk.

Lord Andreas, Duke of Little Egypt, and a hundred men, women, and children, came to Daventer in the low countries. Here they received free lodgings, food and money gifts staying at The Gypsy House in Deventer where the aldermen had to pay 19 florins 10 placks for their bread, beer, herrings, and straw, as well as for cleaning out the barn in which they lay.

At Tournay in 1421 'Sir Miquiel, Prince of Latinghem in Egypt,' received twelve gold pieces, with bread and a barrel of beer. Arrivals are reported in Bruges and Mons, the latter had even been visited twice. On October 8, 80 people, led by "Duke Andreas of Little Egypt", arrived, and produced a letter of safe conduct issued by Emperor Sigismund.

On October 20, a second group followed, whose leader was called Michael and who claimed to be the brother of the aforementioned Andreas. The Chronica di Bologna tells how on 'the 18th of July in 1422 a "Duke of Egypt", Duke Andres, arrived at Bologna, with women, children, and men from his own country with up to maybe a hundred in number.His wife told fortunes and it was said that she could read destiny,fortell the future, divine the present and number of children as well as the qualities of a woman."She told true for so many things".

The story goes that this Duke Andre passed through Bologna and Forli with a large group of Gypsies, declaring that he was on his way to see the Pope. When they arrived at Bologna, they had been journeying for five years with more than half of them dying on the way. They had a mandate from the King of Hungary, the Emperor, permitting them during these seven years to thieve, wherever they might go, without being accountable to the law. This Gypsy 'Duke' told that he had forfeited his lands and possessions to the King of Hungary for having renounced his Christian faith, and that he was obliged to wander for seven years before seeing the Pope in Rome.

Duke Andrea having denied the Christian faith, said that the King of Hungary (the Emperor Sigismund) had taken possession of his lands and person. Then he had told the King that he wished to return to Christianity, and he had been baptised with about four thousand men; and it is said that those who refused baptism were put to death. After the King of Hungary had thus taken and rebaptized them, he commanded them to travel about the world for seven years, to go to Rome to see the Pope, and then to return to their own country.

Another who arrived in Spain well before the main party of Gypsies arrived told them that he was Count Thomas of Sabba.

Some Romanies had migrated from Persia for a chronicler for a Parisian journal described them as"being dressed in a manner that the Parisians considered shabby", and reports that the Church instructed them to leave there due to their fortune telling practices.They journeyed to the German speaking area calling themselves Sinti, which is thought to have its origin in Sindh Pakistan.They then went into countries throughout the length and breadth of Europe where they were seen as being royalty by the authorities, church and state and treated both favourably and accordingly.

Many years later other such groups also visited the Low Countries, where they were said to have astonished the citizens of Arras. At Macon it was explained to them that they were on the kings land and that their imperial letters of protection were now of no value. The ancient Greeks and Romans spoke of these so called travelling Arabic tribes who frightened the population in the bordering lands of their empire Sarakene.

In 1497 Arnold von Harf writes "We headed for the outskirts". "Many poor, black, naked people live there". "Their dwellings are small homes with roofs covered with reeds; altogether about three hundred families live in them". "They are called Gypsies, known in our country as pagans from Egypt travelling through our lands". "They work at many trades such as, for example, shoemaking, cobbling and smithery". "It was very strange to see an anvil right on the floor"."A blacksmith sat at it in the same way that tailors sit at work in our country". "Near him, also on the ground, sat his wife, and she spun so that there would be fire between them". "Two pairs of leather bellows half buried in the ground by the fire lay next to them". "From time to time, the spinning woman picked up one pair of bellows from the ground and worked them. Thus a stream of air moved along the ground to the fire and the blacksmith was able to work".

During the battles with the Turks, many Christians had fled and migrated from threatened areas to Europe along with the Roma and the inhabitants of Methoni, which culminated with the conquest of Methoni in 1500. Around 1501 Gypsy bands were regularly seen travelling in the south of Russia; others were crossing from Poland to the Ukraine

Count Antoine Gagino of "Little Egypt" arrived in Denmark in 1505 on a Scottish vessel. He had been expressly recommended to King John of Denmark by James IV of Scotland. Then on 29th of September 1512, a Count Antonius, who is most probably the same person, entered Stockholm to the great astonishment of the people there.

Shortly after in 1518 Jacques le Saige recorded that "On the island of Zakynthos, there are Roma blacksmiths who work in the manner of those in Methoni". "There we saw an admirable thing, for a blacksmith who produces nails and horseshoes forges right on the street and sits on the ground like tailors in our country"; "the said blacksmith has a small stone near which he piles up coal and lights a fire". "This stone is about two feet long and one foot high. It protects the hearth. In the centre it has an opening and it also has a small iron pipe, to which are attached two pieces of skin not sewn together, and then there is some kind of helper or servant who holds this skin on one end and raises it and lets it go, and a stream of air fans the coal, which is very admirable to see and hard to describe". "Now there are so many people who pursue this profession and they are so skilful".

Gypsies expelled by the Holy Roman Empire and the Holy Catholic church

Previously before the 16th century all Gypsies had been expelled from Germany by the Holy Roman Empire for espionage, and Elector Achilles of Brandenburg had banned the Sinti from his land. Any non Sinti had the right to hunt Gypsies, flog them, incarcerate or kill them, many other countries soon followed suit with similar actions with Switzerland bringing in the death penalty.

When Janos Zápolyai took the Hungarian throne by Ottoman support in 1528, he rewarded his Roma loyalists with the renewal of the "ancient Gypsy liberties" granted by his predecessors. Roma musicians were highly praised by nobility and members of the court at that time.In 1530 the "Egyptians" that danced before the King in Holyrood House and in 1540 gave mocking Romani noinnies de guerre to the officers of the law, Borrows called these "Real Gypsies of the old order."

In a letter from 1543 from the Transylvanian court of Queen Isabella, wife of Janos Zápolyai, the writer states that "the most excellent Egyptian musicians play, the descendants of the Pharaohs'". He goes on to observe that the "Gypsy" cimbalom players "do not pluck the strings with their fingers but hit it with a wooden stick and sing to it with all their might".

In France The Bourgeois of Paris Journal, recorded a visit of these people. Describing in detail how multitudes "from Paris, Pa-I ixova Sainct Denis, and from the neighbourhood of Paris flocked to see them. And it is true that the children, boys and girls, were as clever as could be". "And most or nearly all had both ears pierced, and in each ear a silver ring, or two in each, and they said it was a sign of nobility in their own country". "The men were very black, their hair was frizzled ; the women, the ugliest that could be seen, and the blackest" "All had their faces covered with wounds, hair black as a horse's tail, for sole dress an old blanket, very coarse, and fastened on the shoulder by a band of cloth or a cord, and underneath a shifl, for all covering". "In short, they were the poorest creatures ever seen in France in the memory of man". "They applied themselves to metallurgy being tinkers, furriers, braziers, and goldsmiths; the women told fortunes and gave charms to avert the evil eye".

Hermann Conerus stated that "They travelled in band's and camped at night in the field's outside of the town's"."They were great thieves, especially their women, and several of them in various places were seized and put to death. Various chronicles at that time declared Gypsies as "useless rascals who wander about in our day, and of whom the most worthy is a thief, for they live solely for stealing." I was noted that these Gypsies wore rag's that resembled blanket's, but were well rigged out in gold and silver jewellery. The Gypsy women were known as palm reader's and petty thieves, many were suspected of sorcery and town's throughout Europe actually began to hand out money to these Gypsies to encourage them to go away as soon as they began to appear on their borders.

Gypsies began to appear in Norway in 1544, but they were supposedly prisoners whom the English had got rid of by forcibly embarking them.

Then in 1564 Pope Pius V expelled all gypsies from the Roman Catholic church this was undoubtebly a major event and a means of branding them as non christian.This was particularly so after the Roman Catholic church denounced them. So turning the general public against them as a wicked peoples.In 1603 an Order in Council was made for the transportation of Romanichal from England to Newfoundland. Many travelling folki went from Dorset docks at Poole and Weymouth. As it was a great trading route at the time and made many local traders rich then and during during the Georgian age.

Gypsies in search for employment and their continual harrassment.

During these times Romanichals travelled around for work, usually following set routes and set stopping places (called 'atching tans') which have been established for hundreds of years.

A lot of traditional stopping places were established before land ownership changed and any land laws were in place. Many of these Atching tans were established by feudal land owners in the Middle Ages, when Romani would provide agricultural or manual labour services in return for lodgings and food.

Many Roma in central Hungary were employed or conscripted as smiths for the Turkish army. Others were musicians, barbers, tentmakers, messengers or executioners.

During the times of the plaguesin Europe, Gypsies were eclared to be in league with theTurks(and by default, with theDevil).'This was due to the fact that they never suffered from the plague itself which was no doubt due to their own strict hygiene rules. At this time settled people in Western Europe rarely bathed and even when they did there was no attempts at separating 'clean' from dirty used water. This was the usual practice of the population of the settled community at that time in Europe until the germ theory of disease was eventually fully understood and accepted. At that time Gypsies travelled but also stayed in inns, however the new anti-settlement laws banned this and so they took to the road.

The majority of settled people as always viewed all Gypsies with fear and suspicion and up to, during and after the middle ages.So turning the general public against them as a wicked peoples.Gypsies also earned the reputation for possessing occult powers and throughout Europe were discriminated against and all manner of acts were conducted against them. Many false stories were told about the Gypsies, most of them not at all complimentary. A Bologna chronicle account reads: "Amongst those who wished to have their fortunes told, few went to consult without having their purse stolen"."The women of the band wandered about the town, six or eight together; they entered the houses of the citizens and told idle tale's, during which some of them laid hold of whatever could be taken"."In the same way they visited the shop's under the pretext of buying something, but one of them would steal."

Miguel de Cervantes (1613)wrote the book" La

Gitanilla",which supported the common feeling during that period that Gypsies were a threat to public safety. It reads "It seems that the Gypsies came into this world to be thieves; they are born to thieving parents, they grow up with thieves, they study to be thieves, and in the end, they turn out to be nothing but thieves; and their desire to steal and stealing are inseparable qualities that only disappear with death".

Phillip IV(1635)issued a royal decree demanding that all unemployed Gypsy men between the ages of twenty and fifty years be sent to the galleys.He later changed this somewhat to state that all Gypsy men had to row in the galleys, saying:"There is a great need for galley men and rowers, and everywhere there is an excess of this odious race, who are all spies, thieves, and liars."

 In 1726 in São Paulo, Ciganos were given 24 hours to leave since they were "harmful to the population because they walked around organizing games and other disturbances." (Teixeira 2007a: 33). In 1727 the bishop of Rio de Janeiro complained of Ciganos in Minas "performing immoral operas and comedies that insult the sacred teachings of the Holy Church" (Borges 2007: 28). As a source of goods and animals, Ciganos were tolerated by the wealthy, especially outside large cities, while Ciganos sought out their protection in order to be able to camp or to earn their living.

The prince of Moldovia Constantine in 1776 remarked, "In some parts Gypsies have married Moravian women, and also Moravian men have taken in marriage Gypsy girls, these people have bound themselves to spend all their lives with the Gypsies".In 1780, anti Gypsy legislation had been gradually introduced.

Heinrich Moritz Gottlieb Grellmann, (1787), noted that Gypsies were "an eastern people" and he went on to comment: "they do not seem to have considered, how extravagant a surmise it is, to believe a whole language, an invention, that too of people rude, uncivilized and hundreds of miles distant from each other".Grellman traced much of the language spoken by these European Gypsies back to roots or origins in 'Hindustan.'

By 1790 the King of Prussia had decided that all Gypsies should be conscripted into the military. Very soon after all other European countries followed suit, and so it is that Gypsy men have since served as soldier's for every country in Europe.

At this time European governments attempted to control and limit the presence of Roma, by controlling their movement and often expelling them all together. The first anti Gypsy legislation was introduced in Moraviaand Bohemia , shortly after a series of fires in Prague were blamed on the Gypsies and Ferdinand I ordered Romani's to be expelled.

The Diet of Augsburg declared that "whoever kills a Gypsy, will be guilty of no murder". However the killings which followed as a result prompted the government of that time to take immediate action and they "forbid the drowning of Romani women and children". In France those Gypsies caught were sentenced to three years on the galley's and in Spain they ordered all of the Gypsies out of the country, under penalty of death, except for those who would settle in one place, dress as Spaniard's, and stop speaking in their own common language.

Wherever they went as a result of the Catholic churchs declaration in this century they were often seen as being "a godless and wicked peoples". Gypsy men in Germany could be given life imprisonment, whilst children of Gypsy parents were taken away from them and put into so called " Good Christian homes".

 Though this was not always the case for in some countries such as Hungary,Gypsies were treated with courtesy and much respect. Here they were declared royal servants and were very highly valued as smith's and makers of fine weaponry and called "Pharaoh's people". In a letter from the queen's court in Vienna it stated "here the most excellent Egyptian musician's play". In Provence they were welcomed and were first called "Bohemian's" and many people went to visit them to have their fortunes told and many were hired by nobles to attend to their horses. An English statute of that time, gave the Romani's special privileges which other nomadic people lacked, then France passed a similar law. Often these wandering Gypsies were led by famous Gypsy leaders or families such as the Coopers, Boswells and the Gritano Conde.

In Spain the nobility had protected the Gypsies with their Gypsy women greatly admired for their beauty and seductive ways, whilst Gypsy men were seen as being excellent horse men.Life for the majority of Gypsies in Europe however had over the years been very difficult and had not improved a great deal, with many being branded, expelled, executed, or hanged without trial.

In Bohemia and Moravisa they had their right or left ear cut off and in many places they were still publicly flogged for supposedly lying, divination, magic and casting spells.

Whilst their Gypsy women were employed as spinner's, their boy's as factory workers and the men were also employed in mine's or shipyards'.

Many Irish Travellers had also immigrated, like the Romnichels, from the mid to late nineteenth century, they specialised in the horse and mule trade, as well as in itinerant sales of goods and services. The literature then also refers to this group as Irish Traders or, sometimes, Tinkers and their ethnic language is referred to in the literature as Irish Traveller Cant.

THE GYPSY SLAVE TRADE IN EUROPE

Many Gypsies were now taken as slaves to work the galleys or sold to the many plantation owners to work on their many plantations in the new worlds.

The Romany people had been flogged, burned with lye and made to wear a three-cornered spiked iron collar. Scouts were probably sent across the channel from France even before 1400,which is the date suggested by M. Paul Bataillard.

Slaves and Masters

The heat of the sun and the scorching G on my brow

the cutting of flesh from the irons and chains

the call of the block masters echo refrains

the ships standing by with their sails and their dames

The plantation journeys and the galleys and rum

the price of the slaves and their freedoms to come

the echoes of bargaining and the masters with pen

their waistcoats and breeches and the sun on the decks

The sweat and the pain of the shackles and holds

the cries of the young men and the wails of the old

the watches and purses all to declare a bargain to board

to cries of despair

the handshakes of gentlemen with coins of the dust

black cosseted Gypsies with no one to trust

The hurt and the tears and the screech of the gulls

the histories of mankind without any love

the trades and the barter and the tragedy blocks

all for the Lords and their rubies and luck

far distant journeys and a Gypsies Kushti Bok.

Ray Wills

Many Gypsies were marked with a G on their forehead, as a way of Governments attempts to control and limit their presence they were persecuted, victimized, murdered, deported and taken as slaves. Others had a V on their breasts.

During these times Gypsy slaves were considered the personal property of their masters or owners. They were permitted to put them to work, selling them or else exchange them for other goods or commodities. The slave masters was allowed to punish their slaves physically, through beatings or imprisonment, but he or she did not hold the power of life and death over them. Their only obligation was to clothe and feed the slaves who worked and lived at their manors.

Free men

They hung the poor Gypsies or sold them as slaves
they tortured them daily from birth to their graves
they sent them to prison and to the U.S of A
then they gave them some land but made them work for their pay

They marked them with signs on their head and their breasts
just because they were different and not like the rest
with rings on their fingers and dark shiny hair
their music was rich and they went with the fairs

They gave them sites in the war years when they fought for this land
then they moved them on with after their ponies and bands
they made them take houses and give up their ways
to live in this country for the rest of their days.

Ray Wills

The usual treatment of slaves, Djuvara notes, was demeaning, and local people believed the masters words that "one could not get anything (out of the Gypsies) without using a whip."Gypsy slaves could be exchanged for animals such as pigs. They were made into clowns but were also status symbols. A defective Gypsy slave could even be exchanged for even a jar of honey. They were passed on from father to son and some traders even sold up to 500 of their slaves at a time with many young Gypsy girls being used as property and often such Gypsies were treated worse than animals.

The social standing of a slave master was often rated by the number and kinds of skilled slaves which he possessed, those most in demand were cooks, musicians and embroiderers many of these were prized and fetched higher prices. The social prestige demonstrated the high status of the boyar families. In the 1300s thousands of these Gypsy families had been donated as gifts by the noblemen to the many catholic monasteries in Serbia. 1428 Prince VLad of Wallaice transported 12000 persons who appearance were gypsies from Bulgaria for slave labour

Earlier in 1430 17000 had been transported to Maldac by Stephen the Great for slave labour. A century later in 1547 Edward V1 of England gave orders to brand Gypsies with a V enslaving them for 2 years and if they ran off he made them slaves for life. In 1564 Pope Pius V expelled all Gypsies from the Roman Catholic church this was undoubtebly a major event and a means of branding them as non christian.So turning the general public against them as a wicked peoples.

Oliver Cromwell shipped Romanichals slaves to the American southern plantations and English Romanies were owned by freed black slaves inJ amaica,Barbados,Cuba, and Louisana.

By the first half of the 18th century, a regular slave was valued at around 20–30lei, a cook would be 40 lei. The slave-owners also separated Roma couples from one another when selling one of the spouses. This practice was later banned by Constant inein 1763 and discouraged by the Orthodox Church, which decreed in 1766 that "although they are called Gypsies, (i.e. slaves), the Lord created them and it is indecent to separate them like cattle".Nevertheless, the practice of splitting married spouses was still common in the 19th century.

The Austrian authorities in Bukovina were alarmed to see that the newly settled refugees made a habit of beating their slaves in public, on the streets of Czernowitz.As a result they issued an order specifically banning such practices. A dispute followed, after which the slave owners or boyars, received permission to carry on with the beatings, as long as they exercised these beatings on private property.

Englands -The Sherborne Mercury, reported in April 1833 '-

Petitions to both Houses of Parliament for the abolition of Negro Slavery are lying in the town for signature'.

In fact two petitions were sent one from Lyme generally, and another from 'the ladies of Lyme Regis'. 'The female inhabitants of Charmouth' also sent one. William Pinney, MP for Lyme from 1832, came from the Pinney family of West Dorset who had been involved with the West Indies, sugar production and slavery from the 17th century. The family received more than thirty thousand pounds in compensation when slavery was abolished in 1834. However the freed slaves did not receive any compensation at all.

In Romania in 1839 there were many slave holdings, with up to a quarter of a million Tigani Gypsy slaves. They worked as groom's, coachmen, cook's, barber's, tailor's, ferrier's, comb maker's, and domestic servants. The slave owners could kill them without thought or fear of reprisal.

One reformer commented on the slavery which he had witnessed in Iasi:"human being's wearing chain's on their arms and legs, other's with iron clamp's round their forehead's"."Cruel flogging's and other punishment's, such as starvation, being hung over smoking fire's, being thrown naked into a frozen river and children torn from the breast's of those who brought them into the world, and sold like cattle".The French writer Felix Colson, on his visits to Romanian slave holdings in 1839, remarked of some of the Gypsy slaves he saw : "Their skins are hardly brown but blond and beautiful". Lighter-skinned Romani girls in Slovakia, noted for their beauty, were given the nickname "Papin" or "Papinori" (white goose). It is well recognized that not all Roma are dark skinned many are fair haired with light blue distinctive eyes.

The first Romanian statesmen argued for gypsy slaves freedom and these were eventually freed in 1848. Though they were still called Ţigani and continued living in their poverty stricken shanty slums on the landowners' estates. Kelderars (Kotlyars) are Romanian Gypsies. They made caldrons and baking trays on mobile anvils or mended leaking dishes. Initially they travelled through Danube principalities, but after 1856 headed to neighbouring countries. Soon Kotlyar taborers arrived in Poland, Russia, France, Spain and England.The Roma had been enslaved for five centuries in Romanian util their total abolition in 1864.

The Roma slaves were not included in the tax censuses and as such, there are no reliable statistics about them, the exception being the slaves owned by the state.

Nevertheless, there were several 19th century estimates of their number. According to Djuvara, the estimates for the slave population tended to gravitate around 150,000-200,000 persons, which he notes was equivalent to 10% of the two countries' population.At the time of the eventual abolition of slavery, there were between 200,000 and 250,000 Roma, in the two principality or some 7% of the total population.

Travelling through Minas Gerais in the late 1880s, Gypsy James Wells bought mules from a settled Cigano owning a fazenda, whose relatives used it to camp temporarily. 71 Ciganos travelled in groups composed of several families. When they came close to towns they were often chased away, accused of disturbing public order and stealing slaves and animals. When travelling through Ceará in 1828, Patroni was approached by a group of Ciganos. Thinking he was being assaulted, he told the Ciganos he was a judge and immediately "all of them at the same time saluted me with bows, and pleaded that I provide them with patronage in the town of Icó, where they were going to trade" (Patroni 1851: 44).

Arch Duke Joseph in the 1800s had made it his life's work to compile a detailed study of the Gypsies with an estimated 80,00 in Hungary alone. He gave himself the title "The Royal Gypsy" and supported the theory of Grellman which was that the Gypsies had their origins in Hindustan. "They call themselves Christians but remain heathen preferring and cherishing the traditions of "The Fire Worshippers"." Which they seem to have once been."-(The Aberystwyth Observer 4th January 1890).

Caldcleugh concludes that "this wandering people, whether gold washers in Hungary and Transylvania, tinkers in England, or horse-dealers in Brazil, preserve a character for duplicity and cunning which pre-eminently distinguishes them above their fellow men".

In Victor Hugo's Hunchback of Notre Dame the heroine, Esmeralda, is stolen as a baby, only to grow up into one of the most seductive Gypsy women in European literature. Such enticing Ciganas, at least partially influenced by the European (French) Romanticism, had also appeared in Brazilian theatre at the end of the eighteenth century (Donovan 1992).

The Khashtalo Gypsies who for centuries had lived on church land were now unemployed and homeless and so they began returning to their former nomadic travelling life. Though still not straying too far outside the monastery gates which had been their home for so long. Following their freedom these former monastery slaves settled on the plateau of the village Tiesuri, known as Golisheni meaning "village of the naked". For these were the poorest and most disadvantaged class of Gypsy who travelled searching for food. The government's effort to settle this new and growing population of homeless Gypsies lead to small numbers being invited to settle close to villages. Here they worked in the fields of local landowners or sold items which they had crafted and collected wild fruits, nuts and berries gathered from the nearby forest.

Gypsies in Russia

In Russia during the Russian civil war (1918-1921) Gypsies supplied the Red Army with cavalry horses. During the reign of the czars, Gypsies, in the areas where they were allowed to settle, stayed in camps at the edges of rural village communes. In some places renting rooms or houses in the towns in the winter in exchange for the use of their horses, veterinarians, and metal repair and other services. In the spring of 1925 the first Gypsy collective farm was formed at Khutor Krikunovo, near Rostov.In 1925 the All-Russian Romani Union, led by Alexander V. Germano, was formed, and Gypsies later were to acquire nationality status in 1931, as Gypsies did not, according to Stalinist reasoning, have a territory or a "stable culture."

In 1926 the Russian communist party decreed that the Union republics should set aside land for Gypsies who wanted to farm. Very many collectives were set up all around the country over the next decade. A long with many small Gypsy cartels, or manufacturing collectives in the cities; such an example of thes are the Tsygpishcheprom (Gypsy food industries)in Moscow. The majority of these were eliminated as national cartels in the late 1930s.Throughout the late 1930s, thousands of Roma, under increased pressure to settle and collectivize, were sent en masse to Siberia or shot.

Under Stalin's rule the Roma Gypsies were forced to settle with the wheels of their caravans forcibly removed. In some areas of Eastern Europe they are still living in those vans. Stalin had set up Roma schools throughout the Soviet Union and had Romany written in Russian script to assist in the creation of a Roma communist elite and in some ways he was successful,with so many of the children in these schools in later years becoming respected officials all holding important positions in government and the Red Army.

In the communism era most Gypsies worked in the factories, until they closed.Then they returned to their traditions and skills of brick-making, basket-weaving, woodcarving and working the fields. Though there poor were still to be seen scavenging in the dumps searching for old metals, begging on the streets. Homeless with shanty towns springing up everywhere.

Then unfortunately in later years with the collapse of the U.S.S.R the former soviet union Roma became the target for further racial abuse and this has continued today.

A CHANGING WORLD

Following farming modernization the lifestyle of Gypsies changed drastically. Now they were no longer needed as fruit pickers, or for seasonal work and as a result they had to learn to quickly adapt. Often such new work was difficult to obtain and as a result many Gypsies moved from the rural areas into the growing inner cities.

At this time that Gypsies became popular as musicians playing in many cities throughout Europe, such as Hungary, Spain, and Russia. In Hungary the nobility developed a tradition of having a Gypsy minstrel alongside the host of a banquet to play for his guest's. Gypsy bands became extremely popular growing in number and demand, with many going on the road to perform. They had many imitator's in Europe, entertaining at festival's wedding's or special occasions. Throughout Europe Gypsies were still being subjected to much ethnic cleansing,many gypsy children were abducted with atrocities taking place. However many group's of Gypsies somehow managed to escape fleeing to more tolerant countries.

Bismarck had noted "complaints about the mischief caused by band's of Gypsies traveling about in the Reich and their increasing molestation of the population." In Germany a clearing house was set up in Munich to record their movement's. The Germans felt that the Gypsies used their positions as entertainer's and perfume dealer's, as a cover-up for begging and stealing. Then after Germanys unification Romas who were without German citizenship were deported and their licenses were suspended. The registration of Gypsies permitted first the Weimar Republic and then later the Nazi's to systematically persecuted them. In 1905 the German Gypsy Book was handed out to police around Europe, this profiled some 3,500 Gypsies." At a conference in Hungary in 1909 concerning "the Gypsy problem", there were equally astonishing statements, that today in the light of recent history all sounds very familiar. One speaker said, "Every Gypsy should be branded so as to assist in identification." (Kenrick 1972:56).

By 1926 new law's came into place making it mandatory for all Gypsies living in Germany to have permanent addresses and regular employment. Those who broke these new laws were sentenced to two years in a workhouse. Karl Binding and a Alfred Hoche, in their book, "The Eradication of Lives Undeserving of Life", referred to the Roma people as being "unworthy of life" and "incurably mentally ill".

When Gypsies first arrived in Europe, initial curiosity was followed by hostility towards them, along with xenophobia and troughout Europe, they were subjected to ethnic cleansing, abduction of their children, and forced labor.

 In 1939, Behrendt Racial Hygiene Institute issued a statement "all the 'Gypsies' should be treated as hereditarily sick and the only solution is their elimination with any destination". Johannes.

NAZIS AND THE GYPSIES

Holocaust

The stench and the odors of inhuman life

the corridors locked and the cries in the night

the gas chamber horrors midst barbed wire cells

the treason and horrors of war and life amidst the cries and wails

The mark of the Nazi and the torture they gave

the promise of freedom and yet none to be saved

the line's of the weary and the cries to be free

experimental genocide scream's of an adult- cries of a child

the rag's and the torture's which men freely gave

no heart for the weary no peace for the brave.

Ray Wills

A law incorporating the phrase "unworthy of life" was to be put into effect just four months after Hitler became the chancellor of the Third Reich.

Countless German Gypsies were catalogued by the Racial Hygiene Research Unit, a part of Hitler's Public Health Ministry. Gathering little more than individual names and birthdates, Nazis went from one Gypsy camp to another to survey residents. But the notation of zigeuner, the derogatory German word for Gypsy, was enough to send a person to a concentration camp.Prior to and throughout the

1939-45 war the German Nazis concentrated their efforts on proving that the Roma were not of Aryan race. They worked tiredly on many plans to achieve this, involving their top scientists, party leaders and their so called experts. At this time great persecutions took place all across Europe and Germany began to enforce this legislation against people who they saw as leading a "Gypsy way of life." At that time Gypsies were all classed as 'on persons,' of `foreign blood, 'labor-shy,' and were known as a 'socials, arrested and sent off to concentration camps.

The Romani prisoners wore markings of various shapes and colors ,with either black triangular patches, being the symbol for "asocial," or green ones, being the symbol for "professional" criminals. A great many German nationals were stripped of their citizenship and a systematic genocide took place, they were all marked for extermination and sentenced to forced labor camp's. June 13-18,1938, was declared as "Gypsy Clean-Up Week" (or Zigeunerauf in the documents) throughout Germany which was preparations for the total extermination of the Roma and Sinti people.

In 1938 a law entitled "The Fight against the Gypsy Menace" was passed and all Gypsies had to be registered with the Police. All pure Gypsies were to be provided with brown passes and those of mixed race blue passes. Foreign Gypsies were banned altogether from coming into Germany and many were put to death and vivisection was undertaken in the concentration camps on women and children.

A German child psychologist Dr. Robert Ritter with a specialty in criminal biology was responsible for this. He believed that criminal behavior was genetic and he found and classified and by race all of the estimated 30,000 Roma living in Germany his staff performed various examinations on them all. Ritter believed that the vast majority of them, had been corrupted by freely mixing with lesser people's during their long migration and that the bulk of all Roma in Germany were of mixed blood and were therefore "degenerate" and he recommended sterilization for them all apart from the remaining few pure-blooded Roma, who would be put on a reservation and studied further.

Many but not all Romanichals are noted for a fairer complexion than that of other Romani groups and lighter-skinned Romani are not uncommon, many were conscripted in the 1939-1945 war. A Slovakian Roma called Otto Baláš wrote an account that stated: "They also took my cousin Paľo. He didn't look like a Gypsy—He was white". Other light-skinned Roma were able to pass of as non-Roma and avoid the Romani genocideor orajmos, such as in the case of Vojtěch Fabián, who told a doctor he was a Roma for which he was admonished: "Never say you're a Gypsy, you don't look like one" and consequently was able to hide his Romani ethnicity from the authorities. The Bulgarian Roma, musician Ivo Papazov, stated of the light-skinned phenotype: "I am one of the few light-skinned people in my family but I know I am Romani."

During the second world war, the Nazis murdered 200,000 to 800,000 Roma in an attempted genocide which was known as thePorajmos. Roma were sentenced to forced lbor, imprisoned in concentration camps and often killed on sight, often by the mobile killing units. Some seventy percent of the Romani population of Nazi-occupied Europe were murdered during this time of the Holocaust.

On 16 December 1941, Himmler issued that the Romanies of the West Germany were to be deported at Auschwitz-Birkenau. And three years later, on 4 August, about 2,400 Romanies were gassed and cremated there and the event is remembered as Zigeunernacht.

According to Mrs.De Wick,an eyewitness, Anne Frank, a notable Jewish Holocaust victim, had witnessed the prelude to the murder of Romani children at Auschwitz. In her words: "I can still see her standing at the door and looking down at the camp street as a herd of naked gypsy girls were driven by to the crematory, and Anne watched them going and cried".Hitler had wanted to destroy all Gypsies as a race. They were tortured in pressure chambers, including their children, tested with drugs, castrated, frozen to death, and exposed to a great many traumas.

THE GYPSY CAMP AT AUSCHWITZ II - BIRKENAU

Roma from the Protectorate of Bohemia and Moravia and other parts of Europe were transported to what was known as the gypsy camp in the BIIe section of the Auschwitz II - Birkenau camp. Set up on the basis of an order signed by Himmler on the 16th of December 1942 (link in Czech)its first groups of prisoners arrived in February 1943 from Germany. It measured 150 by 170 m consisting of 32 wooden buildings, tere was no insulation. The buildings were designed for 300 to 400 people, but during the camp's existence 1 000 to1 200 people were squeezed into them. All of the Roma families were herded together with some 15 people squeezed on to bunk beds that were 185 cm long and 280 cm wide.

Upon their arrival at the camp, Roma were driven out of the trucks with cursing and beating, and ordered to form rows of fives, in which they were taken from the train to the camp. On their arrival the were a;ll bathed together . The communal bath was a source of shame for many Roma, since according to tradition a woman should not strip off in front of strange men. After the bath, the prisoners were given the black triangles used to mark asocials, and which they had to sew onto their clothing, since unlike other prisoners they were allowed to wear their civilian clothes. They also had a number tattooed on their left forearm, starting with a large letter Z (German Zigeuner - gypsy). The prisoners were forced to obey orders blindly and to carry out the most senseless wishes expressed by their supervisors. Human beings became mere numbers. Unlike those in other concentration camps, the prisoners in the Roma camp were not included in labour commandos outside the camp. They mostly worked inside the camp, which often meant unnecessary work with no aim. Instead of being destroyed by labour, however, they were killed by catastrophic living conditions and shortage of food.

The Roma prisoners came from various social groups, ranging from people on the fringes of society to traders, former soldiers on the front or even members of Nazi organisations. Their reactions to being in the camp also varied. Some sought to enjoy the last moments of their lives as much as possible, and so prostitution and carousing appeared. Others tried to ensure they had enough food by stealing it, something for which fierce punishments were meted out, often resulting in death. The only hope of survival was to escape, but this was complicated by the fact that most of the prisoners did not go to work outside the camp. Despite this around 80 unsuccessful escape attempts were recorded, most of them ending in death /execution.

The Gypsy camp was one of the focuses of the pseudo-scientific experiments of Dr. Mengele,he was particularly interested in Roma twins he was said to love Gypsy children, befriended them and give them treats of chocolate and candies. He was known by the children as "Uncle Pepe". He took them to a special children's barrack known as "The Zoo" for medical and scientific experiments. Jewish prisoner Dina Gottlieb was ordered to draw portraits of imprisoned Roma especially for him.

 In all, over 20, 000 people were recorded as having

been imprisoned in this camp. Those not recorded included, a group of some 1 700 Polish Roma, in which typhus appeared. These were taken away to the gas chambers without being recorded. The largest group consisted of German and Austrian Roma, followed by Roma from the Protectorate of Bohemia and Moravia and the territory of the General gouvernement. Smaller groups of Roma came from France, the Netherlands, Belgium and other countries. Their one and only hope of survival became transports to other concentration camps.

On the 15th of April 1944, 883 men were transported to Buchenwald and 473 women were taken to Ravensbrück (link in Czech). The last group to leave was 918 men who went to Buchenwald and 490 women who went to Ravensbrück on the 2nd of August 1944. After these left, the remaining 3 000 Roma, of whom were mostly old and ill, women and children were sent to the gas chambers. Then the Gypsy Family Camp was finally closed down.

THE GYPSY CAMP AT HODONÍN U KUNŠTÁTU

The gypsy camp at Hodonín u Kunštátu was used for the forced concentration of Moravian Roma. As with the Lety camp, Roma families were sent to the camp at the beginning of August 1942, in numbers that considerably exceeded the camp's capacity, set at

800 people. The living conditions, food and sanitation were just as terrible as at Lety, and the camp rules were the same. At Hodonín too, the supervisory staff consisted of policemen from the Protectorate of Bohemia and Moravia. The camp was headed by Štefan Blahynka, who went to the Lety camp temporarily in the winter of 1943 to help deal with a typhus epidemic, and to aid in the transport of prisoners to Auschwitz. He then returned to Hodonín, where he was commander of the camp until it was closed. Over 1 300 people passed through the camp in total. Illness (above all during the typhus epidemic) and bad living conditions caused the death of 194 people in the camp itself. Two mass transports were carried out from the Hodonín camp. The first transport of 46 men and 29 women (the asocials) set out on the 7th of December 1942 to the Auschwitz I concentration camp, on the basis of a decree on crime prevention. The second mass transport took place on the 21th of August 1943, with 749 prisoners being taken to the Auschwitz II - Birkenau concentration camp. After the second transport left, only 62 prisoners remained in the camp. A non-Roma family from Olešnice adopted an eight-year-old prisoner from the camp, thus saving her from further suffering, since only a few of the remaining prisoners were released. The rest were

taken to the concentration camp at Auschwitz in winter 1944.

Night of the Gypsies

On the so called "Night of the Gypsies", August 2/3, 1944, the SS rounded up the rest of the Gypsies by luring them out of the barracks with the promise of water and bread. Once the Gypsies realized they fought back with their bare hands but they were no match for the clubs and guns of the SS and were put onto the vehicles and driven to the gas chambers. As most Gypsies at that time were illiterate, many were not registered at the camp's and if they were registered, a plain 'Z" was placed on the form. The vast majority were either killed in transportation or before or where they were captured, there was no record of their deaths.

According to Ian Hancock "The 'family camps' were not created out of any humanitarian motive, but because Roma became completely unmanageable when being separated from family members"."It was simply more expedient and caused the guards less problems, to leave families together for processing." yts referred only to Roma people and not to the Jews.

An Hungarian Roma survivor stated:"They cut off our hair and everything to be hairless. It was done by women, then a doctor examined us thoroughly... they examined, you know, everything. He was the one who gave an injection to me and to all the others, to everybody. It hurt badly. You know, he gave me an injection down there...Everything went black... I fell off that examining table. They kicked me away;

it was time for the next. They gave me an injection like that one in eight months and after that I did not have that monthly thing" .

Turn, turn, turn

The vardo wheels keep turning on the highways of regrets

where Gypsy memories returning to sale flowers on the set

where castanets are playing and the honky tonk parades

within the heather-ed commons where rabbits traps were set

The story tellers gathered and the wheels were still in spin

far off from the distant hills where rhapsodies begin

the wars took all our young men all lost to the great cause

whilst the landed gentry aristocrats counted all the poor

The stories that we were told then where shadowed with their lies

like the king of Germanys great fall and the common Gypsy spies

the grass roots undertaker sold their profits for to spree

whilst hungry urchin children had nowt left for their teas

The fires that were lit there offered sanctuary and good ideals

whilst we sheltered in the birch and briers and lived life misunderstood

the skill's of all our children were scattered to the wind

whilst the sites were sold for profit then and some toffs chosen whim

All the strangers offered monies and homes of brick to tread

whilst country daughter's offered gifts of love and recompense

the young men gave them kisses sweet and held them in their arms

whilst their mothers counted widows left amongst their Gypsy charms

The falling soldiers lost to war were counted on the breeze

where Churchill's foolish armies were gathered in the breeze

a leader of the armies was calling for young men s they signed their lives for God and country poets penned in Zen

The Churches offered sanctuary and the preachers spread the word

one hand on the book of life the other on the sword

the Gypsy camps lay scattered and the hills were rich in blooms

where lovers strolled amongst the thorns on a springtime afternoon.

Ray Wills

THE WAR YEARS

Gypsies have always played an active part in the armed services in the UK. They fought in Afghanistan in the 1870s and members of the traveling community have had the Victoria cross, military medals and DCM for their bravery and distinguished service to the country in both world war 1 and world war 2. During and throughout the war's despite the sensational press reports to the contrary from the right wing, mainly conservative press, the Gypsy young men and women of the UK joined the armed services in large numbers.

Many Gypsies served in the British forces in the 1914 1918 war and 1939-1945 and lost their lives serving their country A very large number of them lost their lives fighting for their country and many areas of the country have sections in local cemetery's where their many gravestone's are marked in respect of this fact.Including with 18 from the first world war and 7 from the second world war recorded on the memorial stone at Thorny hill New Forest cemetary alone.

War to end Wars

It was the war to end all wars

the diplomats declared

the flags were blowing in the breeze

plus all the prayers were said

They said that it was for freedoms
the price of true democracy
with bullets by the millions
then they went home for their tea

The universal soldiers
all lined up in rank
with weapons of destruction
and platoons led by tanks

The captain called for leaders
and the colonels hummed the tune
one was killed in action
and million's killed too soon

The bugle sounded retreat
and the master rang the bell
one went on to heaven
whilst millions rode through hell.

Ray Wills

Flanders Fields

Cannons roar on the last battlefields
memories fade yet never ending
only the tears remain
those hard bitter grounds

Where grass or plant will not take
only the poppy grows there
a gift from God of our shame
its bloody redness decorates our coat's and recollections
the lord Kitchener call
your country needs you in time of war

On the fields of Flanders
the young men died for reasons unknown
for only Honor was bestowed on bravery
the fallen flowers of a generation

Died that we might recall their bravery
the bugle plays the last post
the call to arms has been silenced
only the tears of generations will reflect
on what might have been

What bravery
what reckless call to arms
for king and country
for peace
there but for the grace of God
on the fields of Flanders
we shall remember them.
Ray Wils

Dorsets pride

All along the Dorset coast
men got into their boats
little craft's and dinghys
anything that would float

They rowed into the channel

out to foreign shores

to save the British army

from the German foes

The brave men and the valiant

trapped on Dunkirk shores

all young men trapped next to the waves

in another long lost war

There were sailor's all retired

fishermen and friend

they sailed from Poole and Weymouth

to save the soldier men

When they got the call to rescue

they took it all in stride

they rowed and sailed through turbulent sea n tide

to save the nation's pride

There on the shores of Dunkirk

they saved the countrys best

all good men and noble

they put them to the test

The country folk and farmer

the workers of the land

the brave young men and sons

they sailed against the tide

then gathered in the harvest

the best of England's pride.

Ray Wills

Heroism

John Smith went to school and learned the lines

the maths and calculations and how to read the signs

he played the games on playgrounds and chased the girls a few

he was like lots of other kids played by the golden rule

He was trained in all the skills of life and read the poets too

his diction was first class they said and he made the was head of school

his masters all thought well of him and he played the teachers games

he rose to be a man and loved the girls a few e left school well acquainted with the histories and tools

He rose to be a leader of his community and then he went to war to fight for democracy

he enlisted in the British troops and fought in Afghanistan

he was knighted for his valour and his ways with every man

his rank was well respected and he rose to be a colonel and his life was on the rise

he had seen the wars of consequence and the look in dead mens eyes

All the years they faded and his comrades they all died

hit by a snoopers rounds and the vision in their eyes

he was wounded hurt and dam near died and sent home in the spring

he was welcomed by his family and the bands did roll and sing

when the rabbits ran upon the downs and the lonesome sparrow sings

His medals they all hung on walls and his credits were so cool

he died in loneliness and pride the victor to the cause

he left behind a battlefield for another young mans cause

the flag it flew half mast there upon the village green

whilst a thousand young men signed their names went to war to fight for king or queen

heroism took their lives and democracy it screamed.

Ray Wills

After the 2nd World War

Following the 1939-1945 war the Sinti and Roma Gypsies had to register with the local police and the criminal identification service. By 1948 the central criminal department of Baden Wurttemberg issued 'guidelines, to the police for the fight against the Gypsy menace'. New law's were implemented based on the former 1926 Law for the fight against Gypsies and Idlers.

In 1956 the German Federal Court stated that 'their (the Roma and Sinti) deportation to the concentration camps had not been a persecution out of racial reasons, but a pre-emptive criminal measure'. Compensation and support for reintegration was denied to them and photos and fingerprints were to be kept on file. The Soviet Union decreed that the last wandering Gypsies there should be gradually settled in places of their own choice. Similar measures were introduced and put into law in all the countries of East Europe, where the vast majority of Gypsies lived, and the majority of Gypsies were grateful to find safety there.

In 1984, Simon Wiesenthal wrote "the Gypsies had been murdered [in a proportion] similar to the Jews, about 80% of them in the area of the countries which were occupied by the Nazis". t is now speculated that his spousal of the Gypsy cause   him the Nobel Prize – and was meant to how Elie Wiesel in poor light. Elie Wiesel supporters claim, allegedly, he was more interested in discrediting Elie Wiesel and less bothered about Romany.

On 16 September 1986, Elie Wiesel addressed a wide range of audience in his Nobel Peace Prize speech, he stated "I confess that I feel somewhat guilty towards our Roma friends. We have not done enough to listen to your voice of anguish. We have not done enough to make other people listen to your voice of sadness. I can promise you we shall do whatever we can from now on to listen better" (Tanner 1997).

Most Gypsy caravan's were drawn by motorised vehicles by the 1960s, and their tent's replaced by temporary shack's. The caravan, or living-wagon, was not originally a Gypsy tradition. It was adopted, elaborated, and then fell into disuse over the comparatively short period of a hundred years. Before then, Gypsies used bender tents which was a kind of shelter made from blankets, felts or weatherproof sheets, draped over bent rods of ash, hazel or willow. A donkey could carry the sheets, and fresh rods could be cut at each stopping-place. The floor was covered with carpets or mats, and beds were made from bracken or straw. These Bender tents come in all shapes, and sizes and could be joined together to build homes of whatever size is needed.

The travelling showman had riginally developed the wagons in the 1860s. Carriage makers art was at its peak then although it was demanding to create a light van sufficient to be pulled by one horse and yet strong enough to handle the roads.They needed to have tall wheels, a narrowed high-slung body, and a low centre of gravity so that they would keep stable over rough terrain. They had to endure life on the roads in the British climate.

However in the years after the war many Gypsies in the UK

around the 1960s moved into council housing, with many of the men becoming scrap dealer's, whilst others worked with copper, made ornaments and decorative pieces of art. However the majority of Gypsy women were still viewed by many as being no more than fortune tellers and beggars.

In many countries such as Czechoslovakia, Gypsies were forced into settlement's, their horse's slaughtered and their wagon's burned. Many were not allowed to travel and had all their valuables and money taken from them and all their various groups and independent newspaper's were closed down. Were as in Yugoslavia it was a very different story, the media television and radio stations gave broadcasts in the Romani language and many Gypsies began to participate in regional politics' and hundreds of them gained work as doctor's, lawyer's, and engineer's.

Until 1985 all marriages, births and deaths of travelling people had to be reported to the criminal police and special records of all Roma and Sinti vehicles and their owners were kept. Many settled in small towns, and began buying and selling ready-made good's or surplus and second hand clothing. The federal parliament held its first debate on issues faced by the community and endorsed an apology for the Nazi genocide.

In the UK the new Highway Act introduced in 1959 had made it illegal for Gypsies to camp beside the roadway, if they did camp there they would soon be evicted. Gypsies were unable to get employment or have their children schooled or apply for permanent housing up till then. It was then that local councils started moving the families from the compounds into Council accommodation. These families had no option than to move into this settled housing, for some it offered a better standard of living, but for the elderly it was very hard to adapt to this new life after years of a wandering life. In 1965 a national study was conducted, out of this came a carefully designed scheme for housing travellers and for providing them with permanent employment. Most of the men living in three of the special centres in the forest at that time were employed as general labourer's on building sites, lorry drivers or park attendants.

All across Europe there still appears to be shortage of laws to protect the Romani from violence towards them.The 1989 revolution in Romania changed the country's political economic and social systems, many Gypsies took part in the liberation, and their names are to be seen in the list of martyrs. In a great many European countries during the 1990s Gypsy family houses were burnt down and Gypsies were beaten up.

Roma/Gypsies from the former Yugoslavia, Romania and Bulgaria entered Germany as asylum seekers though many were returned to their countries of origin. Roma Gypsies usually do not have citizenship, many long-term resident Roma in Germany only have temporary 'tolerated' status, or duldung. Often Gypsies freedom of movement was restricted and access to employment or social assistance and their Romani language and music was banned from public performance.

Throughout Europe Gypsies were living in camp's, with poor accommodation with most of them destitute, poor and discriminated against. Some commentators today feel that in many ways little has changed since the earlier times of slavery and persecution.They say however that one important change is that, although in the time of slavery, Romani people could not be killed without the master receiving compensation.

The Roma arrived in Europe from the former communist countries to the European Union in 2004 and 2007 enabling the free movement of people. In Europe today there are tens of thousands of Gypsies travelling westward to flee from the countries of south eastern Europe to escape from poverty and discrimination. According to an Amnesty International report issued of 2011, "systematic discrimination is taking place against up to 10 million Roma across Europe".

Nowadays Romani are found all over the world, but the majority are in central and eastern Europe. Their culture, trades, and language are passed down from one person to the next, the majority being illiterate. Each Gypsy clan is usually led by a Kris, or a tribunal leader who passes laws based on their religious beliefs and customs.

They were eventually forced due to circumstances to give up their Romani language as well as their nomadic lifestyles, though a few of these Gypsy families can still be seen working the circuses and fairground's. In many countries they provide various repair service's or are used car dealer's, sell furniture, antique's, and junk carpet and textiles. Despite all their problems many of them still manage to have kept their old traditions, of hawking, entertaining by making music and telling fortune's.

CHAPTER THREE

Gypsy Life in the UK

"They excite the hatred of the bourgeois even though inoffensive as sheep, that hatred is linked to something deep and complex, it is found in all orderly people" It is the bedouin,the heretic, the philosopher, the solitary, the Poet and there is fear in the hatred".-Gustav Flavbert (1880s).

Silk from the East

I've brought cotton from France and silk from the East

trinket's and goblets and clanking false teeth

old fathers shavers and ladies blue gowns

faded old books you bought for a crown

I've gambled on horses and slept with a few

when times they were hard in a stable or two

the bookies all knew me I was known for my sins

I slept with the ladies in a room in the inn

The cradles they rocked and the poets then penned

the words they were laudy and the themes rolled in Zen
the cock it did crow in the farmyard each day
whilst the pastor slept on and the old uns did pray

The forests were thick then and the rivers were clean
the potters were plentiful and the milk it was cream
the maidens were blossomed and the trees they were tall
where the grass it was high and the peasants so poor

The modern day men with their fine fancy talk
who squandered their riches with long ladies walks
the sun shone so brightly and the stars shone at night
in feather bed lands with a candle to light

The girl's played at hopscotch and the boys kiss and tell
there were pugilist boxers and fairgrounds so swell
the hunchback and midgets and bearded ladies
with peep shows to venture and sights for to see
We oft times go back there in our memories
then ride on the Ferris and hum with the bees
the pastimes and sonnets that tickled my dreams
like the days from the past in the land of the Queen.

Ray Wills

Around every campfire
We looked into the ember's as the sparks did fly and soar
we dreamed of happy memories and those who'd gone before
the scouts sang all the chants there and the children sang a rhyme
the Indians made their camp there before the ranks of time

The cones did sit and crack there and the hedgehog looked so good
as we gazed into the embers and shared our brotherhood
where the vardos hitched daily and the stars did shine at night
beneath that blanket serenade we told our yarn's so right

The old ones told us stories tales of long ago
when the freemen roamed this barren land in summer sun and
winter snows
when the rabbits they were plentiful and the bison was just game
long before the white man took away the right's of Indian men

The fires lit our lives then and the heat was shared so free
from the foothill's of Kentucky to the plains of Tennessee
the English country yokels where the land was open reign

whilst the Aussie bushman lit his pipes and told his tales again. -Ray Wills

The English Gypsies called themselves Romany Chals or Romany Chies, meaning sons and daughters of Rome.When talking to each other they said Pal or Pen which is brother and sister.They travelled in large family groups of between thirty and ninety with carts drawn by ponies or donkeys.This was a period in time when there was little in the way of traffic apart from horse drawn traps, carts and coach and horses. A distinct time in history in a world where folks sought gainful employment out of necessity, for there was not such a thing as a welfare state or social service.

During the middle ages and after, there had been an abundance of busy fairs, shows and markets throughoul England where folks bought, bartered and sold their wares. Many of these were celebration events, religious festivities or holy days, which we now call holidays. These were popular stopping places for travelling people, tinkers, traders, sellers of wares and others. In Britain the road's have for centuries always been busy with traveller's of all kind's, long before the Romani's Gypsies themselves were said to have arrived here.

Despite information to the contrary in the 13th century there were actually many Tinkers living in the UK. James 'Tinkler' Perth Editha le ' Tyne- in Berkshire Huntingdonshire and Ralph Tincler had a house in Morpeth, Northumberland. All of these seem to have had fixed abodes, and not to have been of the same itinerant class with which we now associate all Tinkers. It should be noted, however, that Tinkers often — as was the case with Billy Marshall —

possess a house into which they retire for a few weeks in the dead of winter. That fact may readily account for the Tinkers referred to by a Mr Crofton having fixed abodes. Mr Crofton points out "All may be pedlars, braziers, or Tinkers, but the reverse may not follow." That which used to require the epithet ' wandering ' to distinguish them. But the further and more difficult problems to decide, as to whether or not Tinkers were originally a Romani-speaking race, or the Romani words in Tinkers' cant were introduced by a wave of Romani-speaking Gypsies.A party of Gypsies who had visited Paris in August 1427 had taken a northward direction on leaving, and as the English were then ruling in the French capital, it is very probable that the Gypsies would hear of these English lands and would want to visit them.Roma people are believed to have arrived in the second half of the 15th century, entering Scotland from Denmark. Referred to as 'Egyptian pilgrims' in older sources, they are known to have sought the protection of King James IV of Scotland on a journey to Denmark in 1506, which suggests that contacts with related Roma clans on the continent continued to be maintained for some time.

The first official mention of Traveler's in Britain was in 1505, when it was recorded that seven pound's were paid to 'Egyptians' by King James IV at Stirling. The earliest reference to Gypsies in England is Sir Thomas More's description of an 'Egyptian' woman who told fortunes in Lambeth in 1514. Though Borrow says they first came to England "about the year 1480," and it is known that Christopher Columbus who was rich in slave trading had them working on his plantations. He had also taken four Gypsies on his excursions to the new world earlier in 1498.

Though it is even thought by many scholars that Gypsies were here many centuries earlier, though this matter still awaits to be confirmed.

A subsequent reference from 1687 confirms the wedding of Robert Hern and Elizabeth Bozwell, 'king and queen of the gipsies' at Camberwell.

 It is thought that some Gypsies soon after their arrival in England also adopted the surnames of the owners of the estates on which particular groups of them camped and worked for. Or else they adopted names of those landed philanthropical families nearby who gave them protection from persecution. Whilst others took the name of the town or village where they lived such as the Wareham family in Dorset.

Th Gypsy Winifred Wells was a mistress of King Charles 11.

 In 1522, the churchwardens of Stratton in Cornwall received twenty pence from the 'Egyptians' for the use of the church house; and sometime between 1513 and 1524 Thomas, Earl of Surrey,had entertained 'Gypsies' at his Suffolk seat, Tendering Hall. Tinkers, were already living in Britain at that time and performed the same tasks living similar lifestyles as Gypsies did in other countries: being nomadic entertainers, knife-grinders, pot-menders, woodworkers, and nomadic field workers.

By 1528 it's estimated that up to 10,000 Gypsies were living in England, there were few prosecutions and these laws were not popular and indeed many Gypsies could now prove they were born in England. Giles Hather became head of the regiment or fellowship of Egyptians in the north about that time.

According to Rid,Gypsies travelled in groups of more than a hundred men and women, with horses, their faces blacked, and practiced all manner of fortune telling, delighting the common people with their clothes and Kit Callot "the Queen of the Egyptians" accompanied Giles Hather. However things changed dramatically and soon they were victimised. For by 1530, the new Egyptian Act required them to leave the country or be imprisoned. Aiming to free England of all Gypsies.

By the mid 16th century Scotland too had its very own King of the Gypsies, Johnnie Faa of Dunbar. He was given royal recognition by being granted a letter under the royal Privy Seal from King James 1V in 1540.The letter was addressed to "oure louit Johnnie Faw,lord and Earl of litte Egypt". This established his authority over all Gypsies in Scotland and calling on all sheriffs in the country to assist him "in execution of justice upon his company and folks", who were to conformed to the laws of Egypt".

In 1542 the very first ever written record of their Roma language was produced by a Andrew Boorde a Catholic monk who possibly wrote these scripts down in an ale house in Sussex.

The Egyptian Act

Later the Egyptian Act of 1554, directed that they must abandon their "naughty, idle and ungodly life and company" and adopt a settled lifestyle. In August 1559 in the reign of Elizabeth 1 a very large number of Gypsy wanderers were stopped and detained in Dorchester Dorset.They were sent to trial before the Lord lueutenant of Dorset. He having heeded an order from the Queen.Instructing him that they the gypsies should be made an example with some of them to be executed.In September 1559 they went to trial but they were however aquitted due to the fact that they had journeyed from Scotland and not as originally thought from overseas.Shortly after in 1562 English legislators, brought in an act that would snare also "counterfeit Egyptians" being local people who had married into families of these immigrants.This was shotly followed by the Roman Catholics churches denouncation of the Gypsies banning them from the Roman Catholic church.

The Elizabeth I new law stated, that"if Gypsies did not give up their way of life they would bc put to death and their belongings taken away from them" a great many others were slaves then under her rule. However they managed to survive despite all of these persecutions and eventually became a useful part of country life for the farming community used Gypsies and Travellers' for many years to harvest all the crops. They were useful in that, they were nomadic and so once their work was completed they moved on elsewhere. Gypsies and traveller's moved around England seeking work, selling, providing services or buying. Although their persecution has continued to an extent since that time.

By 1665 Oliver Cromwell was sending many more Gypsies as slaves to the West Indies to work on his and others many plantations. Though at that time most Gypsies were expelled and cruel harsh laws were passed condemning them all to death. There was much unemployment then , prices were high and peasant workers were thrown off the land. As usual people looked for scapegoats. Strangers, immigrants, foreigners, fitted this role so well as of today with Gypsies in particular standing out. These gypsies were scapegoats as being very different in appearance as well as in their ways and custom's.Billy Marshall a famous Gypsy King in Scotland died in 1792 after living 120 years. Billy had fathered over 100 children, some by his 17 wives, and some by other gals.

Brittania Lovell the famous Gypsy fortune teller told fortunes for the King of England,whilst he George 1V was Prince Rupert, for just 5 pounds and a hearty kiss.

By the 1800s Rodney Smith the Gypsy evangelist, had noted on reflection that "Sixty years ago a marriage according to the law of the land was unknown among the Gypsies". The sweet hearting of a Gypsy young man and maiden usually extends over a long period, or, as "gorgeous" would say, the rule is long engagements. Very often they have grown up sweethearts from boy and girl. When the young people are able to set up for themselves they make a covenant with each other. Rodney Smith was of the opinion that "There is nothing of jumping over tong's or broomstick's, or any other of the tomfooleries that outsiders attribute to Gypsies". Rodney Smith estimated at that time that "there were between 20,000 to 25,000 Gypsies in the UK".

Gypsies were portrayed in so called 'factual' accounts as dangerous and somewhat deceitful individuals, with evidence of the earliest glimmers of interest in the Gypsy's culture. The Gypsy was seen as a criminal, though not as dangerous in many songs, ballads and stories designed for entertainment at that time often portrayed as being carefree, and of living a romantic lifestyle.In this so called romantic period. For great adventures stories were the fashion then with Gypsies being most prevalent and popular in them. Although many magazine essays and articles during that period portrayed them as no more than beggars and thieves. It was also popular to portray them as fortune-tellers and this common view of the Gypsy as criminal and scoundrel continued well into the next century along with the public interest in their ethnic origins and the theory of their Hindu origin at the same time was also to gain momentium. Gypsies were written of as being a race apart and for the first time, the concept of the Gypsies' race is used as an excuse for their delinquent nature. During this so called "Romantic period" the concept of the Gypsy race, based on early ideas of genetic origin, enhanced their mystique, along with their fortune telling and exotic appeal.

Not everyone described as a traveler or vagrant was necessarily a Gypsy or traveler. Whether hawker, basket maker, or chimney sweep, but so many of these occupations were none the less undertaken by Gypsies.

The Sherborne Mercury, reported in April 1833 '-

Petitions to both Houses of Parliament for the abolition of Negro Slavery are lying in the town for signature'. In fact two petitions were sent one from Lyme generally, and another from 'the ladies of Lyme Regis'. 'The female inhabitants of Charmouth' also sent one. William Pinney, MP for Lyme from1832, came from the Pinney family of West Dorset who had been involved with the West Indies, sugar production and slavery from the 17th century. The family received more than thirty thousand pounds in compensation when slavery was abolished in 1834. The freed slaves did not receive any compensation at all.

Abram Wood (who was known as king of the Welsh Gypsies at that time) had descendants who included musicians who kept alive many musical traditions. One of them was to became a chief harpist to Queen Victoria. Abram was noted for keeping the Romani language together in Cambria and his family was reputed to be fluent in Romani, English and Welsh. Children in North Wales were told to beware "teulu Abram Wood", the family of Abram Wood (who would like all Gypsies, steal naughty little children). Another common saying at the time was that "an untidy house as being like the "house of Abram Wood".

Revd George Hall- commented that Tom Lee, an English Gypsy, broke up a loaf of bread and strewed the crumbs around his tent when his son Bendigo was born, for some of the old-time Gypsies hold the notion that bread possesses a protective magic against evil influences. Seated one day in the tent of Bendigo Lee on the South Shore at Blackpool Tom Lee when questioned about his father's practice.He commented " In the days when I was born,there were people that could do hurt by looking at you, and I suppose my dadus (father) sprinkled the crumbs lest any evil person going by should cast harm upon me." A distinct survival of the belief in the evil eye.

According to Konrad Bercovici in his book, "Gypsies, Their Life, Lore, and Legends": "English Romanies have divided England among themselves, and an unwritten law keeps every tribe within a designated border line".

"Wanderlust" and skills

For Gypsies, travelling is not a pastime or leisure activity, but a way of life. A common belief of the latter part of the 19th century suggested that this need to travel, known as "wanderlust," was itself of genetic origin and often used as the basis for the claim that "it was as natural for Gypsies to move as it was for the majority of the population to stay in one place". It was in the economic sphere, then, that Gypsies interacted with settled society. It was at that time that the Gypsy caravans with horse-drawn vardos, and donkeys or mules in tow first appeared in the country. Though many Gypsies were still preferring to live in tents, even during the severest harshest winters.

Gypsies provided a valuable service to the community by delivering goods and services to remote towns and villages, long before the arrival of the railways and they entertained at many village festivals. They were seen by many as being very skilful people who were able to fix and repair almost anything, the Gypsy men also harvested hops and the women worked at the many popular carnivals and fairs as fortune tellers. Gypsies attracted huge crowds whenever they gathered they were always a great attraction for all the locals who longed to see the Gypsy women with their colourful dresses gold coins around their necks and bosoms and their plaited hair. Townsfolk would await the arrival of these Travellers with great excitement. anticipation and looked forward to hearing from them the latest news and gossip from all across the country and abroad.

For many Gypsies, their work has traditionally been a means of remaining independent and mobile. All members of a family had worked together,or grouped up with others, as opportunity allowed. Until recent years, Gypsies were able to find a market for crafts manufactured from natural sources. Clothes pegs, brooms, baskets and artificial flowers could be made in the intervals between domestic work, and then sold from door to door. Shopping baskets were woven from willow, or from paper-thin strips of split hazel. Large baskets built from coils of rush, or from strands of grass bound with bramble stems. For making pegs, rods of hazel or willow were cleft and tied with banding strips cut from old tin cans.

Artificial flowers were also popular; chrysanthemum heads from elder sticks, and pink and white roses fashioned from crepe paper. Flowers gathered from hedges or small bouquets of daffodils, primroses, cowslips, violets or snowdrops, depending on season, were gathered and sold. In this way, a number of Gypsies became known by name to people in the settled community. These folk settled well into the local rural communities with seasonal farm work and other skills and manual labour

Gypsies moved in regular routes back and forth across the countryside in the spring and summer months, searching for and obtaining seasonal work, hawking and attending fairs. Due to this industrialization the demand for seasonal manual labour declined during this period and many of them abandoned their rural life for scrap metal work, car dealing and tarmac laying. Although the Gypsy caravan Vardo still became central to the average persons romanticized image of 'the Gypsy.

A major figure for the Romani Gypsy cause in recent years has been Professor Ian Hancock. When he had a private meeting with the Dalai Lama in India. The Dalai Lama informed Professor Hancock that," it was crucial for the Romanies to sustain the strength of the family unit within their culture. To keep their language alive but to lose those customs that are holding them back and keeping them from integrating into the larger society".

According to Professor Ian Hancock, most people are only familiar with the surfeit of romantic fairytale myths that surround the diverse collection of individuals erroneously termed "Gypsies."Novels, poems, plays, films and songs over the past several centuries have portrayed 'Gypsies' as free-spirited, promiscuous, indigent criminals who dance around campfires and are fortune-tellers, thieves and liars. 'Gypsies' are carefree and enjoy an almost childlike innocence and release from duty.Though the common false assertions put about was still that of Gypsies' practice witchcraft, steal babies in the dead of night and are filthy and unkempt, so the stories say. We're as the authorities were actually stealing Travellers children, sending them to the colonies and packing them into homes run by cruel masters, they had their names changed, removing any form of identity.

Camping grounds were denied the scattered Travellers desperately trying to find common ground to maintain their wandering lifestyle and live in peace and freedom. Because of the increase in traffic on the roads house building and growth of population of the UK Gypsies found it more and more difficult to continue their nomadic life and as a result many emigrated with the bulk of them going to the USA. Then from the 1930s onward, Gypsies found that open heaths and commons, previously used by their families for hundreds of years, were now no go areas.

Although there was a brief period following the war when Gypsies led a less troubled life alongside the settled community. So many families had been bombed out, and were living in prefabricated houses or mobile homes, that the Gypsy lifestyle did not look too far from normal. There was lots of employment opportunities in casual work building post-war Britain, and no shortage of stopping places. But soon these sites too were developed and people began to move back into the cities and towns.

As Gypsies followed, searching for work, the largest urban camp in England was on Belvedere Marshes near Erith on the borders of south-east London and Kent, located on land which had been occupied by Travellers since the late 19th century. The camp grew through the early decades of the 20th century until it accommodated approximately 2000 people living in some 400 caravans, sheds, old buses and huts (Stanley, 2002). Erith Borough Council instigated a long and protracted battle to evict the 'marsh people' though eventually it was the effect of the North Sea floods of 1953 that destroyed it dislodging many inhabitants, with the remaining 700 people finally being evicted in 1956.

Gypsies as always came up against unsympathetic treatment by all. All the traditional sites had now been enclosed with fences, banks and ditches. The Gypsies had no choice but to move onto any space available, these were usually car parks, disused factories and other public land, which unfortunately led to further conflict with police and local people.

Rambling Gambling Gypsy

He was a rambling gambling Gypsy
born on the wayward tracks
where the vardo wheels were rolling
and the berries were in the sacks
way out by the heather not far from canford downs
where the yogs were still a burning
on the dark side of the tracks

He was a rambling gambling Gypsy
spent his youth out in the fairs
where the carousels were turning
and the music hit your ears

Where the bumper cars were laden
with young girls on the town
where the young men took their fancy
and the old gals bedded down
He played the cards there daily
shuffled up the packs

where the Gypsy wheels were rolling

laid down the king and jacks

He was a rambling gambling Gypsy

when he met her and they dined

in the shadows of the moonlight

candle light and wine

He was a rambling gambling Gypsy

he bet on every mare

they courted in the springtime

flowers in her hair

He was a rambling gambling Gypsy

but he left her in the shade

to join the British army

for peace he craved to save

She lost him in the battle

but she still stands by his grave

where the sun comes up each morning

to salute that Gypsy brave.

Ray Wills

Campfire Nights

We sat around the yog my good friends and I
we told those old stories and we told them old lies
there were good times and bad and we went on the spree
in the summers and long winters in the hills past the leas

Oh the days they were long then and the nights they were cold
put some logs on the fire friend my bones getting old
pass me the pan and the kettle and tins
put the pot on the yog boy and pass me the gin

Oh the trails they were mean and the weather was cruel
in the time of the yearnings when the mornings were cool
there was food on the table and mats on the floors
when the chavvies were crawling right out of the door

You can look at the stars and tell me you know
the pathways to take by the red embers glow
you can taste of the stew boys and take the gals arm

then you can dance in the moonlight and use up your charm

Tell her your stories and laugh in the firesides hot glow

whisper sweet nothings tell her you love her just so

whilst we can whisper our prayers till the stars start to fade

then wel take off to bed for the chavvies to make

Oh the winters were harsh then and the snow it was deep

we lived on the rabbits hedgehogs and beet

we sang around the yog there till late was the night

went off to get some much needed sleep

then we said our goodbye and left fore the new morning light.

Ray Wills

Travellers today have modernised alongside the rest of society and are not seen as a 'secret people'. This change in their lifestyle has resulted in the removal of that which the settled society understands as the markers of 'true' Gypsies: bow-topped caravans, cob vanner horses and so on associated with the romantic vision of the Gypsy folk.

In 1968 a law was passed stating that all local authorities were obliged to provide a site for all Gypsy Travelers. This promise was never ever fulfilled plus the sites that were provided were totally unsuitable where no one else would ever wish to live. The present sites made available for Travelers in England often portrays the very worst examples of housing to be seen in Britain ever, some are not fit for animals let alone humans. Whilst some

Traveler's do fortunately live on well maintained, well run council sites, there are many who are not so lucky. Many of these sites are often no more than dumps or ghetto's. Some Gypsies out of necessity will choose to live on other illegal site's as yard's of disused factories, or underneath urban motorway's, These are often situated where access to normal facilities usually don't exist at all.

So many Gypsy Travelers today are facing extreme forms of prejudice as they always have done since they first arrived here from the Indian continent. In 1994 the government abolished the Caravan Sites Act and took away the obligation for local councils to provide sites. The Gypsies and Travelers were told that they should look for their own sites and that councils would give them planning permission. Again this never happened and families were forced or obliged to either go into housing or apply for planning permission retrospectively, because no Gypsy could ever get planning permission granted because of local prejudice.

So many local councils across the country, decided that not only that Travelers may not stay on council land, or even in their neighborhood. Such common inhuman, uncaring act's of putting so many Gypsy travelling families onto the highway will be to Britain's shame as a nation. Homeless Gypsies and Travelers who have to stop on unauthorized sites may have uncollected rubbish because public refuse collection does not cover these sites. If rubbish is not collected from settled residents, the local press may not be very supportive of their difficulties. Very often, the presence of Gypsies and Travelers' on an unauthorized site is used as an excuse for fly-tipping by other people in the area, but the

Travelers' will often get the blame.

In recent years many of the old traditional stopping places such as commons, old roads etc, have been sealed up or blocked access. This has made it more difficult for Gypsies to live a life on the road. Whilst many of those who have chosen the settled housing route have often found hostility from the settled population.With many of these folk forced to live in houses, particularly the elderly, have ended up clinically depressed. Whilst many of the young people living on these estates have lost their cultural roots and have ended up with a dysfunctional family life. On top of this each year it costs the British tax payer in excess of over £20 million pounds to evict Gypsies.

Homeward Love

I'm a rough diamond born on the dark side of town

I'm a wandering freelance traveller I don't let nothing get me down

I'm a talking singing freeman with lots of foolish pride

I'm a riding on the highway got a ticket in my hand n flowers for my bride

I'm counting all the stars up there and I'm trying to be wise

my friends and old acquaintance s are numbered one to ten

I'm a poet with a mission and I ride upon those stars again

I've got my dreams to keep me company n a busted old guitar

vie been travelling on this same old road this same ole track so far before

I've got a promise that I'm keeping and my hide is saddle sore

I'm a chewing some tobacco and I'm rustling up some time

got a buckboard n a wagon and I must be home on time

I've been out upon the town drank too much booze n wine

seen a lot of women and I've cursed a lot of times

but my heart is true to my true love and I must be home on time.

Ray Wills

Hearts on the road

She plucked at my heartstrings and begged me to stay

she took all my money and then went away

her tent it was awesome with strawberry wine

we drank till the morning I grew up so wise

The thunder and lightning and the stars in the sky

the ruby red lips of her distinctive young face and that look in her eyes

her wiles and her wherefore and the love in this place disgraced

the minstrel played on his banjo and the Gypsies eyes were wild

I was young and deceitful so was the promise in her eyes

There were vagabond people on the road to the downs

with their wayward lost children neath the silk shrouds

the dusty trails and the tales they told with their copper kettles n pots of gold

the nights of splendor I remember it so well

but things were different then and we compromised

lost in wonder in the Gypsy's eyes.- Ray Wills

Gypsies in the UK have been the subject of much prejudice and animosity throughout history usually followed by the threat of much violence against them. So often stirred up by false stories and accusations such as that that they do not contribute by paying any taxes, they have shady reputations or that they do not respect private property, do not contribute or belong here and are therefore seen as outsiders. Until recent years they were able to become invisible within the black economy and society of many of the UK cities.

There have also been a number of television shows and documentaries over the past few years which have either shown poor representation giving a very false public image of the Gypsy as being both unrepresentative, sensationalized or glamorous and somewhat over the top. Such as Gypsy Child Thieves, The Secret Lives of Britain's Child Beggar's, along with the various Big Fat Gypsy Wedding's series shows and programmes.

Big Fat Gypsy Weddings

It was the big fat Gypsy wedding

all the folks came to see

you could watch it free on you tube

or on that old TV

the people came from miles away

to watch that Gypsy dance

there was music in the air that night

within the Gypsy dance

It was billed as true Gypsy

but they were only didycoy

with not a Roma folki in sight

not one gal was shy

There were costumes made to fit a Queen

and lads to grab your arm

there were local fighters with all mouth

yet none had Gypsy charm

The wind it blew there freely

and the media told its lies

with lots of scenes of church and vows

but none were all that wise

The grass was mean upon the earth

where the warblers sang their tune

but only words were said that night

under the foolish moon.

Ray Wills

These old prejudices against Gypsies still remain, with common usage of old phrases such as, "the dark-skinned Roma sings and steals", "doesn't put shoes on his children's feet and likes living in the dirt","that's their tradition, they can't help it and they do not know no better", so the prejudice goes. Were as, this is so far from the truth. For the traditional Romani's and travelers in fact place a very high value on morality and law keeping and value the extended family. Today when they are married, the woman joins the husband's family, where her main job is to look after her husband and her children's needs, and to take care of her in-laws. The power structure in the traditional Romani household has at its top the oldest man or grandfather, though men in general have more authority than women, women gain respect and authority as they get older and young wives automatically gain more authority they become mothers.

Many Gypsies still retain a way of communicating between themselves which is known as the patinm which is a system of sign's left on the road.They pass these along and is used to keep outsider's ignorant of their movement's and give a clear message to other Gypsies following later. They consist of a handful of grass or a notch on a tree or maybe a simple cross drawn on the ground. This is how Gypsies are able to tell which direction was taken, and how many wagon's or families are in the group or how far ahead they are. They also can be seen on a village wall to show whether or not the village people are friendly or hostile.

Queen Victoria and the Gypsies

Queen Victiria came to know the extended families of Coopers, Scamps and Smiths well, making regular trips to take clothes and food to their tents, and also sketching and painting them on occasion. The young Queen Victoria tried to go out of her way to help the Cooper family camped close to Claremont House in Esher, Surrey, where princess Victoria lived.They were often referred to as being the "Windsor Coopers.The young princess future Queen Victoria was said to possess a great fondness for them.

Sarah Cooper was the Gypsy mother of this gypsy group andfollowing the birth of a baby Victoria sent food and blankets to the family. Throughout her lifetime Queen Victoria had had many dealings with Gypsy members of both the Coopers and the Stanley's during her reign particularly amongst her aristocratic friends in the art and riding world. A Stanley fortuneteller in later years at Rotting dean, near Brighton was to tell the fortunes of the then Prince of Wales for a few pounds and a kiss from the German Emperor. As well as predicting the fall of the Kaiser due to the fact that he mounted his horse incorrectly as a result she became known as "the Queen of fortune-tellers. This era became the era when the Gypsy-ologist was born. Queen Victoria regularly wrote in her diaries of her meetings with the Gypsies camped aside the roadside close to her home. On 1 January 1837, she wrote: "I must say that through what I have seen of their characters they are a superior set of Gypsies, full of respect, quiet, discerning and full of affection for one another." "Such a nice set of Gypsies", "so quiet, so affectionate to one another, so discreet, not at all forward or importune'". "So unlike the gossiping fortune-telling race-Gypsies who turned up out of the blue, camped on commons or byways in their bow-topped caravan, grazed horses, sold pegs, perhaps 'tinkering', 'here today and gone tomorrow'". "How often these poor creatures have been falsely accused, cruelly wrong and greatly ill-treated." Queen Victoria's chief harpist was a himself a Gypsy descended of the Welsh Gypsy king Abram Wood.

Matthias Cooper (1811-1900)the royal rat catcher

"Matty", as he was known, was a member of this group he wore a white hat, yellow waistcoat, black cut-away coat, and white trousers. It was from him that Charles G. Leland obtained most of the materials that he used for his work entitled "The English Gypsies and their Language". Matthias taught Leland to speak Romany, which was the Gypsy language and provided Leland with all his information concerning Gypsies.Matthias was also very well known at the Epsom Races as the king of the Gypsies. At the first hint of rats Queen Victoria would have a servant fetch the rat-catcher Matthias Cooper. For he was one of her most favorite reliable rat catchers. One day he was summoned to Windsor Castle, the Queen's main residence, where he caught 50 rats He used to lay them out on the exspensive carpet at the castle, according to his grand-son Edward Prince of Wales, who paid him half a sovereign for his work which was a large sum of money at the time. Matthias died aged 89 hit by a train in 1900. Following Matthias death Anselo and Wacker Cooper his two sons continued his fathers interest in attending the Epsom races for many years. He declared that he had himself been acquainted with Jasper Petulengro, of Borrows' Lavengro.

The young princess Victoria also often read and underlined the book The Gypsies' Advocate by James Crabb. A book dedicated to judges and clergymen in the hope that they would develop a more benevolent attitude to the Romany people. James Crabb helped Gypsy children – he looked after some at home and paid for their schooling establishing a committee with suggestions for reform. Crabb first worked on changing opinions about the Romanies when he had witnessed a judge saying that he intended to execute horse-stealers, especially Gypsies, even after a convicted man pleaded for his life.

CHAPTER FOUR

Gypsy Life in the New Forest

Nova Foresta."Nevi Wesh" is the name for the New Forest.

"Oh Forest! green New Forest!

Home of the bird and breeze,

With all thy soft and sweeping glades,

and long, dim aisles of trees,

Like some ancestral palace thou stands proud and fair;

Yet is each tree a monument to death and wild despair."

-Smedley:

Forest days

In the forest of England they tethered their mares

they worked on the land from craft to repair

they lit of the fires from bracken and log

where the wind it was brisk and the snow it was deep round the yog

They bedded in benders where hogs once did sleep their gowns they were long and their shawls they were wool from the sheep

where the chaffinch did sing and the man sang the blues

For years they did roam from Boldre to Poole

where the vardos did roll and the weather was cruel

though summer's were warm beneath the starry blue skies

where the birch grew so wild and the heathers and grasses were rye

Their fathers were blessed with the call of the free

here the forests were rich from the village to the sea

their children were many and their old uns were wise

they worked on the land with hope in their eyes

The wheels they did roll and the ponies ran free

where Rufus stone stood there amidst the villagers pleas

the bracken was course and the berries were sweet

with lizards and snakes squirmed just beneath of your feet

They gathered their families and took them to Poole

where the lodge hills of Canford were rich in the dew

where the rabbits and foxes ran free on the downs

where gaffers and landlords were rich by the crown

They settled so freely on the Wimbornes estate where the Guest
family resided and the turves were to waste

they built them their homes there beneath the warblers nests *where the gravel was rich and the clay it was blessed*

From Talbot to Magna and over the down's
they gathered their families and all bedded down
in Kinsons New England and Heavenly Bottoms abode
they ran with the wind in the summers so warm and the winters so
cold
All through the war years they traveled this land
from south to the north with their merry bands
they were branded and moved on like thieves in the night
with landlords and mean men who took of their rights
They fought in the war's like true British grit
worked on the land and the factories shifts
they built the great walls with viaducts and brickyards so tall and
mean
then they were herded like cattle and grounded in teams

Their stories are rich and their histories are keen
from the New Forest walks to the home of the Queen
they talk with a richness and will give you the eye
like a true Romani trooper with a didykoy guise.

Ray Wills

When travelling down from London to Weymouth you cannot miss the beautiful landscape of the majestic New Forest unfolding before you. For it is a large area in the south-west of the county of Hampshire covering some several thousands of acres or to be precise some 30 miles in circumference bordering Wiltshire and Dorset and still is today mainly woodland. It was at one time well over 200 miles in total masse.and was created as a hunting reserve by William the Conqueror in about 1079. The story has it that king William, to make way for this area, cleared some 36 Parish Churches, along with all the Houses in the vicinity which were demolished and as a result left the people living there without a home."Probably no action of the early Norman kings is more notorious than their creation of the New Forest", states H.R.Loyn. For many years after its creation the New Forest was the playground of Kings and the aristocracy, a place where the deer roamed free, and were hunted for pleasure and the table.

The Rufus Stone, Canterton Glen

William the Conqueror's second son, William 11, or William Rufus, as he was also known, hunted locally. Then on a fateful day in August, 1100 whilst in the company of a group of friends and supporters, or so he thought. Whether by accident or design, William met his death the victim of an arrow allegedly shot by Sir Walter Tyrrell, an Anglo-Norman nobleman possibly acting under orders from William's younger brother, who then took the throne as Henry 1.The Rufus Stone is in Canterton Glen, near Minstead, 2 miles south of Cadnam, commemorates the event. It is claimed the stone marks the place of William's death.The stone was erected by Lord Delaware, of Bolderwood Lodge, in 1745, but was so damaged by souvenir hunters, who chipped off bits to take home, that in 1841 it was encased in the commemorative metal surround that can still be seen today. The inscription on the Stone reads: "Here stood the oak tree on which an arrow shot by Sir Walter Tyrrell at a stag glanced and struck King William II surnamed Rufus on the breast of which stroke he instantly died on the second day of August anno 1100".

There are several parishes in the forest, including those of Beaulieu, Lyndhurst, Ringwood, Boldre, and Lymington Beaulieu Abbey, Nearby is Buckler's Hard, where many of the old warships were built, including Nelson's flagship HMS 'Victory' which is in dry dock Portsmouth.

"According to Florence of Worcester,the New Forest was actually known prior to the Norman Conquest as "the land of the Jutes", one of the early Anglo Saxon tribes who once colonized this area. Though it was first recorded in the Doomsday book in 1086 as being "Nova Foresta".
Also known as Nevi Wesh.

"THE FOREST PEOPLES"

Gypsies have always been regarded as being the Forest peoples since the middle ages when they arrived in England from Europe. Though Gypsies were first recorded living in the New Forest in the parish of Alton Hampshire records in 1638.Though by 1528 it's estimated that up to 10,000 Gypsies were actually living in England. In 1555 there was a reference to gypsies living in the forest in the Southampton Stewards book.With much of Britain covered by forest, these great forests of the land was home to deer and wild boar. The New Forest may well have been one of the earliest gypsy settlements in England and the Encloruere Act may well have driven more gypsies than ever into the New Forest to survive,with its abundance of game and its shelter.

For many hundreds of years Gypsies were able to camp anywhere they wished within the New Forest without concern. They had popular places where they would stop and often met up with their family friends and acquaintances. Len Smith notes that 'The first visitors to the Forest regarded the Gypsies as an essential part of the mystique of the scene, enhancing the overall sense of wildness and freedom that a visit 'there was little or no friction between the Travellers' and the commoners or cottagers: no more than occasionally crops up between all neighbours.

The New Forest Gypsies often met up with other Travelers from Surrey, Kent, Sussex, Devon and Wales and vice versa when they all travelled to the various Parishes for the annual Hop Picking/Pea Picking/ Strawberry Picking/Potato picking and so on. This is no doubt how the different families met and married and how over time all the families seem to have relations across the width and breadth of the UK.

Gypsies regularly travelled back and forth from the New Forest to Kinson and other towns in Dorset,Hampshire,Wiltshire,Berkshire and Somerset villages and towns such as Poole, Southampton and Portsmouth in Hampshire, Wiltshire,Berks and Somerset. Some of these Gypsy families such as the Fancys lived in the Wareham area in the 16th century too. There were also many places outside the New Forest which were extremely popular at that time with the Gypsies, such as Bournemouth, Parkstone, Kinson,Turbary,Newtown,Rossmore;Poole,the Purbeck region, Somerset, Blackhill near Wellow and at Eastleigh Southampton. Many Forest gypsy families settled in these areas.

Others lived at Fordingbridge on the edge of the Forest and all of the Cranborne Chase area. Some of these were originally from Sussex, Kent, and Surrey, whilst others had even travelled from as far afield as Wales and Scotland.

Gypsies and the Horse

The Forest Gypsies seemed to be always surrounded by a variety of domestic animals, horses, cat's, and dog's and the dogs were used for hunting of rabbits and hares. In the New Forest a ring plaited from the hair of skewbald or piebald horses, particularly from the stallion's was often used as a good luck charm.

The Gypsies of the New Forest claimed that they were the first to tame the local wild horses to breed them for riding and later to tow their caravan's. Legend has it that the New

Forest's wild ponies are descended from the horse's that swam ashore when most of the Spanish Armada ship's sank.Following the sinking of the Spanish Armada by Sir Francis Drake it is believed that hordes of ponies were saved from drowning by the forest Gypsies and these are now known as the New Forest ponies.

Their horse trading occupation came from many generations of ancestors. A business in which Gypsies excelled, there's a saying that what Gypsies do not know about horses is not worth knowing.The horse is almost a trademark of the Gypsy life and culture with horses often painted or carved on the sides of their wagons, carts and lorries. Many have pictures of horses inside their vans too. Horse-dealing has long been a gypsy sideline a major occupation for many gypsy folk in Britain.

William the Conqueror is recorded as bringing shoeing Smiths with him for his invasion of England in 1066, and by the time of the Crusades in the 1100s, shoeing horses was a much more common practice than in previous centuries.

In earlier times a reliable trade could be looked for from farmers and other private individuals, coaching and freighting businesses, for work down the coal pits or in the Army. Although there may no longer be a demand for working horses, the recreational market for hunts and riding schools has increased to replace them. A living can still be made by a Gypsy with generations of experience and working knowledge of horses behind him, particularly so if he has too has veterinary skills and a blacksmith trade.

Despite moving to motor transport, Gypsies still continue to retain this special relationship with horses. With their children taught to ride at an early age, and a pony may be taken on the road alongside the trailer. Such reliable horses were never sold under any normal circumstances and they became solid and respected members of the Gypsy family. The Gypsies have always had a high regard for their horses and the eating of horseflesh was banned, for to them the horse is a sacred animal and has always been a symbol of good luck and prosperity.

Commoners' cattle, ponies and donkeys roam throughout the open heath and much of the woodland, and it is largely their grazing that maintains the character of the Forest. The New Forest Pony is one of the most famous attractions, they are still allowed to wander about wherever they please in the forest. The ponies are an essential part of the landscape and in order to increase the quality of breed in the forest, many different types of horse were introduced to create the rich diversity desired. Queen Victoria herself lent out one of her Arab horses for 8 years to help improve the breed.

Numerous deer also live in the Forest; though these are usually well hidden.Nowadays many horses and ponies still survive in the forest with the present day travellers and Gypsies being settled in the area living in cottages and in the surrounding areas. The annual New Forest show is still as popular as ever event and has always remained so with the Gypsies, Romani's, traveller's, and tinker's. This event attracting horse dealers among other 'trades'. This was particularly so in earlier years when a horse was such a highly valued commodity essential to the true Romany travelling life.

In Ringwood the Gypsies often gathered to buy and sell their horses; usually these were the New Forest ponies.Those ponies seen today are a mixed variety of Dartmoor, Exmoor, Welsh, and Highland etc. These are intelligent, docile and friendly, making them very popular with visitors to the New Forest. In more recent decades the New Forest has been the setting of the autumn pony sales but these are rare now.

Due to their living so close to nature they developed a skill at making medicines from both the animals and forest plants, their knowledge of such herbal folk cures is very well known. Their dress was also considered to be much different from the norm with their women wearing loud bright colours of floral designs and long heavy cheap jewellery and gold-hooped ear-ring's which contrasted well against their jet black hair. Some of the Gypsy men also wore ear-ring's and sported brightly coloured neckerchiefs.

Amongst the early Gypsy settlers in the forests it is said that there were some most excellent musicians, some of whom played the violin really well.

Many Gypsies were transported as punishment for poaching etc sent off to the new worlds of Australia,Newfoundland/Canada or USA.

The occupation of most Gypsy women then was fortune telling "dunkerin" and Gypsies in the New Forest were often seen locally fruit picking on local farm's during harvest times. Others would be seen loading their cart's and driving off to join in with the seasonal traditional fruit picking trips to Kent, Worcestershire and Herefordshire.

Most of the year then the Gypsies spent their time making

clothes pegs, dairy churns, casks for 'home made wines', straw baskets, beehives made from straw and stringed rabbit nets. Others fashioned crepe paper and rushes into artificial flowers, whilst some of the women would gather daffodils to sell in the market, they usually hawked what the men had made and some of these wares they peddled.They are really clever makers of briar mats and baskets; and rush work of various kinds, and clothes pegs for use in hanging washed linen to dry, are among the handiworks that they practice including making brooms and brushes. They sold their products to any buyers they chanced upon.

Door to door selling was an opportunity for the Gypsy woman to persuade a housewife to have her fortune told too if they 'crossed her palm with silver'. Divination was also well in use by the Gypsies then, along with palmistry, tarot card reading, crystal balls and the reading of tea leaves. My aunt Macey Castle and her sister in law Mary King excelled at this craft of tilting a cup of tea n telling fortunes from the dregs. Which was a unique skill which she had gained from the Castles and Kings tribes of Gypsies.

In the Southampton area close to the New Forest is Sholing Common which was at one time a small hamlet of brick bungalow type cottages which had been built in the 1790s. The first people living there were poor Romany Gypsies who kept to their own tight knit community and many of them kept their caravans there also. They spent the winter in the houses, with their caravans in the garden. Then in the summer they went hop picking or fruit picking and the men would race their horses on the local roads during the local horse sales.

Numbers living in the Forest

At that time there were said to be up to 700 Gypsies in the New Forest, in the Thorney Hill encampment alone as estimated by Eric Winstead. These were living in thatched cottages camped close to Southampton. The late Len Smith a travelers elder once estimated that there were up to 10,000 Gypsies living in the New Forest area at one time. The true figures of Gypsies in the UK were not reflected in the early censuses as in 1841 the enumerators were not expected to record Gypsies or people living in tents or vans and first names or place of birth were also not recorded.By 1851 the figures were surprising in that Dorset had only 37 Stanley's and Hampshire 113.The 1871 census for Holdenhurst gives several families of Travellers living in Sheep House Lane, which is now Woodbury Avenue just off Castle Lane West. Personally based on the numbers who originated in the forest and moved out and married into the wider areas of the surroundings counties I believe the figure is probably substantially more.For the Gypsy family names are still around and prominent in big numbers in this part of southern England.

Encampments in the forest including those at North Godshill Wood, Whinyates, Crock Hill Copythorne,East Ipley, Pennerley, Lady Cross, Norley Wood. West – Poulner Pits, Picket Post, Burley, Thorny Hill. South Bransgore, Shirley Holmes, Pennington, Setley,Central Rufus Stone, Bartley, Buskett's Lawn, New Park,Castle Malwood,Mark Ash,Binstead,Coldharbour.Fordingbridge,Crystal Hollow,Sheephouse Lane,Tin Tin Bottom,Millingsford Bottom,Minstead and Cotshill Wood.
John Richards Wise wrote in 1831 -"They live chiefly in the

various droves and rides of the Forest, driven from place to place by the policeman, for to this complexion have things come". One of their favourite halting-places is amongst the low woods near Wootton, where a dozen or more brown tents are always fluttering in the wind, and as the night comes on the camp-fires redden the dark fir-stems". A favorite Gypsy site then was at Shave Green near Minstead,here there were a variety of poor dwellings of flimsy construction often with just a bed and chairs. The 1871 census for Holdenhurst gives several families of Travellers living in Sheep House Lane, which is now Woodbury Avenue just off Castle Lane West. First names or place of birth are not recorded. Another family living at Redhill Cross was James and Jane Burchell and their two nephews, who were born in Portsmouth.

At Millersford Bottom site near Fordingbridge and Crystal Hollow and other places deep in the forest, the Gypsies still used old Gypsy bell type tents. These were later to be condemned by the authorities and these families moved elsewhere, where some were housed.

Many Gypsies then were and many still are dealers in scrap metal and it was quite usual to see the Gypsy rag and bone man too riding down the local streets on his cart shouting out "rag n bone", "rag n bone". The local Gypsy women were often seen carrying their large sturdy hand-woven baskets over the fields filled brim full of wild flowers, berries or nuts. Although they picked and sold snowdrops the Gypsies themselves were not fond of these flowers and Gypsies often being superstitious would never carry them into their vans fearing it would bring bad luck.

Goldfinches and Gypsies

Goldfinch Days

He was raised at the Mannings where the goldfinch did sing
in long summer months in the thistles from the dawn of each spring
where the orchards was rich in pear trees and fall
where pigs were once kept amidst the good soil

He ran wth the dogs and gave chase to the packs
schoolduys at Branksome and nights playing jacks
in wartime he travelled out to the East
drove generals and captains with his Dorset rich speech

On returning to England he drove for a while
from the docksides of Weymouth to the New Forest wilds
he loved to play darts and shovehalfpenny too
spending days on the farm and night out at Poole

His stories were rich in tone and in depth
with his humourist anecdotes and his lengthly odettes
his dart throwing visions and quick witted speech
though the birds were his fancy with feathers all set

pigeons and doves with canaries his best

His stories he told to children in rhymes

once upon a time when the bees drank the wine

Hel be remembered as the storyteller of the heath

with his own unique brand of humour and his rich dialect speech

Every time you hear a Johnny Cash song or a childs happy laugh

youl see his smile and his unique country ways

itl all come back

not forgotten

in those young springtime goldfich days.

Ray Wills

The goldfinch is a symbol of good fortune and loaded with allegorical meaning since the Middle Ages, often appearing in religious paintings. Such as The Goldfinch, the 1654 painting by Carel Fabritius which inspired Donna Tartt's 2014 Pulitzer Prize-winning novel.The red flash of the goldfinch was a sign to medieval Christians that, like the robin, it had acquired blood-colored feathers at the crucifixion of Christ trying to remove seeds from the thistles in the crown of thorns. The goldfinch was believed to be a symbol of endurance, an allegory of the salvation Christ would bring through his sacrifice. In medieval times thistles were thought to combat the plague and gold was considered a color that could cure sickness. Goldfinches were caught in bird traps and bred with canaries to create offsprings of Minors. Wonderfull singers.

Thomas Hardy Dorsets most famous novelist writer in his finch poems recalls the earlier appearance of a caged goldfinch in The Mayor of Casterbridge (1886)when,in an act of contrition, Henchard visits his stepdaughter Elizabeth-Jane on her wedding day with the gift of a goldfinch in a cage as penitence for his previous bad behavior. When she dismisses him, the bird is left behind and found days later starved to death, prompting Elizabeth-Jane to go in search of her stepfather to forgive him. Too late, she finds he has suffered the same fate as the bird, starved to death in a metaphorical cage of his own past actions.

In 1828 there were attempts by Crabb and others to set up missionaries and a free school in the forest for Gypsy families.But this was unsuccessfull despite a member of the Stanley Gypsies being involved.

The forest Tent-Dwellers

New Forest Tent-dwellers' Night Prayers

The berries they does be turnen' red towards the winter-time,

When hollies be a-shinen' all with rain and misty rime ;

The star that travels the World around^ looks down the leaves

between, When tents is shut and prayers is said, o' night in the Bushes.

Alice E. Gillington

These were often described as being descendants of the old tribes who have made the Forest their home for centuries past. A few families would go in summer for a short time to the hop gardens, then do not return again to the Forest till the season was over. The Van-Dwellers were not seen as fulltime residents of the Forest, and were said to only pass through it periodically. The vardo Gypsies were usually seen as being well-to-do; often "cheap jacks", or hawkers of various wares, at which they ran a successful business. Many of them were extremely very clean and tidy and cared well for their horses keeping them healthy and well groomed, and their children well cared for.

There was a good supply of venison, game, and rabbits, at that time in the Forest, and a some liquor was often smuggled in too. In the warm weather it was a common sight to see a group of women wearing their colorful apron's and headscarves' busy hoeing between the lettuce's and strawberry plant's in a market garden at Gorley.

The New Forest Gypsies used all the pubs in the forest regularly and always received a warm welcome being well remembered for their singing and dancing. They were also well known and respected by the local police, villagers and tradesmen, being very skilled in the making of clothes pegs, paper flowers, the casks and the hives which the foresters used for their bee keeping to produce local honey.

Hutchinson writes 'The sense of family is very strong with the Gypsies', and it is here that we see their kindly virtues most eminently displayed.Their children are bright and happy, their animals, though somewhat starved, which is the result of the Gypsy not having much hay or corn to give them or show that affection for their masters which is the best proof of fair treatment.' '

Len Smith remarked - 'there was little or no friction between the Travellers and the commoners or cottagers: no more than occasionally crops up between all neighbours. Each regarded the other as simply a different type of indigenous inhabitant, and in some cases there were tenuous threads of blood connection. The shared adversity of the struggle to wrest a living by whatever means from the unforgiving environment of the then much more natural Forest and its surrounding commons, would surely have engendered a mutual respect.'

A commoner, who had lived as a child close to the Gypsy camp at Longdown,lamented their confinement in the compounds and the restrictions placed upon their movements. He saw them as an essential element in the Forest's composition. They worked for local farmers on seasonal jobs and 'they were the police force. If there was anything going on that really shouldn't be, they knew about it. All these little things, like catching the rabbits and all that:- well who wouldn't!' In fact, he said, the Gypsies often got the blame for things that had been done by commoners or other Forest residents.

Numbers of Gypsies in the forest would increase when the local fair arrived with many fairground show gypsies coming to the Forest from surrounding neighbourhoods. Their beds were made out of nearby bracken and straw which they called mat grass and bender tents made out of hazel sticks. Whilst chairs were often no more than orange crates or overturned bucket. Their yog or fireplace was often no more than an iron bar in the fire with a hook for hanging the stewpot this was called the kiddle. Most of the men could put their hands to anything throughout the year including rag n bone carts. Their children would all be expected to help with any work.

The Thorney Hills population in 1907 was mainly Gypsy though caravans were a rare sight there. At Thorley's Horney Hill there were at one time up to 400 Gypsies recorded in the 1911 census alone. These included those of the Does, Pidgleys, James, Moores, Williams, Lambs, Smiths, and later the Hughes families. They all lived in thatched cottages.

At the start of the twentieth century new laws were introduced which meant that Gypsy Travelers were no longer permitted to remain on the same piece of land for no more than two days. Most of them would keep to these laws and moved on every forty eight hours travelling on a regular route which lasted some six weeks in total.

Elizabeth Godfrey wrote in 1912 "One of the favorite camping grounds was at Coldharbour, a name accounted for by some as Cold'arbres, During the summer many Gypsies moved farther away going travelling some as far as London or in the outskirts, seeking jobs in haymaking, fruit picking, harvesting and hopping. A number of them would go away for the hopping month only, the rest remaining in the Forest all the rest of the year.

In winter months numbers of them congregated, with their vans, in a field near Fording bridge, which they had bought as a safe place during the cold weather". Hop-picking was a great season for New Forest Gypsies. It usually started the last week in August or first week in September from the early 1910s to the late 1920s. These events in the Gypsy calendar lasted from late August and well into October. There were three hundred or more Gypsies gatherings at Binstead near Alton in Hampshire for the hopping season.These Gypsies and travelling farmhands had followed the harvests and horse fairs throughout the British Isles in 1913.

Munnings the artist in his autobiography wrote "By the "Hen and Chickens" pub at Froyle, we turned, right-handed, over a small stream, finally arriving in a forty-acre pasture, with a fine oak-tree in the middle. Standing along the hedges on each side were caravans of all shapes, sizes and descriptions : round, Romany, bee-hive tents; old Army bell-tents. There were at least two to three hundred souls, men, women and children. not including dogs and horses camped in this pasture". Lurchers and greyhounds lay underneath many a vehicle, travelling families of fowls were making themselves at home around the fences, and smoke from wood fires, shouts of fighting children, and barking of dogs filled the air.

'"Never in my life have I been so filled with a desire to work as I was then". "For all my painting experiences, none were so alluring and colourful as those visits spent amongst the gypsy hop- pickers in Hampshire each September". "More glamour and excitement were packed into those six weeks than a painter could well contend with". "I still have visions of brown faces, black hair, earrings, black hats and black skirts ; of lithe figures of women and children, of men with lurcher dogs and horses of all kinds. I still recall the never-ceasing din around their fires as the sun went down, with blue smoke curing up amongst the trees".

In a report to a House of Commons Select Committee (see Hansard) Lord Arthur Cecil was asked about grievances against the Gypsies. He replied, '"They are a great nuisance to everybody. I am specially troubled by Gypsies myself. I have two instances which I cannot turn them away from within 100 yards of my house".

Due to growing concerns about the problems that Gypsies were said to be causing, and in response to a police authority request, in 1926 the Forestry Commission in 1927 had found an answer to the problem of the hundreds of people who were living wild in the forest. Its solution was to confine them to compounds, where, like native Americans on reservations, they could be corralled within the forest in which they had once roamed free. Forbidden from building any permanent structures, these were issued with six-month licenses which could be revoked instantly should their behaviour upset the Commission. Their compounds were, in effect, no more than concentration camps.

John Augustus the artist lived in Fording bridge in the Forest area at Fryern Court which became an open house for travelling artists and he was highly regarded by the New Forest Gypsies, who called him Sir Gustus. John Augustus "Although nobody so far has proposed to liquidate these nomads after the Hitler style, is it possible that, in his own country, John Bunyan's people have been sentenced to a lingering death"?' asked Augustus John.

Movements between these compounds were not restricted

but Gypsies were forbidden to camp outside of them. There were no toilets and limited water supply, living in the compounds interfered with the Gypsy normal way of life because they had preferred to live in small family units rather than a community. This often led to trouble, disagreements and many arguments between families.

The system also restricted the Gypsy Travellers earning potential because they were no longer able to travel and earn an honest living as they had previously. This system in many aspects was not unlike the native American reservation or the German concentration area. Rather than live in these compounds some families actually moved out of the New Forest altogether. By the 1930s, the population of the seven compounds had reached nearly one thousand, swollen by the effects of the Depression.

In 1937 film star Henry Fonda made and starred in a movie called Wings of the Morning about an American who falls in love with a Gypsy woman. Gypsies were hired as extras and Uncle Moocher was a horse wrangler for the film; he appears in the movie holding horses with his wife Aunt Sarah walking between the wagons resplendent in her feather hat. Wings of the Morning (the race horse's name) has a place in film history as the first Technicolor movie shot in the British Isles.The Gypsy's particular knowledge of the Forest was taken advantage of and very many of them were employed locally in forestry work. In the 19th and early 20th century, many members of the new forest community were granted special licences to provide a mobile shop service to the soldiers stationed at nearby Borden Camp.

War years in the New Forest

The new forest was used as a staging post for British troops during the first world war 1914-1918 prior to them going to France. There was a Grenade School at Bolton's Bench, Lyndhurst, and a War Dog Training School in Matley Wood. The airfield on Beaulieu Heath at East Boldre was bought by the War Department and from 1916 training squadrons were based there. Charcoal burning once again returned to the Forest providing absorbers for gas masks.

At Beaulieu Heath, the New Forest Flying School was taken over by the services, and in 1920, RAF Calshot became a training unit for flying boats and one of the coastal stations which helped to defend the Channel during the war. Many pilots learned to fly there with an excellent war record. Generals Eisenhower and Montgomery took over the Balmer Lawn hotel as their operations HQ for the invasion of Europe in 1944. Anti-aircraft emplacements were dug and Hurst Castle was a good observation post for any invasion from across the Channel.

As usual the Forest provided thousands of tons of timber for the war effort and crops were grown to help with food production. The Normandy Landings began on the 6th June 1944, when 130,000 troops set off from the south coast of England (including some from the port at Bucklers Hard, where Nelson's ships had launched 150 years earlier) and landed on the beaches of Normandy - Operation Overlord had begun. A

At the end of the 1939-45 war some of the new forest Gypsies found shelter in these disused huts which were former Air Force bases. Then in 1947 the Report of the New Forest Committee stated that "the Gypsies in the New Forest were living in most terrible squalor and unhygienic conditions, many without water or sanitary facilities with no proper shelter". This Report put Gypsies on trial without being allowed to defend themselves. They were thus found guilty of a crime they were not responsible for. They had been herded into these compounds which had no water or sanitary arrangements. In 1949, it was reported that there were still about five hundred Gypsies living this way when Arthur Lloyd wrote his report for the Picture Post, illustrated by the photographer, Bert Hardy with pictures, taken in the aftermath of war.

Housing of the Gypsies

Some of these Gypsies were housed by the various councils in prefabricated bungalows in the 1950s with some attending classes on household skills and literacy. However at that time no provision was made for their trauma. These Reports made the Gypsies bad news in the media as never before. Though Ralph Wightman in Abiding wrote that "One class of people who know all the old rights of way are the Gypsies. They very seldom do any bad harm and they are better than most as far as litter is concerned, The irony is that they were disliked just because they were a nomadic people".

Around a hundred families were settled in council houses from Gypsy camps and it was so successful that two of the camps were shutdown. Many local folks married into the Romani's from the New Forest at that time and throughout the surrounding areas. Many of these had found casual occupation dealing in scrap metal, but this was now discouraged in favour of regular employment. Local Gypsy families were fairly static or occupied permanent winter homes and wanted to be housed, but groups still existed who lived in sub standard camps. The Centre for Holocaust and Genocide Studies recognizes that: "It is hard to believe that civilized Britons would herd innocent people into compounds because of their race, just as Nazi Germans would a few decades later".

On the northern edge of Southampton County Borough and on the eastern border at Eastleigh two such camps existed. With Gypsies left to their own devices and traditional ways, dealing in scrap metal and hawking their wares, until they were also permanently settled.It was quite a common sight in those days to see Gypsies camping in these places in their traditional ways with their tents and carts and the occasional yard.

Previously there had been opportunities for Gypsies to live off the land and find self employment and local farmers had been glad of the extra help during busy seasons.There had also been a good living for the gypsies in horse trading and breaking. However, as demand lessened, Gypsies turned to their old trades of selling crafted objects and hawking. Whilst this door to door "hawking" had been welcomed by the community during the war years when household goods and labour had been in short supply, but after the war attitudes had begun to change. Door knocking was no longer considered to be acceptable. One commentator remarked "In the Gypsies we meet a problem of more than local significance while the standard of living in this country is steadily being raised; a group is allowed to live in the area which has hardly reached the standard of the Stone Age.

The growth of road traffic in the main lead to Bournemouth road being fenced off and car parks and picnic areas were arranged and placed throughput along with designated camping sites. Today, with motor cars and mechanized industry, the Gypsies are classed even more so as misfit's or outsiders. Considering their numbers and family names which are so prevalent across the south of the country, this makes it extremely confusing and difficult to understand why.

David Essex singer has been a regular visitor to the New Forest over recent years. David himself comes from a travelling family his Mother being from the Kemp clan. David first came to the New Forest to prepare for his film Silver Dream Racer in the mid 1970s when he spent time with our family friend Scott Mitchell(World champion dart player) family home and farm in Bransgore, learning to ride the motor bike for the film Silver Dream Racer and being shot for the film. David returned again more recently to complete excerpts for the film The Traveler.(David kindly made a poetry contribution Tinker Man to my previous book which I edited entitled "Gypsy Storytellers").

When the yellows on the broom

When the yellows on the broom and the heather decked the floor
when the travelers on the road and well sing the Gypsy reel
when the birch tree shed its branches and the warbler sings his tune
I'll be wandering down that highway beneath that old new moon

When the yellows on the broom and the furze is rich with dew
where the lizards warm their bodies and the adders bake in June
where the fir trees shed their harvests with Coneys rich in tar
where the wandering Gypsies travel playing that old country guitar

When the yellows on the broom and the wheels they turn once more
where the vardos bless the hillsides from north to sandy shores
where the Gypsy boys lay sleeping whilst the rabbits hunt and play
across the moors and valleys where the wise ones sit and pray

When the yellows on the broom and the gal she tells her cards like
fortune tellers do
there be lots of zunners laughing and yokels playing tunes
where the benders blessed the heather and the fox did hideaway
whilst the caravans rolled on towards the light of day

When the yellows on the broom and the brackens rich in black

where the berries are sweet in fruiting and the horses rode bare back

where the dogs all run in packs and the accordions still play

where the wise man knows the Gypsy song and the hares do dance.
in May.

Ray Wills

True Love Stories and Tales

We looked in the embers and he told us those tales

there were many a long year and I remember it well

the fire cracked and spat then and the kettle whistled through

whilst the yog it was burning red and the moon it shone too

He told me of times the good and the bad

the life on the roads then and the people so sad

he talked and his story though was painfully true

as the chavvies all listened to the wise one they knew

Their vardos were tall now and the drapes they were red

with the cushions of wool and the warmth of their beds

He smoked of his pipe and he spat in the fire

whilst the logs they did hiss and burn and the young men desired

the women were frisky I heard him to say

when the times they were hard and the men earned their pay

The cobs they were wild then but their coats they did shine

the locks of their hairs and their manes they were strong

like the men folk who rode them on the banks of the drom

he told us of gaffers and gorgas so fine

Of men who lived only for a bottle of wine

of pasture so rich and of woodlands so free

where the hares and the rabbits ran over the leas

He told us of the deers and the pheasants and the grouse in the dell

the lord of the manor and the surround high walls as well

the homes they were stately and the master was rich

he owned all the land there in the country and ditch

whilst the homes of the traveler was built in the mud

consisting of nowt but benders and bracken

and yet was full of true love.

Ray Wills

Smuggling country

This area of England was also at one time great smuggling country and no doubt there were many well known and respectable people involved in these activities, including lords, clergy and business men. Many used their lofty positions in business and society in which to cover their illegal practices. Given that for centuries all the habitat of this terrain was mostly desolate heath lands and the vast New Forest being so readily available and easily accessible in which to hide these activities. The rising food prices saw the onset of smuggling and highway robberies. The numerous natural creeks and inlets around the coastline made life easy for the smugglers to get their contraband into the secrecy of the Forest. The most popular routes were at Chewton Bunny, near New Milton, and up the Beaulieu river. If caught both smugglers and highwaymen would be hanged from the Naked Man, an oak tree, part of which still stands today at Markway on the A35.

Coastal smuggling took place at all the numerous coves, bays and chines of Dorset and Hampshire. All of which was a source of inspirational material for writers such as Robert Louis Stevenson who wrote much of Treasure Island and Kidnapped whilst living at Westbourne' Bournemouth and also no doubt in later years for the children's writer Enid Blyton.

In 1748 one record stated   'We hear from the New Forest in Hampshire that Smugglers have got to such a height in that part of the country that scarce a week passes but great quantities of goods are run between Lymington and Christchurch and during the same period every labourer was regarded as either a poacher or a smuggler, very often both". Favourite smuggling centre's then were at Fordingbrige, Lymington, Christchurch, and Cranborne Chase.

Warner says that he had then seen twenty or thirty wagons laden with kegs, guarded by two or three hundred horsemen, each bearing two or three "tubs," coming over Hengistbury Head, making their way, in the open day, past Christchurch to the Forest. At Lymington, a troop of bandits took possession of the well-known Ambrose Cave, on the borders of the Forest, and carried on, not only smuggling, but wholesale burglary. The soldiers were at last called out, the men tracked, and the cave entered. Booty to an enormous extent was found. The captain turned King's evidence, and confessed that he had murdered upwards of thirty people, whose bodies had been thrown down a well, where they were found. At one time every forest labourer was said to be either a poacher or a smuggler. The local saying runs 'Keystone under the hearth, Keystone under the horse's belly' since these were two favourite places for hiding contraband which were under the stable floor, and under the hearth, with a fire burning innocently above it.

 According to legend,smugglers who lived in the village of Cranbourne Chase pretended to be stupid or crazy as a way to hide their activities, and told foolish tales such as that they had spread manure around the church tower to make it grow taller.

 Another tale they told was that all of the village folk had once walked to Devizes to watch an eclipse of the moon. But the most told yarn of all tells how several villagers were caught one night in the act of raking the village pond to haul out tubs that had been sunken in the brackish water. The excise men demanded to know what was going on were told by the smugglers, who pointed at the moon's reflection in the water, that they were raking the pond to recover the 'big yellow cheese' that was floating in it. Smuggled spirits were concealed either below the fireplace or in the stable, just beneath where the horse stood.The expression of "Hampshire and Wiltshire moon-rakers" had its origin in the Wiltshire peasants fishing up the contraband goods at night, brought through the Forest, and hid in the various ponds.

Many of the church cemetarys in the locality contain some old gravestone bearing witness to the murderous carrying ons between the Revenue men and the smugglers. One at Kinson Dorset at St Andrews church which is dated 1765 (where I at one time managed the renovation of the church grounds) is of a certain Robert Trotman. He was shot dead in the act of smuggling tea. St Andrews cemetary has around 6 smugglers buried there.

A little tea one leaf I did not steal

For guiltless blood steal I to God appeal

Put the tea in one scale

human blood in another

And think what it's to stay thy harmless brother.

– Epitaph Kinson St Andrews church cemetary

Bucklers Hard

The New forest was also used for boat-building, and some areas often to the amazement of outsiders are still known locally as 'the Boatyard'. The port of Bucklers Hard was built on Beaulieu river by John, 2nd Duke of Montagu, to land his sugar from the West Indies. Many of the old warships were built there some 50 ships were built there from New Forest oak for Nelson's navy in 1781.With timber used for Nelsons flagship HMS Victory, including Nelson's flagship HMS 'Victory' which is in dry dock Portsmouth.

Bucklers Hard is a great tourist attraction with gift shops,inns and restaurants situated in the heart of the forest.

Travellers' school

Dorset had its own Gypsy travellers school at Farnham in the forest.

The school was opened on 5th October 1847 and, as well as the children from the cottages, Gypsy children were taken as boarders and listed in the 1851 census: These included Unity Ayres, Britannia Barney, Mary Ann Mills, Lucy Bowers, Rhoda Barney, Mary Bowers, Amberline Barney, Henry Barney, Dangerfill (Dangerfield) Barney, Henry Mills, Henry Martin, Samuel Martin.It was not to be the success hoped for, however, and by 1855 the decision was made to close the school, where only five pupils remained.

Travelling School

I went one day to the travelling school

there were bridles and stirrups and how do you do

baskets of flowers with sweet violets

cheerful real laughter and from the people one met

The talk and the banter and the zunners run free

with no sock's on their feet and candle's to see

there was food on the tables and rabbits hung high

a sparrow to sing and an old apple pie

The grass it was green and the heather was thick

with furze bush and broom and old maidens witch

there was room around the fire and songs for to sing

with tales of the old folks on the first day of spring

The ponies and chestnuts were rich and so proud

there were travelling men from abroad and music so loud

with the cards on the tables and the banter so free

when the Gypsy gal danced it was music to me

The piano accordion did play and the fiddle soared free

with history tales from cradle to sea

there were vardos and vans to glorify your eyes

with hand crafted garments and pegs split near by

The talk and the banter where the children ran free

where daisy chain's spread and the buzzing of bees

the wagon wheels turned and the folki did bless

the good lord in heaven and their travelling ways.

Ray Wills

Chewton Glen times.

We rode the lanes near Chewton Glen

where Captain Marryat put ink to pen

where forest children laughed again

where leaves were rich on bended boughs

where hedgerows grew so wild and proud

With clotted cream and tea for two

in summer suns and morning dews

we gathered our thoughts and paid our dues

buttons on dress and and buckles on shoes

Dusty roads and springtime's breeze

chaffinch songs and hidden leas
forest lanes and chattered talks
common folki eyes alert.
Ray Wills

Gypsy rides

Down some quiet country lane where oak trees stood so proud
where chaffinch sang amongst the fern and poppies grew so proud
where honey bees they blessed the thorns where Rose petals bloomed
the travellers trotted down the lane where sun did beat at noon

The crowd' did gather on the grass and the tractor turned the soils
the geese did fly across the downs and the lassies looked forlorn
where cocks did crow at early morn and farmer kissed his wife
beneath the chimneys thatch with hope and the labourers retired

The Gypsy travellers used that lane where the children sang their
rhymes
alongside grass and heather down's where country folk resides
the language it was rich in tone and the vardo tall and gay
whilst children danced upon the green just a little ways away

The Gypsy crowd that walked the road alongside vardos decked

with good things crafted in their hand's and windows with neat net's

the steps were hard and mighty there and the Gypsy boy he sang

whilst gals did dream of long off days a courting in the sun

The walks and rides to the village fairs where ponies trade was free

whilst landed gentry smiled that smile from hilltop o'er to sea

the gaffer's talked of far off days when land was open fields

where Gypsy gal and Gypsy boy was part of brotherhood

The lessons learned around the fires and the dogs they barked t'was
true

whilst old uns told of olden days and ate their mushes stew

the sailors sailed to far off land' and the soldiers went to war

but the poor old Gypsy worked the land and never knew what for

The nights were dark and the stars were rich with jewels set to see

from common lands where travellers roamed too far off liberty

whilst story tellers told their tales to poets like you and me.

Ray Wills

Where Salisbury stands

Grandiose dreams in Purbecks spire
with walls of stone and stain glass attired
histories of conflicts etched in stone
horrors of war mans wealth atoned

Beauty in art personified
wars of lost causes uninspired
organ of architectural enterprise
beauty of man in some fools eyes

The spire with devils curse on tap
images of man in life trapped
enchanting town with Tudor gates
waters of beauty where loneliness waits

Wars of man and God's own grace
two faces of life
what a waste.
Ray Wills

Crossing Over

We crossed the Iford water down upon the Stour

we stayed a while my folks and I for many happy hour

the swans were on the river then and the sun was on our backs

*the boughs were rich in blossom then and the downs were full of
sacks*

The birds were singing peacefully that life it was so grand

*the Gypsy lady told the folks their fortune as she gazed into their
hands*

the trials and tribulations their joys and ecstasies

their zunners running on the grass and the songs upon the leas

*The cob was tall and proud that day and the towns we passed were
true*

*not far from Ringwood Christchurch and just miles a ways from
Poole*

the sky was blue and beautiful and the gaffers they were kind

*my mates were common mushes then and just like the girls I left
behind.*

Ray Wills

Christchurch Priory legend

On the south-west borders of the New Forest there's still the legend that the Church of Christchurch Priory was originally to have been built on the lonely St. Catherine's Hill. Instead of in the valley where the people were and it was most needed. The stones, however, which were taken up the hill in the day were brought down in the night by invisible hands. The beams, too, which were found too short on the heights, were more than long enough in the town. The legend tells that when the building was going on, there was always one more workman—namely Christ.

CHAPTER FIVE

New Forest Gypsy Families

There were hordes of Gypsy families and Gypsy characters with roots in the New Forest and surroundings areas. In this chapter I present a glimpse into many of these along with some of their stories and traditions.

The New Forest was home to a great many Gypsy and non Gypsy families many of these people led a hard life and their stories are very interesting and their lives full of character. The following is a brief glimpse into the lives of many characters who roamed the forests over the years along with others of fame and those who made a distinctive impact upon the lives of the local area and its communities. Shirley Holmes, Pennington, John Richard Wise wrote in 1863- "The principal tribes round Lyndhurst are the Stanley's, the Lees, and the Burtons; and near Fordingbridge, the Snells". "They live chiefly in the various droves and rides of the Forest, driven from place to place by the policeman, for to this complexion have things come".

One of their favourite halting-places is amongst the low woods near Wootton, where a dozen or more brown tents are always fluttering in the wind, and as the night comes on the camp-fires redden the dark fir-stems"."The kingly title formerly held by the Stanley's is now in the possession of the Lees". "They all still, to a certain extent, keep up their old dignity, and must by no means be confounded with the strolling outcasts and itinerant beggars who also dwell in the Forest". "Their marriages, too, are still observed with strictness, and any man or woman who marries out of the caste, as recently in the case of one of the Lees, who wedded a blacksmith, is instantly disowned". "The proverb, too, of honour among thieves is also still kept, and formal meetings are every now and then convened to expel any member who is guilty of cheating his kinsman". Surprisingly by 1851 the census figures only recorded Dorset as having just 37 Stanley's and 113 in Hampshire.

The Gypsy Charcoal burners of the New Forest

Many new forest Gypsies were also skilful in the art of charcoal burning as many of their great ancestors of the East were charcoal burners.Hutchinson stated that, "when the Romans came to the New Forest, they made use of the charcoal produced in the area to fire their pottery". In the 19th century De Crespigny and Hutchinson describing the charcoal burners of the New Forest and their huts as 'A quaint feature of the Forest almost hidden beneath the tangle and the greenwood tree, in the midst of a circle of blackened, charcoal strewn earth".The charcoal burners of the Forest are well documented and drawings etched and displayed in local taverns such as the Swan.

The most famous charcoal burner of all time was undoubtedly Purkis.who transported the lifeless body of King William 11 in his cart from the fatal spot near Stoney Cross where the arrow pierced the monarch 's forehead, from where the Rufus Stone now stands to the town of Winchester, which was then the capital of England." A familiar journey for Parkis, for the burners often used to travel to the City from all parts of the Forest to sell their charcoal. The trade was practiced by the Purkis family at

Castle Malwood right up to the end of the 19th century when another local family the Tinsley's, took over most of the production. Ringwood is Saxon name meaning the Edge of the Forest. Vesey Fitzgerald-called the inhabitants of the new forest "A race apart" and said that "There is here in the New forest a people that has never been conquered".

Eric Holme wrote-in Wanderings of Wessex-"The observant stranger will notice a large proportion of small dark folk amongst the inhabitants of the New Forest".

Now, however, the old encampments at Castle Malwood (near Stoney Cross) and Mark Ash have long gone and there is a new era of burners with their mode of life more in keeping with the present century. Large, caterpillar-wheeled tractors today heave the oak trunks to the kilns in place of the old carthorses, and the kilns are all metal cylindrical structures instead of the old, conical shaped logs covered with turf. Philip Blake, the village blacksmith at Broughton in Hampshire made most of these modern burners. In earlier decades these burners in the forest lived in a tent, made of a framework of poles and heaped with sacks and turf. No doubt that many of these burners were in fact Gypsies who were skilled in the art from their Eastern origins.In more recent decades they lived in their cottage homes and during the week whilst at work in caravans on the site.

In 1847, the railway link from Southampton to Dorchester brought the first visitors to the New Forest. It also brought Queen Victoria's army to the area, needing more room for manoeuvres.

Forest Day's

Life was hard in the forests
where few strangers passed bye
where the rabbits ran free
where the old uns did sigh
Where the fires that were lit
lead to smoke in your eyes
where the old mum smoked pipe
and the rivers ran bye

The ferns they did grow there
so tall and so wild
where the foxes gave chase
and the old uns were wise

Where the trees shed their branches
in autumns rich lanes
where the ponies were tethered
where it snowed and it rained

The chestnuts gave sustenance

whilst the blackberrys grew

all over the waysides

for me and for you

Where the dew it was rich on the ground in the morn

where the chaffinch did sing and the babies were born

all through those days when the vardos did roll

beneath the blue skies which we all called home

There were songs and tales told

for many a day in the heart of the forest

where the young uns did play

the gals told your fortune in the palm of your hand

The old men did wander and the young men did gain

rabbits and work there with their bridles and reins

the life it was hard yet their spirits were rich

close by the heathers next to the ditch

Where the traps they were many for the ponies to bear

whilst the wind it did blow and did mess up your hair.

Ray Wills

Rambling Gambling Gypsy

He was a rambling gambling Gypsy
born on the wayward tracks
where the vardo wheels were rolling
and the berries were in the sacks
way out by the heather not far from Canford downs
where the yogs were still a burning
on the dark side of the tracks

He was a rambling gambling Gypsy
spent his youth out in the fairs
where the carousels were turning
and the music hit your ears

Where the bumper cars were laden
with young girls on the town
where the young men took their fancy
and the old gals bedded down

He played the cards there daily
shuffled up the packs
where the Gypsy wheels were rolling
laid down the king and jacks

He was a rambling gambling Gypsy
when he met her and they dined
in the shadows of the moonlight
candle light and wine

He was a rambling gambling Gypsy
he bet on every mare
they courted in the springtime
flowers in her hair

He was a rambling gambling Gypsy
but he left her in the shade
to join the British army
for peace he craved to save
She lost him in the battle
but she still stands by his grave
where the sun comes up each morning

to salute that Gypsy brave.-Ray Wills

New Forest Families

The names of the principal Gypsy families in Southern England as compiled by Charles Leland, With their characteristics. Supposedly prepared for him by Marty Cooper. Though Leland confessed that the following list may not have been totally perfect.

Ayres, Barton- Lower Wiltshire, Black- Hampshire, Broadway and Somerset, Burton -Wiltshire, Chapman, Clarke. Half-blood. Portsmouth. Cooper-Chiefly found in Berkshire and Windsor,   Hare- Chiefly in Hampshire. Hicks - Half-blood- Berkshire, Hughes- Wiltshire, Jenkins- Wiltshire. Lee-. The same in most respects as the Smiths, but are even more widely extended, Lewis-   Hampshire, Locke- Somerset and Gloucestershire.

Lovell- Known in Romany as Kamlo, or Kamescro, that is, lover. Petulengro, or Smith- The Romany name Petulengro means Master of the Horseshoe that is Smith. Smiths came from France Normandy invasion of 1066.

 The following families are also some of the many listed family surnames who are all known to have travelled in Southern England during these times.

Ackleton ,Alexander, Allen, Ayres, Baker, Ballam,Bales, Barnes, Barney, Barnett's , Barton, Bath, Bellows, Bint,Black, Blackman, Blake, Blythe, Bonds, Bosneys, Boswell, Bosvil, Bowers, Bowring, Brazil, Broadway, Brewers, Bridle, Broadway, Brixeys, Bryer,Buckland, Buckley, Bullock, Bundy, Burtons, Bushell, Cannon, Carter, Carey, Charman, Cherretts, Cheeseman, Church, Churen,

Clark, Cleft, Coates, Cole, Colen, Collins, Cooper, Corrie, Cox, Create,Cruthchers, Day, Davis, Dibben, Dighton, Doe , Domineys, Donovan, Dorrington, Drake,Draper, Ducketts, Dunk, Dunkett, Eastwood, Emmett, Evans, Glove, Gray, Faa; Fancy's, Fishers, Fletcher, Frankham, French,, Gardiner, Gardner, Goble, Goddard, Griggs, Green, Greening, Gregory, Hardy, Harris, Haynes, Halls, Hansford, Hayward, Heron, Hibbard,Hicks, Hilden, Holloway, Hooper, Hughes, Ingram, Ivall, James, Janes, Jeff's, Jeffries,Jerrard, Jerrim, Johnson, Johnston's,Joles, Jones, Keat,Keet, Kelly, Kings, Lakey, Lamb, Lee, Light, Limburn, Lock, Loveday, Lovell's, Loveridge, Mabey, Macdonald,Manley, Martin, Messenger, Miller, Millis, Mills, Mitchells, Moore, Morris, Newman, Nippards, Oliver, Orchards, Ostler, Page, Packman, Parker, Parson,Pateman, Pearce, Pedlows, Penfold, Penfeld, Perren, Peters, Phillips, Pickard, Pidgeley, Pike, Pitcher, Proudley, Puttick, Rawlings,Rickman, Roberts, Rogers, Rolph, Rook, Ropers, Rose, Ripley, Sands , Saunders, Saxby, Scamp, Scarrett, Scotch; Scott, Scriven,Seller, Sherred,Sherwin.Sherwood, Small, Snells, Sopers, Spencer, Squires, Stanley's Steer, Stevens, Stokes,Stone,Streck, Strickland, Strange, Targett,Tapps, Taylor, Thatcher, Thick, Tomkins, Trowbridge, Tuck, Turner, Wallis, Ware , Wareham, Waters , Weeks, Welch, Wellings, Wells, Wellstead, West, Westlake, Westwood, Whale, Wharton, Wheelers, White, Whittle, Williams, Willett, Wills, Witte, Wittel, Witt's, Wood,Woodman,Young.

Barneys,Dears and Lights

These families married into nearly all the New Forest Travelers and also into the large Black or Blackman family who originated from Inkpen Berkshire. With cousin marriages being the norm among gypsies this was inevitable as with all Romany families.Their many descendants are said to be still living in and around the Forest in recent years having married into many of the old Romany families like the Blacks,Coopers,Hughes and Keets. They travelled back and forth many times in a year on their yearly circuit throughout the Country on foot or horse travelling greater distances than we do today by Car !

Dangerfield Barney married Sophia Light.

The Blacks.

The Blacks originally owned three houses in "Black Latches" 1836. They were well thought of as horse traders and hawkers selling their wares wherever they went. Their families travelling as far south as Beaulieu, Hampshire; as far east as Farnham, Surrey; as far west as Pewsey, Wiltshire; and as far north as Chievely, Berkshire.These families travelled together and married within the group.

Amos Black (1801-1875)

Amos married Mary Jane nee White in 1826.

They were married at Ink Pen church (she was just 16). Both of their families no doubt knew each other well and travelled together. They traveled around the country trading horses and doing business. They had 14 children who were born in scattered places. Though they lived at Bonfire Lane for over 50 years. On leaving that village the couple lived for a time at Newbury .Their oldest son, Amos was born Thatcham Berkshire he became quite influential in the community.

Amos Black died in 1875 at the age of 74.

Mary Jane White Black

Mrs Black was brought up in the neighbourhood of Burbage.

Mary walked the three miles to church every Sunday to worship until she was in her 80s. She was a faithful, religious woman who lived during a time of sickness and hardship. Here, in the ink pen parish graveyard she and other members of her family are buried.

Maurice (Morris)Black

Maurice, the youngest of Amos and Mary was christened on the 2nd of June 1858 at Inkpen. He married Annie on 21 April 1877 in Inkpen. Two years after Amos death.Then Jane lived with him and Annie till her old age.

Maurice and Annie only had one child, Rhoda, who was born 11 January 1878 at Inkpen and christened 10 February of the same year. They lived at Rose Cottage in Inkpen just down the street from Black Latches and other members of the family all their married lives. They were the only ones who kept in contact with Rosanna in American. Annie could read and write and would correspond with her, while Rosanna had no schooling and had to rely on others to read her mail and write her responses.

Maurice died 2 May 1940 and Annie in February 1950. They are buried in Inkpen.

Jane Black

When Amos, became ill in 1863, Jane cared for the family and earned a living by going from house to house and place to place selling her wares. She had a large apron that she had sewn pockets on and she would fill these pockets with things to sell. She read people's palms and they in turn bought what she had to offer. Rosanna, Arabella, and Maurice were at home, the girls staying until they married.

Jane died in 1900 at the age of 90 years.

Henry Black

Henry was born at Kintbury, Berkshire on the 24th April 1844.

Henry married Rosa and by 1881 they had seven children and were living at 155 New street Andover.

John Black

John Black was born 29 March 1846 at Speen (Stock Cross), Berkshire, England.

John married Mary Ann Doe of Rotherwick, Berkshire on 17th November 1864 at Inkpen.

Walter Willis Black

Walter was born 21 June 1842 in Kintbury, Berkshire.

Walter married Eliza Hughes, 1st October 1877 at Bentley, Hampshire they had 8 children.They lived in Inkpen. Walter died the 16 May 1918 and buried there in the Inkpen churchyard on the 20th May 1918.

Rosanna Black

Rosanna was born 19th January 1848 in Inkpen, Berkshire, one of 14 children. 7 girls and 7 boys. Two boys Thomas, age 7, died 21 March 1857; and Matthew, age 8, died 6 March 1858.

Rosanna married Edwin Spackman when she was 17 on the first Monday in August (8th) 1865.Their marriage certificate dated 24 July 1865) they were married after Banns had been published, in a parish in Burbage. The marriage certificate was witnessed by Henry Black, brother of the bride; and Sarah Ann Spackman, a sister of the groom.

Arabella or Bella Black

Arabella was born in 1852 in Mortimer (Inkpen), Berkshire. She was Rosannas sister, and they raised their children together when they lived close together as neighbors. She married Henry Hamblin 6 May 1872 at Kintbury where they were to raise their children. Rosanna's brother, Henry did business with the horse dealer Henry Spackman.

Blackney

William Blackney

William married Clemintina Ayres

Their son Amos Blackney was born about 1804, and christened

23rd February 1806 in Boxford, Berkshire.

Bowers

Noah Bowers

Noah married Lavina whose family had established the Gypsy colony at Botany Bay 100 years before. Lavina lived to 75 years of age.

Betsy Page nee Bowers.

Throughout her writings Gillington the artist mentions meeting up with many Gypsy families in the New Forest, including those of Betsy Page.

Burchells

Jane and James Burchell lived in the forest with their two nephews, who were born in Portsmouth.

The Burtons lived in Lyndhurst in the new forest.

Churens

Amos Churen

Amos was the New Forest Gypsy who provided the writer Brian Vesey Fitzgerald with most of his material for his books on the new forest Gypsies.

Coles

The Coles were show people who worked with elephants at circuses and at fairs. They were a dark race said to originate from Spain. In the present age they operate very successfull fairgrounds businesses in the area.

The Coopers

The New Forest was known as "The Cooper Country".

These were one Gypsy family amongst others, popular with royalty, particularly Queen Victoria and they were often referred to by her. In 1836, princess Victoria made friends with a family of Gypsies who became the subject of some of her work.They were travellers who had set up camp near Claremont from December 1836 to early January 1837. She records her every meeting with the family and even drew pictures of them."We saw our Gipsy friends peeping out of their frail abode of canvass. They certainly are a "Hard-faring race"."alas! I too well know, its truth, from experience, that whenever any poor Gipsies are encamped anywhere and crimes and robberies &c. occur, it is invariably laid to their account, which is shocking; and if they are always looked upon as vagabonds, how can they become good people? I trust in Heaven that the day may come when I may do something for these poor people, and for this particular family! I am sure, that the little kindness which they have experienced from us will have a good and lasting effect on them!"

Eliza Cooper -Gypsy Prophet. She was known as Black Liz.

At Abbots Well Eliza called on the locals occasionally to collect rags and old clothes.   She claimed to originate from the Black Coopers.   (The term, black blood (Kaulo ratti), means the purest type of Romany). Eliza possessed the gift of prophecy and also a belief in charms. (A charm which was worn only by the New Forest Gypsies was a ring made from

202

plaited horse hair). Eliza Cooper told a fascinating story as to how she would spend hours trying to approach the wild ponies close enough to pull strands of hair from their manes and tails. But the ponies had to be either skewbald or piebald, as rings made from the hair of this color were believed to bring good luck to the wearer's. The common custom among all Gypsy women who went hawking from door to door was to ask for a drink. It is said that Eliza was no exception and that she always came in for a cup of tea. When drinking her tea sipped from the saucer she would tell her stories of the old days when they could camp out on the forest.She would often tell how she would sit by the campfire smoking her 'baccy' and would weave her nets for the men to use rabbitting. Sometimes she said these nets would be over a hundred yards long.

Joshua known as Jesse Cooper

Joshua lived at Fordingbridge he was the 'original Gypsy King 'of the New Forest. Joshua died near Picket Corner, on the edge of the Vet, and is buried at Fordingbridge.

Annie Cooper

Annie lived in the village of Hyde where she followed her old way of life though lived in a modern caravan, as opposed to her vardo hid away on a piece of common land adjoining the Forest. she drew her water daily from a well on the nearby common and collected dead gorse wood for her stove.

  John Cooper known as "stumpy"

John camped on Mrs. Messengers land at Bonham's, attending to the occasional odd jobs on the farm, for around twenty years. An accident in early life depriving him of his right hand (one brother had lost a leg, another an eye). However despite his handicap Stumpy was able to use the other hand to cook,sew and write earning sufficient money to support his family. Then unfortunately he dislocated his shoulder and after that he really was helpless, being too frail and old for it to be set. Stumpy died in 1923 and is buried in the grounds of Wimbornes Roman Catholic church cemetery.

Charlie Cooper, Maurice Cooper,Mable Cooper,Marti Cooper,Nelson Cooper and Louis Smith were members of the last two families to resist eviction from the New Forest.

Tommy Cooper

Tommy was known for his fine playing of the squeeze box.Tommy always said that he was the last baby born at Shave Green compound prior to the authorities finally closing it in 1963.

Granny Wells nee Cooper

 Granny was said to have a remarkable gift of fortune telling and the story has it that she once read the hands of a Salisbury ploughman and his wife, and predicted that the couple would soon become rich and the man would not have to work again. Some days later while ploughing his field the blade struck something solid. He dug away the soil and found a crock that was filled with gold coins. Granny Cooper was handsomely rewarded and the couple lived the rest of their lives in comfort.Granny Cooper was a wise and clever old lady who fostered countless children and lived to a grand old age." I am proud of my heritage I can trace my family back to 1546 in the New Forest". Granny died November

2012.

Susannah Cooper born 1826 at Stockbridge Hampshire.

Drakes

These were gypsy horsedealers in the forest and used by Munning the artist.

Does

Albert Doe

Albert was known as the singing Gypsy

He was born in Wiltshire in 1856. Albert married Caroline Hastings Emily Mitchell.

Caroline was born in Hastings 1861.

Albert and Caroline lived at Netley Marsh, Lower Bartley and had 11 children.

Bert Doe

Bert served in the cavalry compound at Denney Lodge before the widespread move of all New Forest Gypsies to the new housing estates following the war years.

Ted Darkie Duckett

Ted married Bert Does daughter. He was a bones player and step dancer who lived at Marchwood at the Bold, hanger corner on the Beaulie road. during the 50s and 60s.He was well known locally and originally came from Wootton Bassett in Wiltshire.

Grays

Nobbie and Charlotte Gray

These were travelling show people well known in the forest.They were also employed as models for the artist Munning in 1912.

Greens

George Green a Chair Bottomer married Eliza nee Wilkins.

Priscilla Green

Priscilla was born on the 27th November 1874 at Horton Heath near Wimborne in Dorset.She was the daughter of George Green and Eliza. Her birth was registered on the 15th December 1874. She was baptised on the 10th January 1875 in the Parish of Horton it is interesting to note that the previous entry in the Parish Register On the 5th January was the baptism of Caroline Wells who was to become her sister in law.

Priscilla married Benjamin Wells on the 29th September 1890 at the parish church Boldre Hampshire.Benjamin was the son of William Wells and Eliza.

Priscilla was made famous in a portrait painted in oil by Sven Berlin who also did a pencil drawing of her husband. The couple were known to have lived at Shave Green.

The Gritts

James Gritt married Sarah Harris.

William Gritt their son married Mary Gritt (nee Sherred) known as Granny Gritt.

Mary Sherred Gritt

Mary the gypsy pedlar was born in 1842 at either Cranborne or Winterbourne in Dorset. She known as Granny Gritt the Gypsy peddler and she would be seen peddling tape in exchange for rabbit skins at Fawley.

Job Gritt

Job married Emma nee Rampton (born around 1849) She was Milly Gregorys widow.Job died in 1907.

After his death Emma his widow continued managing Jobs business.

The Gritts, Harris's, Ramptons,Rawlings, Ayres and Sopers. All seem to have intermarried and were chimney sweeping families.

Hills

Vince Hill

Vince lived in the forests with his team of holly cutters. He had a horse and cart and shortly before Christmas each year during the holly cutting his team travelled from Frogham to Linwood around mid November. Then later in December they all travelled to the city of London to sell their holly. The Forest holly is blessed with a rich supply of bright red berries, Many of the butchers' shops in London owed their brightness at the festive season to the New Forest holly.

Hodges

Charles Hodges .

Charles married Mary Hodges 1839.

They had 9 children. Alice,1851 Mary 1855 Lucey 1857 Sarah, 1859 Jane, 1861 Charles, 1863 John 1866 Joseph,1868 George 1870.

Hughes

Noah Hughes 1852-1927 also known as Sandy Cooper Known as the Chief Traveller.He had 13 children.

The Jeffs

Job Jeff married Nancy Crutcher

The Jeff's sold flowers on the streets of Christchurch for very many years their baskets famous for being very large and full. Many of the Gypsy woman like those from the Jeff family would travel to Bournemouth from Christchurch every Tuesday, Thursday and Saturday with their big heavy baskets full to the brim to sell flowers in the town centre which they all referred to Bournemouth then as being Bourne.

Lakeys

G Lakey

He married Hannah Mason Lakey nee Benson (1818 -1903)

Hanna was born in Andover. Hannah was married to G Lakey and was known as Hannah "Queen of the Gypsies," For a number of years she lived in the forest with her husband, G. Lakey, camping in many places. During the later years of her life a local charity persuaded her to move into a small cottage close to Beaulieu payng her rent and bought her groceries and tobacco. She was considered to be the last person able to speak true Romani. She had spent most of her life living in a bender, living until eighty-five years of age. Despite all the money she received in her former years she died penniless. It was said that for many years, one kind clergyman in the Forest was most Liberal to her and would give her half-a-crown every week when she made her regular call, and it is said she was never sent away without it. Many wealthy upper class people were also said to visit her regularly at her camp in the forest bringing her gifts. She was said to be the last of the New Forest Gypsy Queens.

The Lambs

 The Lamb sisters sang to huge crowds at the Forest Inns, wearing very colourful clothes often decorated with pieces of heavy picture chain when they had no other jewellery to wear.

The Lees

The Lees became the most prominent gypsy family after the Stanleys left for the new world.

Joseph Lee

Joseph known as Gypsy Joe (King of the Gypsies). His occupation was as Razor Grinder. He was a native of

Brockenhurst in the New Forest. He travelled mainly around Southampton, Ramsey, Lymington, and Ringwood. He was reputed to be a wealthy man and is reported to have left a great deal of money. He was friends with the notorious smugglers Peter Warren and Billy Dear, the two great contraband adventurers. It's said that he assisted them with their smuggling, deer-stealing, poaching, and on occasion sold a few ponies at various fairs. Joseph died aged 86.When Charity Lee his daughter was married to one of the Stanley's. Joseph Lee presented her with one hundred spade guineas, along with trinkets and several pieces of plate furniture.

Jack and Walter Lee

Reputed to have broken the forest strict laws,for damaging undergrowth at Thickthorn were known as Hampshire Mumpers. Oliver Lee played fiddle.

The Loaders

Loaders had strawberry farms in Frogham and would collect sedge grass for the beds there.

The Lovells

Morrish and Jasper Lovell

These were uncle and nephew/ musicians. Both were pure-blooded Romanies. The old man Morrish was the boshomengro (fiddler), the younger Jasper was the unskilled musician, both wore Gypsy style clothes. Patched and ragged garment, diklos (neck scarves) of red and of green, shapeless, brimless hats of olive felt upon their head's of bushy hair, which showed in hanging locks black of hue.

Jasper wore a peacock feather which poked out from a tear in his hat crown.

Mundays

Bill Munday

Bill Munday was a well known Gypsy who became even more famous as one who murdered another shooting him with a pistol at point blank range. He was said to have got off the murder charge under the grounds of self defence. The incident occurred across the River Stour on a rough patch of ground that was a Gypsy encampment.

Patemans

Tom Pateman

 The Patemans were often the most prominent family in the forest with often up to three generations living together in the same cottage. They kept cows and tended the forest ponies. Their main occupations being strawberry picking, stick making and farming.

Alice Louise Pateman married Frederick White in 1905.

John Pateman married Sarah White 1923.

Rose Pateman married Leonard White 1930.

Patemans also lived at Wareham in the Purbeck.Maurice his wife and his 2 sons. Many Patemans served in the British forces during the first world war 1914-1918.

John Pedlow

John Pedlow was a famed Gypsy herbalists, who had

travelled Somerset for many years. He was particularly well known for his skill working with horses and had possessed a secret cure for the healing of fistulous withers, an ailment even today considered as generally incurable. He died suddenly a bachelor and thus his secret was never ever to be told.

Patchy

Patchy was an old man who served in the army all through the Crimean War and the Indian Mutiny, eventually returning to the old life, to wander in a van with the rest.

Gypsy Peters

He was a horse dealer who lived in the Abbots Well area. During harsh weather he could be seen daily coming up the forest lanes with his sacks full of gorse. He would pound this furze with a mallet to make a forage for the ponies.

Pidgleys

Oliver Pidgley

Oliver married Edith nee Sheen and they had 8 children.

Edith regularly sold flowers to the owner of the Bournemouth Dormy hotel who helped her to obtain a council house to prepare for the birth of her child Raymond Pidgley.

Raymond was born on the 12th of May 1935 at 22 West howe road Bournemouth. The family moved to Godshill, near Fordingbridge, where they stayed during the war.He served 23 years in the Royal Marine Commandos, becoming a Sergeant, and was Admiral Mountbattens bodyguard. He was also the Light Welter Weight Champion of the Royal Marines and 3 Commando Brigade.

Irene Pidgley

Irene whose real name was Edith was the oldest girl of her family. She gained work in Lymington, and married a pilot who had escaped from a prisoner of war camp, and made his way back, and later met her at a dance in Fordingbridge. They had four children, including Tony who became a Sergeant Major in the SAS, and was presented with a bravery medal by the Queen.

Patricia Pidgley

Patrcia married a Corporal in the United States Army Air Corps who was in this country preparing for the war, and altogether they had fourteen children, and lived in Cincinatti, Ohio.

Lily Pidgley

Lily married a German, who was formerly a prisoner of war. Their name was Waue.

Oliver Pidgley

Oliver was in the Royal Artillery he married an Egyptian girl who worked in the British Military Hospital in Egypt.

George Pidgley

George married May Turner from Romsey.

May was a corporal in the Royal Army Service Corps.

Michael Pidgley lived near Southampton he was a Royal

Marine, and served in 40 Commando, and 3 Commando Brigade Head Quarters.

Rosemary Pidgley

Rosemary had three children and lived near Downton, Wilts.

Richardsons

Many Stanleys left behind in England took on the Richardson name to avoid trouble with the law.

Rogers

The Rogers family were brick makers (the authors relatives). They have their roots in Ringwood the New Forest then moved to Kinson Dorset. Many of the Rogers came from and still live in Ringwood.Many of their descendants moved to the Parkstone Newtown area.These were members of the Stanley tribe of Gypsies, cousins of the Stanley's and also other new forest families including the Scotts and the Cherretts.They had brick yards and industries in the area as well as small holding farms,piggeries and transport companies.

Slippery Rogers

Local smuggler so named as he kept getting away from the eluding the coastguards.

Granpas days

My Grandpa was a farming man and brick maker by trade

his family were travelers he took it to his grave

they came from the forest glades and surely had it rough

travelling on the beaten tracks amongst the mire and muck

My grandma was a Sally Army maid

plaited hair growing long told stories of the bible

n sang those salvation songs

took them to her grave

She was from the travelling mould

lived to 96 she was rare and dignified

lots of stories she once told always truthful n never lied

talked of heaven on the other side

They lived upon the common lands lady guests estate

had eight children and ganders running at the gate

they planted trees of fruit n briar

worked long hours and expired

they were rich in virtues grace

always a kind word n smiling face

They knew the Gypsy folks as one

Stanley's, Lees, goldfinch song and rabbiting

they worked hard all their lives

grew fine fruit and bred strong sons

they were wise in Gypsy song

roll those wheels and roll along.

The Scottts

The Scotts were often the most prominent family in the forest with often up to three generations living together in the same cottage. They kept cows and tended the forest ponies. Their main occupations being strawberry picking, stick making and farming.

Sherreds

Moses married Harriet Sherred.

They were the Parents of Mary Sherred

Priscilla Sherred (known as Trembling Polly).

Priscilla was a well known great Gypsy character of the New Forest, known as Trembling Polly as she suffered from the St. Vitus' dance. Despite being almost ninety years of age, she was still managing to get around in spite of her ailment. She was often to be seen walking for many miles daily, smoking her pipe and she always wore the same familiar large coal scuttle bonnet with a big curtain falling over her shoulders. She spoke with a high pitched and shaky voice and would tell a sad tale or two to any who would bother to stop to hear it. She lived at Bull hill in a small thatched house with a garden in a quiet area, close to Lymington. Till her final days she walked the Forest as she had done throughout her life. Then in her last days she moved and lived in the Workhouse.

The Smiths

The Romany word for Smiths is Petulengro which means "Master of the horseshoe". Many smiths first came to England with the Normans towards the end of the 11th century.

Len Smith

Len was a gypsy elder who lived in the forest in Thorleys, Horney Hill and was renowned for his recordings of the Gypsies and their lives.

Rodney Gypsy Smith the preacher (1860-1947)

Rodney was born in a tent, raised in a Gypsy camp, he never attended a school and yet influenced the lives of millions of people through his powerful preaching. He was converted at the age of 16 and worked with General William Booth founder of the Salvation Army prior to ministering as an itinerant evangelist, working with a variety of organisations all over the world, but particularly in Britain and America.

Spackman

The Spackmans were dedicated Christian people.

Henry Edwin Spackman married Ann Bond Hibbard. They had 9 children. One child, a twin boy named William, died soon after birth. The other children Mary Jane, 1848; Henry 1850; Elijah 1852; Brigham, 1854; twins Naomi Emma & William 1856; Sarah Marie 1859; and Annie 1861 were born in Burbage.

Edwin Spackman

Edwin was born 28 June 1846 at Burbage, Wiltshire, England he was the oldest child. He was a horse trader and before leaving England he was a caretaker of some stables with beautiful horses owned by a rich man and lived in Coldrey, Hampshire.Edwin Spackman married Rosanna Black when she was 17 on the first Monday in August (8th) 1865.Their marriage certificate dated 24 July 1865)they were married after Banns had been published, in a parish in Burbage. The marriage certificate is witnessed by Henry Black, brother of the bride and Sarah Ann Spackman, a sister of the groom.

They had twelve children, nine of whom survived. They were: Amos Spackman(Of Butte, Montana), Mrs. Charlotte S. Sullivan and Alma Spackman (Richmond), Henry Edwin Spackman (Salt Lake City), Mrs. Alice Leavitt (American Falls, Idaho), Albert Spackman, Mrs. Jane Hodges, and Hyrum Spackman (Preston), and Brigham Spackman (Lewiston). There are 59 grandchildren and 47 great-grandchildren. when their first child, Amos, was born in 1866. Then they returned to the Inkpen area for the births of their other children; Ann Marie 1868, Charlotte 1870, Henry Edwin 1872, William George 1874, Alice 1876, Francis Albert 1879. They were all baptized 16 November 1877 and were members of the Reading Conference. Then the decision was made to "come to Zion" and gather with the Saints in the tops of the mountains. They set sail 5 June 1880 with their six children from Liverpool on the ship "Wisconsin".

Annie Black Spackman

Annie was born 8 November 1868 in West Woodhay, Wiltshire, England, to Edwin and Rosanna Black Spackman. She attended a church school in England where she received an award for being an honor student.She had a beautiful singing voice and sang in the church choir. After emigrating she came to the Lewiston area at the age of 12, Annie attended the public school there and was very industrious and was always willing to help her neighbors in time of need. She became self-supporting at a very early age.

Annie married Andrew Lee Allen as his second wife one month short of her 16th birthday on 8th May 1884.

Granny Black had not been happy with the family leaving England for they had all been very close. She kissed the grandchildren goodbye but when it came time to say goodbye to her daughter, Rosanna Spackman, it was said that she spat in her face.

The family traveled by rail to Salt Lake City, and by 29th June 1881 were in Richmond for the birth of their daughter, Sarah Jane. Followed by Alma 1883, Ellen 1886 (who died when two months old), Brigham 1887 (all born in Cove, Utah), and Joseph Hyrum 1889 (born in Provo).

  Two brothers, Brigham Spackman of Bancroft and Henry Spackman, Richmond and three sisters, Mrs. Emma Hall, Salt Lake City Mrs. Sarah M. Yeates and Mrs. Annie Humphreys, of Logan survived.

Rosanna Black Spackman

After her husbands death Rosanna moved from Richmond Cache County Utah to Preston and lived close to some of her family. Later she stayed for a while with Hy and Iris Spackman in Preston and with Alma and Clara Spackman in Richmond. She died in Preston at the home of Hy after a brief illness on September 18th, 1935, and was buried in the Richmond cemetery next to her husband Edwin Spackman.

Amos Spackman

Born 27th September 1866 in Coldrey, Hampshire, England, Amos was the first child of Edwin and Rosanna Spackman. When growing up he had travelled the countryside in England with his mother and father.

Amos married Francis Wilson from Logan. The 3 children from the previous marriage were raised by other people. Halverson was later killed at 7 years of age when he fell under a harrows. He was living with a Beckstead family in the Preston, Idaho area.

Amos and Francis stayed in the Logan area until after their 6th child was born. Then they moved to Butte, Montana where Amos was a timekeeper at the Mountain View mine and a watchman at the Lexington mine. Amos and Francis had 12 children , Con, Arthur, Wilson, Vanetta, Florence May 30 May 1902, Vernon 1 Feb 1904, Maurice 1st Mar 1906, Violet 13 December 1908, Ruby, Lee Roy 2nd September 1911, Howard Delmos (died age 24 of tuberculosis), and George Clyde. Francis had poor health in her later life and passed away after suffering from a stroke.

Amos later remarried a Mrs. Odgers. She passed away about a year later. He then married Ada Hodges but he died shortly after on the 22nd of December 1946 and he is buried in the Mountain View Cemetery in Butte.

The Stanleys

The Stanley's are one of the most extended Gypsy clans and said to be the most prominent Gypsy family in England. Gypsies recognise the Stanley's as being of the royal blood line Stanleys were regarded as The Royal family. In the early days they camped at Marl-pit Oak and Gally Hill.The Stanley family or to give them their old name "Beshlie"or Beshaley which is thus described by George Borrow in his book Lavo Lil" There are two renderings of this name into Romany; one is Baryor or Baremescre, stone-folks or stonemasons, the other is Beshale that is, Sit-Down, from the word Stan, suggesting standing up in connection with lay.Thus "Stony-lea" was likely to have been their first name. Also called Kashtengrees.The Stanleys regarded themselves as the true traveller compared to the inferior Lees.

Boxing, especially bare-knuckle boxing, was particularly popular amongst the Gypsy fraternity and perhaps it is not surprising that many such exponents of the sport came from the travelling population. A particularly famous one being George 'Digger' Stanley, the son of George and Cinderella, grandson of Diverus and Naomi, and great grandson of Peter and Rebecca. At his death newspapers recorded the event, the Dundee Courier of 8th March 1919 reported that the first "outright winner of a Lonsdale belt" had passed away in

Fulham, after a long illness. He was, it reminded its readers, "the ex-England and World's bantam-weight champion." He was also a descendant of an ancient Romany tribe. That we know his antecedents as far back as his three times great grandfather with a certainty, and in all probability one generation beyond, owes something to his fame, but much more to the settlement and removal records of his Romany ancestors, dating back to the early eighteenth century.Other famous local gypsy boxing champions have included Ted Sherwood,Freddie Mills and Abe Stanley.

The Stanley vardos and black tans were often stationary in the forest, but most of them possessed good forest ponies and dogs. They were very skilled in most of the Gypsy trades, particularly brick making and could speak well their own Romany language.They were a prolific tribe, favouring Berkshire, Hampshire, Dorset and Wiltshire and they were also to be found in the West Country. The Hampshire connection continues to be significant for those Stanley's who considered Dorset as their home territory. The Stanley family were recorded very early in Dorset, Hampshire and at Lyndhurst in the New Forest. Many made their homes in Portsmouth in later years whilst others lived permanently in Dorset.

Aaron Stanley

Aaron of the new forest "King of the Gypsies" born 1863.

Mercy Stanley

Mercy the daughter of Owen and Harriet Stanley was baptised at Broadwindsor in 1824.

Solomon Stanley was a peddler known as Blind Solomon.

Solomon married to Repentance Ayres at their encampment in Copner Lane,near Portsmouth. They had one child a daughter Caroline baptised 8th May 1836 in Widley, Hampshire. Shortly after her birth in June Repentance was found dead and Solomon was indicted accused of her murder him being just 19 years of age. The case caused quite a sensation at the time and on 24th June 1836. (Following a post-mortem it was clear that Solomon was innocent and that Repentance had died of natural causes).

Solomon married Sarah Alexander on 20th December 1842.

Solomon had built his one roomed house on the heath with his bare hands, out of mud and stone, and thatched it with furze. By 1881 Solomon was a widower and lived with Clara his daughter along with her family at Mr Holder's brickyard, School Road, Hound, in Hampshire.

Richard Owen Stanley(1794–1860)

Richard was a Razor Grinder he married Harriett nee Worden (1793–1857). They had 15 children.

Harriet died on August 30th 1857. Aged 63 years of age.

On her monument is the epitaph

> *Harriet Stanley was her name,*
>
> *England was her nation;*
>
> *In any wood her dwelling place,*
>
> *In God was her salvation.*

Levi Owen Stanley (1818 — 3 December 1908)

Levi married Matilda nee Joles

Levi and Matilda had 17 children. Paul, Levi (Jr.), Missouri, Martha Louise, Lilly, Michael, Sofia, Loving, Johanna, Benjamin, William, Edward, Elizabeth, Gentillia, Algenny, Matilda and Levi

Levi was head of the American branch of the family who emigrated to the U.S.A from Berkshire arriving in New York November 14th 1856. Levi once told a reporter that the honorary titles of King and Queen were an indication of their peoples' love and trust for them, nothing moreL Levi Stanley had brought his family from England. He was the King of all the Gypsies in USA and he traced his ancestry back to his royal Gypsy blood of Hungary. Levi directed the affairs of the Gypsies from the old home place here, but he encouraged his followers to invest in Miami valley and Dayton as they created wealth through their horse trading.

Their families moved to the United States leaving England "when Buchanan was king," as they put it along with others of their people and soon settled near Troy Ohio as their home for the summer months.It became the centre for the Gypsies of that country.

After Owen Stanley called together his followers and told them that he had chosen Dayton as his permanent home. He would invest money in farmland so that his children, their wives and husbands and their children would have houses to live in during the cold winter months. He purchased a large lot in Woodland Cemetery where all the tribesmen and women could be buried when the time came. He bought a small farm northeast of Dayton, and there he lived with his wife.

They pastured their horses there during the winter, and although they had somewhat peculiar lifestyles in the opinion of their neighbours, they never gave offence.Others of the tribe bought land in Dayton, Harrison, Wayne, Mad River and Butler townships.Initially the Stanleys were agriculturalists and over time became horse traders and did some metal work whilst the women told fortunes and the family acquired sizable wealth. Their prosperity lured others to the county, making the Miami Valley during that period America's Gypsy capital.

Matilda Stanley, she was the daughter of Ephraim Joles.

She was born in Reading in Berkshire, England and was said to be a gifted fortune teller with remarkable powers of clairvoyance said to be handed down to her as being the eldest daughter. She was described in the press as a "plain, hardy-looking woman, with a touch of Meg Merrilies in her appearance, and a manner indicative of a strong and pronounced character." Meg Merrilies was a Gypsy queen in the Sir Walter Scott novel, Guy Mannering, made famous on the American stage by Charlotte Cushman. She was highly regarded by the tribe, being wealthy and having a great deal of influence.

Matilda Stanley died childless in Vicksburg, Mississippi aged 51 on January 16, 1878.

Following Matildas death her body was embalmed, shipped

to Dayton and for nine months lay in a receiving vault so that word of her death had time to reach those who wished to arrive and bear tribute to her worth. More than 25,000 Gypsies from the United States, Canada and England arrived in Dayton to pay their respects. The cemetery was packed with an estimated 1,000 horse-drawn carriages were turned away at Woodland's Romanesque gates. No one in Dayton had ever seen the likes before.

Levi Stanley died in December of 1908 in Missouri and was buried on Tuesday, April 13, 1909 in the Stanley plot.

The body, according to Gypsy tradition, being previously kept in a vault at Woodland until the springtime. Around 40 members of the tribe were in attendance at the burial they came from all over the west and south, where they had stayed during the winter, and from where they had started migrating several weeks before the funeral.

At the grave were Levi Sugar Stanley, the king of the Gypsies, now an old man and the other sons of the deceased, Paul and Adam, along with their wives and children.Among notable Gypsies present were Vally Harrison and family and the Joles family, from Illinois; John Bryce and family, from Vermont; the Jeffries and Cooper families, from Virginia, and the Gray families, from Michigan.

The Stanley's rest in a large subterranean vault in what was then the central part of the cemetery. An angel tops the 20-foot granite obelisk surmounting the site. Stanley Avenue is named after the Stanley Gypsy tribe as it is the route they travelled from their campsite along the river north of Dayton.

Levi Sugar Stanley Jr. (1835-5th March 1916)

Levi Sugar Stanley succeeded as King of the Gypsies when his father became weak in old age. Levi Sugar became ruler of the tribe following the death of his father having been directing the affairs of the nomads for several years previously. Though his people recognized his inability to counsel them as in his earlier days, the Gypsies would not deprive him of his title of "King." "Sugar" Stanley, also had several sons and daughters, all born in America. All the Gypsy children were bright and intelligent were literate and most attended local schools.

Levi Sugar Stanley died in 1916 his funeral took place at Woodland Cemetery Dayton USA.

Mary Stanley

Mary was the granddaughter of the Gypsy Queen. She became famous for having had her portrait painted in oils by the famous New forest artist Amelia Goddard and entitled "Mary Stanley in the Forest". Amelia records that the Marchioness of Waterford wrote from Highcliffe Castle in 1883 thanking her for the charming picture of a Gypsy which she was very glad to possess. The work was passed to Major Wortley on Amelia's death.

Jimmy Stanley's Grandfather

A legend that has been passed on from father to son, tells that the first Romany to arrive in the Isle of Wight was Jimmy's Stanley's grandfather. It is said that he had journeyed there from the New Forest with a fine batch of ponies and spent his first night sleeping in a churchyard, with 500 gold guineas on his velvet coat and breeches. This forefather of the last Isle of Wight Romany died at the age of 104 years. He had settled in the Island as a toll gate keeper. Jimmy Stanley's father gained fame by winning a hurdle race at the age of 70, damaging his knee and it is said that he never recovered from the shock.

Elizabeth Jane Stanley

Elizabeth previously Elizabeth Castle a member of the show fairground family and she died in 7th July 1969.

The kingly title once owned by the Stanleys is now held by the Lees.

Smalls

James Small was a Gypsy from Blandford.

He married Susan Wareham. They lived at Shroton and had two sons born before their marriage James Crib Small and George Wareham.

Squires

Country folk have long called the Gypsies by the name of "broomstick" or broom squires", hence the surname of Squires (My brother in laws Ron Squires people).There's no doubt that the use of this name was acquired by the Gypsies from their hawking of broom's and brushes. Gypsies may also have got the title of "broomstick squires" from their supposedly marriage tradition of leaping over a broomstick by the wedded pair. Such events as broomstick marriages are usually taken place outside of the church, and are not an official marriage. A large percentage of Gypsy weddings were once believed to be of that kind, though many such as Rodney Smith the Gypsy evangelist of the 1800s doubted the authenticity of such claims.

Warehams

 The Wareham name took the maternal link as George and James are both recorded as being Mr Small's offspring. At that time Shroton was well known for its fair and its common land which would have attracted travelling Gypsy families.The Wareham name was often used throughout Dorset by travellers who no dount had their origins in Wareham itself which may well have ben a Gypsy site of some importance in the 15th century.

Susan Wareham

Susan married James Small a Gypsy from Blandford. They lived at Shroton and had two sons born before their marriage James Crib Small and George Wareham born 7 years later.

The Waters

Granny Waters

Granny and her two sisters earned around fifty pounds a day dancing at numerous horse race meetings. For Gypsies were great entertainers with a fondness for music and dancing. Often the women danced and sang for money at local fair's and horse races and one old New Forest Gypsy woman remembered when she and her sisters were asked to dance for King Edward VII at Epsom races. To the sound of tambourines the women swirled about in their colourful skirts performing for the king while his friends threw coins for them from the grandstand.

The Wells family members included William, Benjamin, Jesse and James.

Benjamin Wells.

William Wells, Benjamin Wells, Jesse Wells, James Wells were convicted for various minor or pardonable offences as were Job Lamb, Joseph Williams, Job Williams and Jack Stacey.

Benjamin was the son of William and Eliza. He married Priscilla on the 29th September 1890 at The Parish Church, Boldre, Hampshire. Priscilla was made famous in a portrait painted in oil by Sven Berlin who also did a pencil drawing of her husband .The couple were known to have lived at Shave Green.

The White family

All members bear very strongly on their dark features which are the signs of their Romany blood. So dark are they, that some of them are nearly black. One of the women of the family occasionally sat as a model of the ideal Gypsy or "gipple," as the foresters call them with the gorgeous handkerchief that Mary White always wore on her head.

Mary Jane White (1810-19000)known later in life as Granny Black Mary.

Mary was born 1810.married Amos Black at Ink Pen church in 1826 and they had 14 children.(she was just 16). At their wedding a loaf of bread was broken and a thorn was used to prick the thumbs of both persons and a drop of blood was dropped on each half of the loaf, this was then eaten by the couple, each one eating the half with the others blood on, the rest was them crumbled over their heads. A day later they came back to the camp to took part in feasting, drinking, singing, dancing and celebrating. Jane too was a woman well loved by many in her community.

Mary had lived for a time at Newbury where she first became known as "Granny Black Mary". She was often seen travelling the neighbourhood with her basket of small wares looped across her shoulder showing all of the articles she had for sale. She lived at Bonfire Lane Easton Royal and was well-known throughout the neighbourhood as a hawker of small wares, and was a highly-respected woman.

She was said to be a very active for her age, walking many miles every day. Long after she had reached 80 years "Granny" was still remembered by the locals as being very agile and was seen frequently walking 3 miles to church and back on a Sunday morning. Mary was famous for telling romantic tales to whoever would listen to them, whilst puffing away at her short clay "piple", which she referred to as her companion'. Towards the end of her life Granny lived with her youngest son, Maurice, and his wife Annie. Mary died on 14 November 1900 leaving some 200 grandchildren to the third generation, some of whom emigrated to the USA. Many of her descendants followed her to the grave, but her eldest son regretted that he was unable to attend, being extremely ill with dropsy.

Frederick White married Alice Louise Pateman 1905.

Sarah White married John Pateman 1923.

Leonard White married Rose Pateman 1930.

Betsy Smith nee White 1890-1960.

Betsy was born on ist March 1890 to George and Louisa White(nee Crutcher) in a wagon on common heath land which is now part of Queens Park Golf Course, Bournemouth. Betsy was raised and spent most of her childhood and youth with her mother father and 11 siblings at Heavenly Bottom Gypsy encampment in Parkstone,Poole Dorset.When she was barely 10 years old her father George passed away. Leaving the family with no income and Mother Louisa had to find ways of making money as there was now no breadwinner. As a result the attractive little girl known as Betsy was chosen as the one who would be sent to Bournemouth Square to sell bunches of white daisies.

 The first day she went to Bournemouth, she sold every bunch, as a result her Mother(Louisa) instructed Betsy to do this every day and so it was that every day she sold all her bunches of flowers in the square. Family legend has it   that the Bournemouth Gentry purchased her flowers from her because she was so pretty. It wasn't too long then that her other sisters and cousins   followed suit and so that was how the Bournemouth Flower girls were born.

Betsy was the longest flower seller amongst all of her relations and the best known flower seller of all her family. For many years her photograph was displayed in the Debenhams store restaurant, along with a photo of her long time friend Ciss Anderson (born Lucy Old and who was married to Jimmy White). Jimmy White was Betsy's first cousin. The family held a double wedding for the two couples at St Peters Church, Parkstone. where Betsy married Charles Smith on 24th February 1908 . Betsy was only 18 years old at the time when she married Charles. but her marriage certificate says she was 21years old. (It was easier to change ones age on the register then, as no proof of age was required).Together Betsy and Charles had nine children, two died in infancy. They had 42 grandchildren. Betsy continued to sell flowers in Bournemouth Square well into her early seventies but she had to stop as a result of a bad fall. When she died in 1960 she had a massive funeral, the procession of which went throughout Christchurch and Bournemouth. It was watched by hundreds of people including many who knew her well. It was reported in the Bournemouth Evening Echo as the biggest funeral ever recorded in the Bournemouth area. There were several funeral cars for her large immediate and extended families. A great number of her lifelong friends were present. There were very many flatbed Gypsy lorries in the procession to cope with the transporting of the hundreds of floral tributes.

Williams

Joseph and Job Williams both were Hampshire Mumpers.Many other Gypsy families were prominent in the forest including the Does,Pidgleys,James and Moores.

Jerry the scissor grinder

Jerry was an old well-liked character who lived rough summer and winter in the hedgerows and thickets nobody knew his real name, he roamed the villages sharpening knives and scissors on his contraption.

The Witt's

The Witts had strawberry farms in Frogham and would collect sedge grass for the beds there.

Len Witt

Len carried the filled baskets on his horse and cart to a reception depot at Romsey. Here he was given payment sometimes as much as seventy pounds to take back to the Gypsy workers.

Gypsies travelled back and forth from the New Forest to Kinson and other Dorset villages, Poole, Southampton and Portsmouth in Hampshire. Some living at Fordingbridge on the edge of the Forest and all of the Cranborne Chase area. Others resided in Sussex, Kent, and Surrey with others travelled from as far as Wales and Scotland.

Many Gypsies from the New Forest settled in Bournemouth and surrounding areas or went back and forth between Wiltshire and Berkshire as well as Somerset, even as far as Cornwall. and Hampshire. Whilst some members of these Gypsy families were known to have lived in the Purbeck in the Wareham area as early as the 16th century.

Wills

Walter Charles Wills born 1864. Recorded as living under Canvas at Setley Hollys, Brockenhurst, Hampshire 1911.

Walter was Married to Caroline (born 1865).They had 5 children- Walter 1896,Mark 1900,Luke 1903,Eliza born 1906, John born 1908.

Wingfelds

These were farm hands and hop pickers.

Kathleen Wingfield was Ken Boyd the film makers Mother.

Bill Moocher Wingfield himself was a skilled horseman.

Whilst both Ocean and Comfort Wingfield were models for the artist Munning in many of his paintings.

At Thorley's Horney Hill in 1911 up to 400 Gypsies were living in thatched cottages. These included those of the Does, Pidgleys, James, Moores, Williams, Lambs, Smiths, and later the Hughes families.

GYPSY MUSICIANS

John Roberts and his 9 sons played harps for Queen Victoria in North Wales.

The Woods family were harp players, fiddle players,step and clog dancers.

James Allen was personal fiddle player to the Countess of Northumberland.

Whilst Winifred Wells was royal mistress to Charles 11.

.

CHAPTER SIX

New Forest Characters and the famous.

As well as gypses of the forest the area became home to a great many artists, writers, poets and statesmen. Such as Thomas Hardy, William Barnes, John Turner and Augustus John. They spent time here for inspiration and the area also boasted great natural sea ports such as Poole which was world renowned for its Poole Pottery and trade to Newfoundland link. Particular families made a great mark on the area including those of the Guest, Talbots, Bankes, Welds, Frampton's, Russell Cotes, Tregonwells and Gulliver's.

Augustus John (1878 – 1961)

One cannot talk about local Gypsy travelers without mentioning Augustus John the artist who was in the 1920s Britain's leading portrait painter and a great defender of New Forest Gypsy rights. John spent much of his life painting and etching the local Gypsies and was regarded with much respect by both the Gypsy community and the wider art world. He developed a nomadic lifestyle and for a while he lived in a caravan and camped with and amongst the Gypsies. He moved to Alderney Manor in Parkstone, Poole, Dorset in 1909 where he spent much time with local Gypsies and painting his famous portraits in his art studio at Manor Avenue.

John moved to live in Fryern Court at Fordingbridge in a 14th century friary turned farmhouse in 1927. Housed on the edge of the New Forest it was a stopping-off point for artists travelling to the West Country from London and developed into more of an open house than bohemian commune. John was involved in politics becoming active in the National Campaign for the Abolition of Capital Punishment and supported the Voluntary Contraception League. He pestered MPs on behalf of Gypsy & travellers' rights, and was honoured to be elected president of the Gypsy Law Society in 1936.

John launched an attack on hedges. `Hedges are miniature frontiers when serving as bulkheads, not windscreens. Hedges as bulkheads dividing up the Common Land should come down, for they represent and enclose stolen property. Frontiers are extended hedges, and divide the whole world into compartments as a result of aggression and legalised robbery. They too should disappear'.

Charles Leland-Romany Rai.

Charles Leland was called "Master" by the Gypsies and was an American folklorist, from Philadelphia, Pennsylvania U.S.A. He was a lecturer, and prolific author who wrote several classic texts on English Gypsies as well as being the founder and first president of the Gypsy Lore Society.He studied Gypsy society and lore in England mainly through his close friendship with Marty Cooper. The Gypsies accepted Leland as one of their own, and giving him the title of Romany Rai, which means someone who is not a Gypsy but one who associates with Gypsies. Leland wrote to his niece Elizabeth Robins Pennell on November 16, 1886, "I have been by moonlight amid Gypsy ruins with a whole camp of Gypsies, who danced and sang."

Ken Boyd

The film maker ken Boyd was a regular visitor to the forest. His mothers family were the Wingfield Gypsies.The film maker Ken Boyds mother Kathleen Wingfield was herself a Gypsy who lived in Horton and then Datchet until 1947. Where she once made wooden flowers, baskets, coloured candles from wax and crayons, and sold fire wood door to door. In the painting titled Hop Pickers from the 1930s Ken's Boyd film great gypsy aunts Ocean and Comfort are seen in their feather hats. Whilst Uncle 'Moocher' (Bill Wingfield) holds the mare and Aunt Ivy, aged seven, sits on the steps of the vardo.

Revd. W. Bullen

Revd Bullen and his wife managed the Gypsy Mission in the New Forest for many years. They moved about from place to place in or near the Forest, visiting each Gypsy encampment and having an individual acquaintance with every member of it. They tended the sick, provided the poor with many comforts and held services in the different camps, instructing the children, as well as adults.

Sir Alfred James Munnings (8 October 1878 – 17 July 1959)

Alfred Munnings one of England's finest painters of horses, He describes in his autobiography, "An Artist's Life", how as a boy he came upon Gypsies in the lane leading to Middleton Hall near the family mill at Mendham, running in 'scared flight back to the governess. 'As I stood there painting, I recalled the dark man with clay pipe making baskets I smelt the wood-smoke from his fire as plainly as I smelt the rotting poplar leaves in the grass around me when I was making my studies twenty years later'. Gypsies were familiar figures in Munnings's youth, as owners of fairground rides and horse dealers. In 1910 Munnings bought his own blue Gypsy caravan for painting expeditions, scrawling 'Jasper Petulengro' across it in homage to George Burrow's immortal Gypsy. In 1911 he sought out the travelling fairground-man Nobby Gray and his wife Charlotte as models, along with others who were not in regular employment and were a focus of several of Munnings compositions. The Grays were independent minded and were grateful for the money thus inspiring works like The fairground, 1912.

Shrimp became Munnings Groom after being introduced to him by the horse- cooper Drake.Shrimp slept under his caravan.Munning said of him 'the best model I ever had'. Shrimp, was 'an undersized, tough, artful young brigand', who joined him on his expeditions in the Ringland Hills near Norwich. Munnings copied the Romany lifestyle on his journeys with Shrimp in the caravan, Though Munnings often slept in nearby comfortable inns. The spectacle and the communal life style entranced Munnings, who returned regularly over a dozen years.

Munning felt well accepted amongst the Gypsies when he was able to persuade several of the older women to bring out their brilliant shawls, boldly coloured aprons, and flamboyant ostrich feathered hats that were for special occasion wear for the women.With Ocean and Comfort Wingfield used as models for Munning in many of his paintings.

Munning states in his autobiography "Among these travelling farm hands and hop pickers were the Wingfield and Gregory families". Munnings bought a collection of ponies and horses from the Gypsy horse dealer Drake.

Other artists at this time painted the Gypsies yet few with Munnings's countryman's understanding. These included Augustus John and Laura Knight. John dressed his womenfolk and children in Gypsy garb and travelled around by caravan, relishing the romance of Gypsy life. Whilst Laura Knight made vivid portraits of Gypsy women at Epsom races, fascinated both by their exotic dress and powerful personalities.

Munnings always viewed Gypsies from a distance, within the context of their setting. Both Munnings and Olive Branson spent much time here painting these Gypsy families. Who willingly posed as models for 'Mr Money' as Munnings was called. Many had travelled up from Bristol and Dorset, Salisbury Plain and Herefordshire. With most of their families these included the Grays, Lees, Stevens, Gregory and Lovedays.

Munnings was later to remark "The families that I got to know had picturesque children, dogs and horses. The women had, somewhere in the back of each caravan, great black hats with ostrich feathers, laid away for gala days, or to be worn when selling baskets or brushes on the road". "Nobody could beat their style of dress, with black silk apron over a full-pleated skirt, a pink or mauve-blouse showing off a tough, lithe figure; strings of red beads, and wonderful earrings glinting under blue-black hair, came into their make-up, and sure enough, if I needed it, the large black hat complete with ostrich feathers was produced and worn. Mrs Loveday was one of the most dressy of these women who enjoyed being painted and posed in all her finery for the picture, holding a black horse".

Olive Branson painter 1885-1929

Olive travelled in a magnificent, carved and gilded Gypsy caravan, drawn by two well-fed horses with an able attendant. She met up with Gypsies at Binstead near Alton in Hampshire for the annual hopping season in late summer where she invited Munnings. Here Two to three hundred Gypsy families, and their animals camped around in a very large meadow. The Gypsies lived in a variety of tents and elaborately decorated caravans that resembled rolling ships.Gypsy adults and older children worked among the hop vines, gathering the bitter flowers used to flavor beer. Olive was a talented artist who made a good living with a London home and another in Hampshire. She travelled with Mark Stevens who also modeled for her and addressed her as "my lady". Munnings the artist had first visited her at a farm near Evesham. After she had journeyed down with her van and horses, over the Cotswold's and eventually into Hampshire.

Juliette de Bairacli Levy (1912 – 2009) Juliette of the herbs.

Juliette was known as 'the grandmother of herbalist', author of "Wanderers of the New Forest." In it she describes the simple way of life of commoners and Gypsies that has gone forever from the Forest. She had a strong bond with the Forest Gypsy community and lived a nomadic lifestyle travelling all over the world with Bedouins, nomads, Gypsies and peasants. She travelled a lot and befriended Romany

Gypsy folk in UK and Europe and New York. She wrote many books on herbs and she healed humans dogs cats and farm animals.

From her travels she learned from the gypsies how they used plants and herbs to treat the ailments of both people and animals. Juliette soon came to believe that these ancient methods of treatment might be lost forever as vaccines and chemical medicines were developed and she became a pioneer of holistic animal care. For three years she lived with her two small children in a tiny cottage at Abbots Well, near Frogham, in the north of the New Forest. It was a simple way of life with daily naked bathing in Windmill Hill Pond which has long since disappeared. During her life in the forest she gained many Gypsy friends.

Amelia Goddard(1847-1928)

Amelia was a gifted portrait artist particularly of New Forest Gypsies and their camps in the New Forest. She lived at Larks gate Thorney Hill, close to a large Gypsy settlement of some 600 Gypsies. Amelia lived in the forest for many years and was accepted by Gypsies as one of their kind. There is a mystery as well. It is of a silver ring worn by Amelia and a secret kept for sixteen years. Amelia Goddard records that the Marchioness of Waterford wrote from Highcliffe Castle in 1883 thanking her for the charming picture of a Gypsy which she was very glad to possess. The work was "Mary Stanley in the Forest" which passed to Major Wortley on Amelia's death.

Henry Gibbins

Henry operated the new forest Good Samaritan Society

providing rent free housing and groceries to needy families most of whom were Gypsies and in 1909 he produced a map showing some 24 Gypsy encampments or stopping places in the new forest. He was also author of many books including "Gypsies in the new forest".

Alice Elizabeth Gillington (1863-1934)

Alice was a pioneer collector of songs from English Gypsies and an active campaigner for Gypsy rights. Her best known collection was "Songs of The Open Road" based on her contacts amongst the Gypsies at Thorney Hill. Alice first encountered Gypsies in the New Forest in 1903 which was entitled New Forest Gypsy folk tales. She and her brother, John Gillington lived in two caravans, the Brown Caravan and the Yellow Caravan and followed the Gypsy way of life throughout their lives. They stayed together, but they did not always camp with the Gypsies. "We could easily find camping ground where the Gypsies do, but my brother doesn't care to be out in the open for various reasons, one of them being the cut-throat ruffians that infest the Forest roads". "We have a gun, but no dog."

Throughout her writings, Alice mentions meeting up with many Gypsy families in the New Forest, including those like Betsy Page(sometimes referred to as Betsy Bowers), Tom Pateman and Walter and Eliza White. Along with the Wheelers, Sherreds, James, and Willetts.

Alice died of a stroke at 27 Balmoral Road, Poole, Dorset, on 22nd of May 1934 though her address was 'The Caravans in Lilliput, Parkstone, Poole, Dorset'.

David Essex

David is perhaps best known for his popular records, Films and TV fame and his warm personality. He has been a regular visitor to the New Forest over recent years. David himself comes from a travelling family his Mother Olive being from the Kemp clan. his mother, Olive (née Kemp), was a self-taught pianist and an Irish Traveller, descended from Romany Gypsies.His grandfather, Thomas Kemp, was nicknamed "Philimore", which was the anglicised version of "Philly Mor" – being Irish for "Big Philly".David first came to the New Forest to prepare for his film "Silver Dream Racer" in the mid 1970s.When he spent time with our family friend Scott Mitchells (World champion dart player) family at their families farm in Bransgore.Learning to ride the motor bike for the film Silver Dream Racer and being shot for the film. David has returned again more recently to complete excerpts for the film The Traveler.(David kindly made a poetry contribution Tinker Man to my previous book which I edited entitled "Gypsy Storytellers").

Sven Berlin and Jenny Vize (1911-1999).

Sven was a famous bohemian artist who followed the Gypsies to the New Forest from St Ives in a gypsy caravan,where he spent over 10 years paintings them. He produced an immense amount of work during these years. Including paintings and books on the new forest gypsies.He wrote Dromengo which meant "man of the road" in 1971

245

about his experiences in the Gypsy compound of Shave Green.He was a close friend of Augustus John."When i see Rosie Smith selling flowers i think of how i made the journey from Tafalgar Square to Christchurch Priory and to discover Shave Green".He became famous for his painting of the boxer and Gypsy Henry Cooper who Sven described as "Old Henry or Tuvvy and his raven-voiced wife Amy.

Godfrey Edward Charles Webb (1914 - 2003).

Godfrey settled in Southampton as a young man he was employed as a cartographer for the Ordnance Survey. As a boy he was fascinated by travelers in tents and caravans who appeared on the heath near his home, seemingly from nowhere, stay for a while and then disappear. He read everything he could get his hands on about Gypsies and befriended the Romanises in the New Forest. In 1960 he published the book "Gypsies, The Secret People".

Henry Brusher Mills (1840–1905)

Henry got the title of Brusher by the enthusastic way he would sweep the wicket of the New Forest cricket ground at Balmer Lawn whenever a match was played there. Henry was also known as the "New Forest Snake Catcher "though locals called him Harry. He lived as a child in the village of Emery Down first job was as a general labourer. Later in his forties he moved into an old charcoal burner's hut in the woodlands near Spore lake Lawn, just north of Holland's Wood campsite.A conical shape hut with a bed inside made of dry bracken, chair and a biscuit tin that held firewood, a homemade spoon and a tobacco tin. Harry loved tea parties and he would quite often ask visitors into his hut for a cup of tea.

Brusher was extremely upset when his hut was vandalized and he was left homeless, some say that his home was destroyed to prevent him using squatters' rights or ancient Forest law to claim the land. He moved to live in an old outbuilding at his favourite hostelry. He was a most popular figure in Brockenhurst, often seen having a pint at the local Railway Inn which now is called the snake Catcher in his memory. This was one of Brusher's favourite haunts and he would often be seen here with a glass of "two or three pennyworths of rum" which was his favourite tipple!. Sadly though this was also the place where he died. On the afternoon of 1st July 1905 he was sitting drinking and after finishing he had some bread and pickles and left.

Purkis

The most famous charcoal burner of all time was undoubtedly Purkis.Of whom it was said transported the lifeless body of King William 11 in his cart from the fatal spot near Stoney Cross where the arrow pierced the monarch 's forehead, from where the Rufus Stone now stands to the town of Winchester, which was then the capital of England. ."This would have been a familiar journey for Parkis, for the burners often used to travel to the City from all parts of the Forest to sell their charcoal. The trade was practiced by the Purkis family at Castle Malwood right up to the end of the 19th century when another local family the Tinsley's, took over most of the production.

William Gilpin (1724 – 1804) writer, artist, clergyman and schoolmaster

William was the vicar of Boldre (devoted his life to improving the conditions of his parishioners). He bought the vicarage in 1777 and whilst living in the New Forest he published more sketches and thoughts in "Remarks on Forest Scenery and Other Woodland Views". He improved conditions in his parish by supporting a project for a new poor house. William had radical views on educating and disciplining the young, and he personally built and provided an endowment for a parish school which bears his name. He used the proceeds from his writing and an auction of his original drawings to fund many of his good works. There is a monument commemorating his long and productive life in the Church of St John at Boldre where his tomb is in the churchyard.

Mary Dore

Mary lived in Beaulieu in the 18th century in her rented house along sides the Beaulieu Mill. She was of humble origins and later in life she was said to be a witch. The archives of the Beaulieu estate tell that, on her return from Winton (Winchester) Gaol, she was angered by the demolition of the house she had previously lived in, and refused to live in the house, also at the mill, which was assigned to her in her absence.

However, the Beaulieu Estate Rental of 1729 shows Widow Dore occupying a house by the mill some 3 years after her release from prison. Richard Warner, describes her and her grave in the Parish Church of Beaulieu, in the following way: "Among the many 'frail memorials' of human dissolution, erected within its cemetery, was one which perished a few years ago, raised to the memory of Mary Dore, the parochial witch of Beaulieu, who died about half a century since. Old John, Duke of Montagu, covered her remains at his own expense and surrounded her grave with a neat railing. There he ordered an inscription of a curious nature which alludes to her possessing magical powers. .

The estate's archives do not include any information on the crime for which she had been imprisoned, and she is not generally well documented in the Beaulieu estate papers of her time. In his "History of Hampshire" (1795), Richard Warner, describes her and her grave in the Parish Church of Beaulieu, in the following way:

"Among the many 'frail memorials' of human dissolution, that have been erected within its cemetery,was one which perished a few years ago, raised to the memory of Mary Dore, the parochial witch of Beaulieu, who died about half a century since". Old John (1690-1749), who seems to have entertained a great veneration for this wonder-working female. This monument was removed and the remains of Mary Dore lay under a green grass turf, undistinguished by any discriminative mark from the common herd that sleep around her.This gifted female on reflection does not appear to have been a malignant witch, 'a black and midnight hag', that exerted her Canidian powers to the injury and discomposure of those around her. Her spells were chiefly used for the purpose of self-extrication in situations of danger

Mary Ann Girling

Mary was a farm labourer's daughter from Suffolk, She had

a vision that they should move to the New Forest and She arrived in Hordle, in 1871 with her one hundred and sixty followers. She had promised them eternal life and they were to live together in New Forest Lodge, Vaggs Lane, in Hordler like the apostles. A property she had aquired with the help of a wealthy patron. Due to their strict rules which prohibited the members from working as a result the mortgage remained unpaid and in December 1894 many of them were evicted. They lived by barter and the Word of God, and threw strange shapes when they walked the streets of Lymington. The Shakers, as they had become known, ended up living in bare wooden huts on an encampment nearby. Which was a cross between a village hamlet and a concentration camp. And there many of them succumbed to consumption. Those remaing continued to live in the Hordle area for a further 11 years, leasing fields, or camping by the roadside, and using an old barn as a chapel. However, Mary Girling's health was also in decline and she died of cancer in 1886.

She was buried in Hordle churchyard, amongst her followers, each grave having a yew tree planted at its head. Today nothing remains of the sect except a few yew trees and a small plaque fixed to the church wall, which reads 'Mary Girling Leader of the Hordle Shakers.

Jane Austen (1775 - 1817)

Novelist Jane Austen was born on 16 December 1775 in the village of Steventon in Hampshire. She was one of eight children of a clergyman and grew up in a close-knit family. Her first novel was 'Sense and Sensibility' in 1811 followed by 'Pride and Prejudice', which she described as her "own darling child". With Mansfield Park' published in 1814 and 'Emma' in 1816 when Jane suffered from Addison's disease. She travelled to Winchester to receive treatment, and died there on 18 July 1817. Her two other novels, 'Persuasion' and 'Northanger Abbey' were published posthumously. Jane had visited Lyme Regis in 1804 and her novel Persuasion is partly set in the West Dorset resort.

Slippery Rogers

Slippery was a smuggler and celebrated adventurer in contraband articles. He gained his nick- name of Slippery Rogers, due to his eel-like faculty of escaping the grasp of his maritime pursuers. He operated along the coast with his remarkable vessel which was rowed by forty daring mariners. Onboard he stowed up to two or three thousand ankers of spirits.

Tom Johnston

Tom is Lymington's most notorious smuggler. He was brought up as a fisherman by his smuggling father and by the age of 12 he knew the south coast of England like the back of his hand and by the age of 15 he had become a smuggler himself. It was said that 'Women, children, dogs and horses adored him. His life story includes spells in prison, injuries and personal disasters. He worked for both for the French and English governments, playing both the roles of smuggler and revenue man. He was easy going and popular so was able to gain the loyalty of the roughest seamen, yet at the same time enabled him to mix freely with the wealthy and titled in Europe.

Lucy Kemp-Welch: The artist (1869 – 1958)

When Lucy was a young girl she sketched the ponies which roamed the New Forest and in later years she went on to become the foremost painter of horses of her time. Her best known work Colt-Hunting in the New Forest is in the Tate Gallery, and some of her other paintings are in the Imperial War Museum. She also became famous for her illustrations for Black Beauty by Anna Sewell. Her Grandfather was Peter Kemp Welch who was a bussinessman who provided monies to establish Bournemouth Sanitorium. Lucy opened the parkstone Kemp Welch secoundary school in Herbert Avenue Parkstone Poole in the 1940s, it was a school attended by many of the local Gypsy children. Close to nearby heathland gypsy encampments of Rossmore and Parkstone.

Eric Ashby (1918 – 2003) Film maker

Eric Ashby loved the New Forest and shared this love with the world through his wildlife films. He believed that wild animals should be filmed behaving naturally, and his high standards of still photography and film-making in the wild became his hallmark. Eric worked for the BBC natural history unit and was a keen conservationist. His home was in Linwood which became a haven for some 30 wild foxes from rescue centre's. Visitors from around the world visited him there to see how both he and his wife Eileen cared for them. They raised a cub called Tiger and told his story in a book entitled My Life With Foxes (2000).

Brian Vesey Fitzgerald

Brian was an Author who wrote about the Gypsies. He obtained the majority of his Gypsy material for his books from the new forest Gypsy Amos Cherin.

Heywood Sumner (1853 – 1940) Artist painter, illustrator and craftsman.

George Heywood Maunoir Sumner lived with his family at Cuckoo Hill, near South Gorley.Spending his life researching and recording the archaeology, geology and folklore of the New Forest. He illustrated an edition of J.R.Wise's The New Forest and designed and built his ideal family house at Cuckoo Hill where he lived from 1904. In 1910 he published "The Book of Gorley" containing many anecdotes and illustrations of local characters and the history of the New Forest and its nearby commons.His famous "Guide to the New Forest" was published in 1923 and is considered to be one of the finest guides to be written about the woods of the New Forest. He died at Cuckoo Hill in 1940 at the age of 87.The family house is now a care home for elderly people.

Captain Frederick Marryatt -The Author.

During the 1840s he stayed for long period at the charming Chewton Glen House home of his brother on the edge of the New Forest. Where he wrote his famous novel "The Children of the New Forest". Chewton Glen has many of its rooms named after his classic book The Children of the New Forest along with his many other novels and book characters.

Sir Walter Raleigh

Walter Raleigh explorer and buccaneer lived at Sherborne Castle and was very popular with Queen Elizabeth I who gave him the lands of the 12th Century Sherborne Castle where he built Sherborne Lodge. He journeyed to America, where he famously brought back and introduced potatoes and tobacco to the British. He was later to have a fallout with the Queen and was sent to the Tower of London and he was later beheaded by James 1st for treason.

Alfred Lord Tennyson (6th August 1809-6th October 1892).

He was Poet Laureate of Great Britain and Ireland throughout much of Queen Victoria's reign. He spent much time in the New Forest. He wrote "My admiration of the Forest is great it is true old wild English nature and then the fresh smell of the air is so delicious" and the Forest is grand." The poet, diarist and Lymington customs official William Allingham, recorded all his visits to the New Forest in the 1860s.

Piccadilly's charitable angel

Theres a statue in London which folks all adore

it's a monument crafted for lovers amour

it's a of a Christian angel with Charitys wings

with an arrow that's pointed and a message that sings

Some say its Eros some say it's cool

it's a tribute to Shaftesbury s visions and rules

to the children who suffered down mines in factories bleak

its there to remind us of his goodness and meek

The lovers all say it's a reason to kiss

under the moonlight in heavenly bliss

its a statue thats pointing to Dorsets fair plains

a reminder to keep the laws rich and sane

Lord Shaftesbury was famous -for children he cared

he was one in a million to the good lord he prayed

he brought in the act's through Westminster's halls

he was wise and so charitable and the kids he adored.

Ray Wills

In recent times the New Forest itself has become a Site of Special Scientific Interest granted special status as the New Forest Heritage Area in 1985 UNESCO World Heritage Site in June 1999 then becoming a National Park in 2005.

Jumping the broomstick

Rosie jumped the broomstick upon a frosty morn

whilst bird's were singing in the trees and wishes all were born

a frog he croaked his story and the springs did run on bye

*there were squirrels a rushing up the trees and a lonesome tramp
passed by*

*There t'wer day's of merriment and gay- long afore
the days of war*

when soldiers fought for what was right upon old Flanders shores

they fought for king and country then with rifles tall n mean n bored

*there were sparrows in the hedge grow then and the pots were full of
beans n more*

the vardos were so splendid with steps up to the door

*Twas a splendid scene with ornate lamps and tapestry like you'd
never seen afore*

*the dogs were barking down the lanes where heathers stretched to
Poole*

where local men and gentle folk all said how do you do

The mushers went to market then and the gaffer took you in

with jobs for the lonesome vagabonds and pennies to buy your gin

the market's were full of hectic pace and all loud hawkers cries

*there were rows of clothes and stalls of cows and things to catch
your eye*

The church bells chimed and the groom did sigh as he kissed her on the green

where wild roses grew upon the trees and the past was left behind and been.

Ray Wills

Mrs 'Witchy' White

In the early nineteenth century Mrs White was a charwoman at Palace House. She was said to have occult powers and to be the author of a paper entitled 'Beaulieu Abbey. A letter from the Beaulieu Steward dated 02-01-1726/7 was told a story by 'a lady born and bred in Beaulieu, and the youngest, they say, of a "long family"' about her father's experience of her when a young man. He was courting a girl from Fawley at the time, and they were enjoying the festivities of the Beaulieu Fair. They forgot how late the hour had got and the girl, having promised her parents that she would be back at a certain hour, was very upset. At that moment old Mrs. White was passing and asked what the problem was. On hearing the story, she 'promised that if a start were made without an instant's delay, and the now benighted traveller just kept 'jogging along,' that she would arrive home in time.' She followed the old lady's guidance and 'never to her dying day could she account for the fact that somehow she did cover that four and a half miles from Beaulieu to Fawley within the allotted time.

CHAPTER SEVEN

Canford Days

Much of the New Forest region and surrounding counties came with vast estates. One of these which was then known as Canford. The area then and since has had its fair share of poets, writers, heroes and villains. Here are just a few of the famous names associated with this region of southern England during those years.During this period 18th/19th century much of the art and literature produced in this part of the country marks it out as being a most unique period from all that which had gone before and which is known as the Romanticism period. At this time there was a marked emphasis on the arts, and away from the previous structured, intellectual age of reason or enlightment. This was based on particular ways of looking at the world which recognized the importance of the emotions and the imaginations. Romanticism was in many ways a revolution in the arts, alongside the political, social and industrial revolutions of that particular age.

William Wordsworth and Coleridge were among the first British poets to explore the new theories and ideas that were sweeping throughout Europe then. The poetry of Wordsworth's and others initiated this new era by putting the emphasis on feeling, instinct and pleasure. Their poems displayed many aspects of Romanticism, with an emphasis on the emotions and expressions. This meant having, or cultivating, a sensitive, emotional and intuitive way of understanding the world around them. It stressed the importance of personal experiences and a desire to understand what influenced the human mind, with a belief in the power of the imagination such as could be stimulated by the pleasure of seeing a splendid and picturesque landscape.

Local Gypsies

 It was during this period that many of the Gypsy Travellers from the New Forest settled in Bournemouth and the surrounding areas. Although its believed that many were here in the area well before then as well and that they had most probably gone back and forth between the Forest and Bournemouth and surrounding areas for very many years. The Gypsies chose to live in and around the New Forest both within and in close proximity to an area of England which at that time and since has boasted very famous land marks. Such as Stonehenge, the present Jurassic coast, the Purbeck hills and the Isle of Portland(where Sir Christopher Wren took the stone for the rebuilding of London).

As early as the 1850s there were a great many Gypsy campsites scattered throughout Dorset and Hampshire. These included those at Beresford road Parkstone, Poole, Dorset where the Does and Jeff families resided from 1870s.Others were at Gallows hill Bere Regis from the 1850s,at Red hill common Bournemouth and also at Holdenhurst common where the Sherwood's, Bonsais and Coopers families lived.

Bournemouth then was known as Poole Heath, being an area of acid sandy soil and gorse criss-crossed by tracks, with a stream called the Bourne draining into the sea and wooded dells (chine's) cut by other streams. The only settlement of the area was by cows, Gypsies, and a few fishermen living in timber-framed cottages. Much of the land was in the possession of Sir George Iveson Tapps-Gervis, Lord of Christchurch Manor.Tapps-Gervis was responsible for the landscaping of some public gardens, but the only other home of any size recorded nearby by 1762 was Decoy House, which was a haunt for smugglers.

In this world the local heath lands of Canford which covered most of southern England were vibrant and colorful with an abundance of wild flowers. Heaths unspoiled by the later pollutants or artificial sprays, diesel and chemicals about to be belched out from the local drug house companies and traffic. Here there was rich foliage and secret nooks and leas for children's imaginative play. This was a time of the travelling tinkers, hawkers and vagrant workers much sought after by the rich land owners and farmers for laboring work on their large country estates, or for seasonal farm work.

Many of the local Gypsies who frequented this area of southern England originated in the main from the New Forest, South Wales and Surrey. Whilst a great many travelers were of Irish tinkers or navies descent who had emigrated here for necessary work to build the new railways, bridges and viaducts at Bournemouth/ Branksome. All labor intensive work, they crafted the finest handmade bricks from the local brickyards of the locality. Situated close to the famous racecourse at Redhill,the sanatorium hospital at Alderney, the Brick makers Arms pub at Bear Cross now Bear Cross and the art studio of Augustus John at nearby Manor Avenue.

The only main route through Parkstone had been the lonely coach road heading east from Poole, and it was beside the road at Brown Bottom and Ashley Cross that the small population of the area was centred. Some local people made woollen clothing, boots and shoes and fishing nets for export to Newfoundland. A few were tradesmen or inn-keepers and most of the rest were farmers and agricultural labourers. A lone traveller on this coastal path in the 19th century would have found a wild and mostly unpopulated area between the towns, inhabited only by nature and some large gypsy camps.

After the war years new council housing estates were built at Rossmore/Trinidad, Alderney and Kinson/West Howe to accommodate the growth in the local Gypsy population. There were stories of bare knuckle fighter's who attracted hordes of folk's to their illegal gathering's and contest's at Bear Cross. A great many local people today are in some way related to the Gypsies and Travelers who frequented the area during those early years and many of these have their roots in the New Forest area. Many of these families worked in the local factories in Wallisdown. Some had originally worked in the many brickyards and clay pits which had been around for many years whilst others worked casually at the large Poole fairgrounds. Whilst many would take sprigs of heather, created artificial paper crape flowers or floral bouquets and wreaths and sell them privately or in Bournemouth square and in Poole high street outside of Woolworth store. Newtown Gypsies and places

From a very early age I had the good fortune to freely mix with numerous Gypsy families who frequented the heaths and common land's close to my childhood home. I was raised on a small holding farm at the Manning's on the Manning's heath within the area known then as Canford and now known as Tower Park. In those days of the post war 1945 -1960 a great many Gypsy families roamed the area with their Vardos wagon's, horses and dog pack's. Gypsy site's were scattered through the terrain from Newtown to Canford Magna.

I was told by my close relatives not to go near the Gypsies, but like most kid's of my generation I was adventurous and inquisitive. In those days children could walk miles in safety with little traffic. As a child I would spend hours accompanied by my Airedale dogs visiting the Gypsy encampments of Canford Heath, old Wareham road and Alderney. At that time many of these people were regular occupants of a vast variety of numerous campsites scattered throughout the large expanse which was then all within the parish of Kinson at Parkstone, Branksome, Alderney, Wallisdown and Rossmore neighbourhoods.

There were many other Gypsy sites like the one at the rear of the Saunders Home of Rest on the Ringwood road, run by mr HoopermAlso at Cuckoo Bottom and Bourne Bottom, Pembroke road and Wolseley road. Though most of these were flimsy homes cut out of the mud with basic bender roofing. Often these sites had their own particular names which they were known by the Gypsies and travellers. Such as Cuckoo Bottom, Heavenly bottom,sugar knob mountain, monkeys hump lane, cinders town, frying pan, wallywack, high moor, Hemley bottom, bribery island, New England, top common and many more.

These Gypsy camps stretched the whole length of the old Wareham road and caused quite a storm and local reactions. The Poole council built one of the very first official Gypsy sites next door to us at the Manning's. The local Gypsies frequently dropped in on us at the Mannings smallholding and I gave them pails of water for themselves and their horses. They were always very polite "thank you sir". A list of Gypsy family names in Upper Parkstone in 1920s-1930s.included Sherwoods, Whites, Saunders, Phillips, Lights, Kings, Comptons, Trents and Stanleys- "A History of Upper Parkstone to 1939" by Patricia Wilnecker, Poole Museum Services 1988.

Flower Girls

Kinson in recent history also had its Gypsy flower girls including Nancy Crutcher and the Jeff's family who lived in the big house on Millham's lane and for many years these along with members of the wider Gypsy families were seen regularly selling flowers outside of Beale's store in the busy Bournemouth town square.

The most famous of these was Betsy Smith(nee White) 1890-1960.

Betsy was one of 11 children.Six daughters and 5 sons born to George and Louisa White(nee Crutcher) 2 died at birth. She was born on 1st March 1890 in a wagon on common heath land which is now part of Queens Park Golf Course, Bournemouth. Betsy was raised and spent most of her childhood and youth with her mother father and 11 siblings at Heavenly Bottom Gypsy encampment in Parkstone,Poole Dorset.When she was barely 10 years old her father George passed away. Leaving the family with no income and Mother Louisa had to find ways of making money as there was now no breadwinner. As a result the attractive little girl known as Betsy was chosen as the one who would be sent to Bournemouth Square to sell bunches of white daisies.

The first day she went to Bournemouth, she sold every bunch, as a result her Mother(Louisa) instructed Betsy to do this every day and so it was that every day she sold all her bunches of flowers in the square. Family legend has it that the Bournemouth Gentry purchased her flowers from her because she was so pretty. It wasn't too long then that her other sisters and cousins followed suit and so that was how the Bournemouth Flower girls were born.

Betsy was the longest flower seller amongst all of her relations and the best known flower seller of all her family. For many years her photograph was displayed in the Debenhams store restaurant, along with a photo of her long time friend Ciss Anderson (born Lucy Old and who was married to Jimmy White). Jimmy White was Betsy's first cousin. The family held a double wedding for the two couples at St Peters Church, Parkstone. where Betsy married Charles Smith on 24th February 1908 . Betsy was only   18 years old at the time when she married Charles. but her marriage certificate says she was 21years old. (It was easier to change ones age on the register then, as no proof of age was required).Together Betsy and Charles had nine children, two died in infancy. They had 42 grandchildren.

Betsy continued to sell flowers in Bournemouth Square well into her early seventies but she had to stop as a result of a bad fall. When she died in 1960 she had a massive funeral, the procession of which went throughout Christchurch and Bournemouth. It was watched by hundreds of people including many who knew her well. It was reported in the Bournemouth Evening Echo as the biggest funeral ever recorded in the Bournemouth area. There were several funeral cars for her large immediate and extended families. A great number of her lifelong friends were present. There were very many flatbed Gypsy lorries in the procession to cope with the transporting of the hundreds of floral tributes.

Jimmy White

Jimmy married Ciss Anderson (born Lucy Old)at St Peters Church, Parkstone on 24th February 1908.

Smiths

Charles Smith

Charles married Betsy White on 24th February 1908 at St Peters church Parkstone. This was a double wedding.

The flower girls dreams.

You'll see them there on Saturday's outside the towns great store

baskets full of daffodil's and roses by the score

their braided hair and darker look's with dresses oh so gay

from heather sweet terrain they came

to while the hours away

Their dialect course with melody

though their words were plain

they spoke the true Romani like children once again

They promised wealth good health and more to people passing by

with smiles to warrant fortunes gain and wisdom in their eyes

Their homes of vardos on the heath and songs of yesterdays

with accordion playing songs of love and rabbits in the hay

with ponies small and dog packs calls

heathers sweetly laid

amongst the hills where mix mitosis killed

the food of yesterday.

Ray Wills

The Bonds

Mary Bond (nee Hughes)1921-2015

Mary was affectionately known as Queen of the Gypsies.

Born in Sherborne in a bender tent on September 9, 1920, Mary Bond became a well-known figure in Britain's Romany Gypsy community.Born to Caroline Hughes and Johnny Cooper, she was the eldest of eight children who grew up in rural Dorset.Her childhood was tough but fondly remembered, she and her brothers and sisters working on farms alongside her parents.Mary and her family moved to Mannings Heath in the early 1970s, She often travelled into Bournemouth with her friend Tilly Johnson selling lucky heather and charms in the square. Being part of the famous Gypsy lady flower sellers.

It was said that Mary loved cooking, often making bacon and meat puddings in her two-gallon pot. She was also a regular visitor each year to both the Great Dorset Steam Fair and the Epsom Derby. Later in life she lived in homes in Bedford Road and Farwell Road, Poole, and with her sister Celia and Frank Benham in Stourpayne.Mrs Bond loved her family, attending their parties, christenings and weddings, and accompanying them to fairs across the country. She died a great great-grandmother in January 2015. In February 2015, hundreds of folks turned out to bid farewell to Mary Bond who passed away at the age of 94. A large funeral cortege, including three horse-drawn carriages, wound its way from her Alderney home to St Clement's Church, Newtown, for the funeral service.

Harold Bond

Mary met her husband Harold Bond, a dairyman, while the family were staying in Blandford.They married on January 9, 1939, at the parish church, shortly before he embarked for Europe during the Second World War, fighting in Belgium and at Dunkirk.Their first child Caroline was stillborn, but they went on to have John, born at Hungry Down, Rosie, born at the Boggs in Wallisdown, Lovie, born at Carters Down, and Jimmy, who was born in Thornicombe.

The Bonds travelled with her parents when they first married. Mrs Bond would work hoeing, hop picking and fruit picking, and the family travelled to Bridgewater to work on the pea fields and cut sugar beat.In the 1950s, they settled at a house in East Street, Blandford, for several years, but were soon on the move again.They travelled on to Carter Down where they lived in a shepherd's hut while Mrs Bond worked on the land there.Her son John made a wooden horse-drawn wagon which became their home on the side of Old Wareham Road until it one day caught fire, and then they moved to Canford Heath.There Mrs Bond worked hawking lace, heather, scrap metal, rabbit skins and more, travelling as far afield as Winchester.

Harold Bond died in 1965.

Brixeys

Brixeys cousins of the Rogers had a contractors/construction yard in Newtown.Brixey road took its name from this family.

The Burtons

Basil Burton was employed at the Mannings gypsy site as

Gypsy Laision Officer for Dorset County Council for 15 years.

Coopers

Horace Cooper

Horace Cooper grew up on the heathlands of Wallisdown commons campsite the Dip in Poole. Horace lived his later years next door to my sister Jo and her hubby Ron Squires at Fraser road in Wallisdown Poole Dorset. Where he was regularly seen driving his pony and cart along the highway or leaning on his garden gate telling stories to neighbours the local kids.For he was a great storyteller and a kid magnet and he would often tell me stories about when his folks lived on the heath on the Gypsy encampment. When Horace passed away just a few years ago the vicar read out one my poems at his funeral. Horace Cooper one time rag n bone man in Wareham he was grandson of Louisa and grew up at what was known as the Dip encampment in Wallisdown.

Horace Cooper

Ole Horace Cooper was a good friend of mine

He could tell you a yarn and spin you a line

When they lived on the heath Annie and he

In old Wallisdown just a stone's throw from me

He would lean on his gate and talk to the kids

carve out his script upon the branch of a tree

in the days of the brickyards in old Alderney

we were cousins of Castles friends of the Kings

the Whites were our history with Stanley's thrown in

Mary and Maisie made the flowers so grand

the wreaths and the baskets from both their fair hands

Ole Horace had a picture that hung on the wall

the storytellers of history and its traditions and lores

when by the ditch was their home in old Wallisdown

where the Gypsies did roam not far from Poole town

The haunts of the smugglers and the pen of the free

Augustus paintings were sketched in ole Alderney

where the goldfinch did sing upon the thistle n broom

*where the heathers were rich and the Gypsies all sang by the light of
the moonmany did live by Arne avenue*

the Johnston's and Mabeys and Joker from Poole

Ole Horace was rich but poor in the hand

but he had the ways of a good travelling man

He rode a good cart all through Wallisdown and smiled at the ladies

on his way to Poole town.

Ray Wills

There were so many Gypsy and Traveler sites and encampments in the area, some of them there from early pre war days going back to the mid 1850s. These included Heavenly Bottom,The Bogs,New England, Wally wack,monkeys hump.Bourne Bottom, Bourne moore,Bourne Hill Camp, Wolsey road,Top Common, Fox Holes and Cuckoo Bottom. Some of them contained caravans that were spotlessly clean with polished brass lamps glass and trinkets inside.Often the women were to be seen sitting on the van step's smoking their clay pipe's.

Castles

The Castles came from Surrey Previously Hitcin HERTS

Mary Mabey nee Castle

Mary married Frederick Mabey

Mary lived in Newtowns Terrace with relative show people the Kings and Castles.(Jean Castle became Pooles beauty Carnival Queen in the 1960s) prior to moving into nearby council housing.

Groups of these Newtown Gypsies were regularly seen selling flowers and lucky heather at their spot outside of Woolworths store on the streets of Poole.

Maceys final curtain -Tribute to Aunt Macey Castle nee Rogers.

They pulled the final curtain down on Macey

this was her last parade

as she counted all her blessings

long friendships she had made

she married into the Gypsies

the King and Ccastle clans

She was a loyal custodian

took her charms and loyal bands

you could see her making flowers

selling heathers too

from the foot of Beale's in Bournemouth

across Waterloo to outside woollies store at Poole

Her kids all talked the diddy

her chavvies were on call too

one danced for Zena Martelle

the others danced the ballroom halls

She offered tea and biscuits

could chat away the hours small

knew the knowledge and the flowers

she walked the fields and commons

worked upon the land

services to war efforts

shed have you understand

As she knew everyone that mattered

the common and the grand

She was a dandy lady

lover of the common land.

Ray Wills

The Cherretts

Harriot Cherrett ,George Cherrett and Mary Cherrett were recorded in Canford from about 1803/1806.

Benjamin Cherrett was recorded about 1769 at Charlton Dorset.

John Cherrett, born in Mordon Dorset in 1779

Ann Cherrett born about 1780 at Shapwick Dorset.

Marcy Cherrett, Benjamin Cherrett, Ann Cherrett,Joseph Cherrett,Eliza Cherrett,Daniel Cherrett were recorded at Corfe Mullen.

 Dorothy May Cherrett was born 23rd May 1901 in Basingstoke and died on 31 March 1968, Parkstone, Poole.

The Crutchers

Louisa Crutcher.

Louisa married George White.They had eleven children 6 girls and 5 boys, 2 died at birth. They lived at Heavenly Bottom Gypsy encampment in Parkstone, Poole Dorset.

Brian Crutcher

International speedway star from Parkstone Brian (Nipper)Crutcher)arguably the best English speedway rider never to win the World Final, rode for Poole Speedway at just 16.In later years managing his own motorist shop in Newtown.Brian was born in Poole on the 23rd August 1934 he finished second at the 1954 speedway World Championship Finals finals. Crutcher made his debut for third division team the Poole Pirates in 1951 at age 16. He made his first World Final appearance in only his second year of racing in 1952, finishing in twelfth place. At the start of 1953 he moved to first division team the Wembley Lions and appeared in the next four World Championship finals, Wembley closed down in 1956 and Crutcher moved to the Southampton Saints until he retired from the sport at the end of 1959. For a number of years he managed a car repair business in sea view parkstone before retirement.

Bill and Daisy Dibben

Bill of haskells road Newtown did the the rag n bone around the Newtown area. He was tragically killed crossing on the first evening of the newly built zebra crossing outside of the Albion hotel in Newtown. Bill Dibben

Joe Fudge (Preacher Gypsy) Joe was born at Heavenly Bottom gypsy encampment Parkstone Poole before moving to the Monkey's Hump site at Parkstone Poole.

Hughes

The Hughes family were one of the largest Romany families in Britain.

Arthur Hughes was married to Lavinina Frankham they had 17 children.

John Hughes

John Hughes had been injured in the Great War and spent time in Dorchester Hospital, his brother was killed in the same conflict. His wife Caroline and the children would work on local farms, picking potatoes, peas and fruit, pulling sugar beet and hay making. Living in the caravan and in bender tents, they would eat from the land, rabbits, pheasants and chicken and plenty of vegetables cooked on an open fire in a two gallon pot. Clothes washing was done from water taken from the stream that once ran all the way through the heath.

John Hughes married Caroline nee Bateman in 1918

> Caroline was registered under the name Caroline Frankham.) 1900-1971 Queen of the Gypsies.

Caroline was one of seventeen children of Arthur Hughes and Lavinia Frankham. Bateman was actually the surname of her paternal grandmother. Caroline was born in a horse-drawn caravan in Bere Regis, Dorset' and registered in the Wareham District which was well used by Gypsy travelers. In common with a number of her siblings, she was baptized twice on 24 November 1900 in Childe Okeford, north of Wareham, and on 4 January 1901 at Lychett Matravers.Caroline's mother was a member of a south country Gypsy family and Carolines father was a 'rat-and-varmint destroyer', but his skill set was much broader as 'Laborer', 'Peddler','Hawker of Tin Wares', 'Tin-Maker' and 'Basket Maker'. Her parents never married. The family mainly travelled in and around Dorset and went hop picking in an around Hampshire during the early Autumn.One of Caroline's younger sisters, Deliah, was baptized (on 1 March 1904).

John and Caroline had 8 children. Diana, Mary, Annie, James, Thomas, Louisa, Caroline and Celia.

 In later years they often watched over their grandchildren Penny McPhillips, her sister Susie and baby Carol Warren.

Meeting with Ewan McColl

In the early 60s Caroline Hughes (Gypsy Queen wife of John Hughes) parked in a layby near the old Wareham road when discovered by US Folk singer Ewan Mc Coll.Ewan tape recorded the collection of Carolines songs. Which she had learnt as a child from her mothers lap and around the yog. Ewan took these back to the USA where they were sang by recording artistes worldwide.

Caroline was sat in her horse drawn caravan in a lay by on the A5 near on Canford Heath old Wareham road in Dorset surrounded by children and paperback books. When she was discovered by American Folk singer and scholar Ewan Mac Coll' in 1963. Caroline was well known for her singing. Her voice was recorded on two visits in 1963 and 1968. Her songs were published and can still be heard today from records held in the national archives. Ewan took a great interest in Gypsy lore, travelling around the British Isles with his tape recorder and a notebook. Preserving stories and songs that were in danger of being lost as the Gypsy way of life was threatened by modernization. It was while he was searching out Gypsies to record and talk to. When he was writing one of his radio ballads, called The Travelling People he stumbled across Caroline. These were hundreds of songs which Caroline had first learnt from her mother at a very young age. MacColl took these songs back to the U.S.A and they were recorded by the Seeger's along with very many popular folk and beat groups of that/ era both in the U.S.A and in Britain. During 1963 and 1966 recordings made by Ewan McColl, Peggy Seeger and Charles Parker.

Gypsies absorbed their songs bit by bit from their mothers' singing around the home whilst performing routine domestic chores, or from their male relatives around a yog after a session in the pub. Some other songs were learned from other Gypsy families at the fairs and meetings which used to form an integral part of the Gypsies' life, or at the occasional chance encounters at traditional camping places.

Caroline Hughes

Do you remember the Dorset Gypsy poet Queen

with her words of love she set the scene

the caravan's gathered on the old Wareham bye pass

with their homes of freedom and their wheel's on grass

The view of Canford hills of lodge

the windy track's on the land of God

she wrote the anthem's and the folk trail ends

where the Dartford warbler thrilled around each bend

They came to visit her the young and wise

with the dust of love within their eyes

she played and sung the word's of rhyme

memories of another age another time

The Seeger's and Ewan Mac Coll came to bend their ears

the sixties vogue in the protest years

the traditions stretched and the words were wise

they crafted melodies and turned the tide

The Dorset Gypsy queen of poetry

sat and talked amongst birch white trees

the guitars strummed and their voices thrilled

amongst the campfires lit and the rolling wheels

The Manning's heath just a stone throw away

where as a child I ran and played

the music lived within their heart's

the Gypsy song and the horse and cart's

Then the master artistes performed her songs

the Gypsy queen with lilt so strong

the heather's bend and the lizard's squirmed

amongst the adder's and fast slow worms

Gone are the Travelers who played that day

amongst the gorse on the great highway.

Ray Wills

Kings

The kings were show people related to the Castles and Mabeys.

Bill Knott

Bill Knott developed his international caravan empire locally which he called Bluebird Caravans/B K Caravans. His mother being a Gypsy lady. They originally lived in a bungalow in Broom road Alderney before he became an entrepreneur and millionaire. My aunt Ivy Rogers was at one time his housekeeper and child minder. Bill Knott started his road to self employed selling shoe laces and match boxes on the streets of Ashley road Parkstone Poole which locals called up on hill. His caravan industry the biggest in the world which was based on the Ringwood road at Newtown Poole grew out of the Gypsy caravan concept locally, for the mother of Bill Knott being herself a Gypsy lady. Bill Knott who originally lived in Broom road Alderney had a close working relationship with the inventor of radio Marconi. Marconi who first sent wireless messages across the channel from Sandbanks Poole.

279

Bill Knott

When I left Kemp Welch fine Rossmore Poole school
I worked for ole Bill Knott with his vans so cool
he had the biggest industry in the world
he turned out those vans so self assured

I painted the kitchen's and spayed those chassis so keen
I was on peace work in the bluebird factory scene
the wheel's they did roll and the till's they did chime
when old Bill Knott made those van's so prime

Those caravan's in Newtown's heath land's
were based on the Romany vardos I understand believe
they sold them to Germany, Ireland and France
the finest van's like true romance

I worked long hours with brush and spray gun
I sprayed those colors oh how such good fun
I was the highest paid lad in the factory
they sold those vans and sent them overseas

They stored those vans on the heath

where I grew up and cut my teeth

where goldfinch nest's were well in reach

and Gypsy still roamed the heather's sweet

where view's were rich to Waterloo and Fleet's

ole Bill Knott was quiet a guy a millionaire they say with the Gypsy eye.

Ray Wills

Mitchells

 Mitchells ran a local haulage concern and local bussiness man Eddie Mitchell became Director of Bournemouth soccer club in recent times.

Kelly Mitchell

Kelly was know as "Queen of the Gypsy Nation," died in 1915 while giving birth. As many as 20,000 Romanis showed up for her funeral in Meridian, Mississippi,USA flooding the small town to pay their last respects.She was buried in the Rose Hill cemetary in Meridian USA.

The Phillips

Percy Phillips

Percy carried on the family tradition of horse grazing despite the local authority taking him to court on a number of occassions where he cited the grazing rights and won the case on numerous occassions.He carried on the family tradition of horse grazing on Turbary Common heathland in West Howe known to the gypsy as New England. His forefather had razed horses and kept pigs there for centuries.Despite the local authority taking him to court on a number of occassions where he cited the grazing rights as confirmed in the Doomsday Book and won the case.

The E F Phillips family of Edward, Frank and Ron operated a very successfull sand and gravel haulage enterprise after the war years 1939-45 and later in the 1970s a continental haulage company. They started from early humble beginings from a small sand and gravel pit on the Mannings heath Parkstone Poole at the rear of Reg Rogers property.

They were Grandfather Reg Rogers cousins (the Phillips family)related to the Fancys in earlier times.The E F Phillips family of Edward, Frank and Ron operated a very successfull sand and gravel haulage enterprise after the war years 1939-45 and later in the 197os a continental haulage company. They started from early humble beginings from a small sand and gravel pit on the Mannings heath Parkstone Poole at the rear of Reg Rogers property.

Rogers

Charles Rogers born 1862 he used monies raised by his wife's (Emily Elizabeths nee Fancys pigs to start his first brickworks.Known as Charles was born 1862 at Kinson, Canford, Poole, Dorset son of Joseph. He married Emily Elizabeth Fancy on 6th September 1887 in Kinson Dorset. Her father was Gideon Fancy from Bourne bottom Gypsy campsite at Parkstone Poole and her mother was Elizabeth Cherrett. The story has it that Charles built his brickyards from monies made by his wife's Emily Elizabeth pigs.

William Charles Rogers died in July 1935 at age 72. He was buried at St Clements Church, Parkstone, Poole Dorset with wife.

Rogers builders were renowned for creating the red Rogers brick from their brickyards at Manning's Heath and Wimborne these were sold worldwide. Brick making was a craft in much demand. The bricks were originally hand made in a wooden mould from clay dug from the clay pits. When finished, they were dusted with sand and stacked on racks in the open air but with a light wooden shelter to keep off rain, and they would be left here to dry for several weeks. When thoroughly dry they were stacked inside the dome-shaped kiln with air spaces between the stacks. The kiln was built of bricks, too, and had a central opening in the roof to act as a chimney, and four small arched entrance doors around the sides. When all was ready, a very small fire was lit in the centre and this was gradually increased by feeding in wood faggots from the entrance doors until the whole kiln was red hot. Then the four entrance doors were blocked up with clay and bricks, and the whole left for several days to cool slowly before the doors were knocked open and the red bricks removed on flat-topped wheelbarrows and stacked for use. The reason that so many Gypsies and Travellers were involved in brick- making was that many of the kilns could be found on the commons, frequently the poorest land in the locality.

This meant that the topsoil was thin and therefore easy to strip away, in order to dig out the clay necessary for making the bricks; in addition there was local woodland, gorse or brush, for firing the kilns. This made the sites, where Gypsies often camped, perfectly suited to this, and the Travellers provided a ready workforce, some acting as sand-carriers, as well as brick-makers and brick burners.

These brick kilns were a common sight throughout the countryside, supplying local needs, and the census records show several well-known Romany and Traveller surnames connected with the business of brick-making. There is a certain irony that a people "who lived abroad and about in Gypsy tents," as the Leicestershire Chronicle as early as August 1860 had remarked, were often to be found labouring in the brickyards that supplied bricks and tiles for the permanent dwellings of the gorjer population,

Their bricks were made at their brickyards at Manning's Heath,Fancy road the Dell Parkstone and Colehill Wimborne these bricks were sold worldwide.The Rogers family were related to Stanleys,Scotts,Brixeys and Cherretts, they were brickmakers involved in building of both the Newtowns, Weseleyn and Evangelical churches.William Charles Rogers

Reginald Rogers (1892-1969)

Reginald was a brick maker. He was the son of Charles and Emily Elizabeth Rogers

Reginald married Alice Wardle. Reginald Rogers called his wife Daisy a common Gypsy name after Daisy Fancy though her real name was in fact Alice.They lived in a rented Lady Wimborne house "Heather View" on Mannings Heath before moving into their newly built house by cousin Harold Rogers and called "The Mannings" on the Mannings Heath Canford.Here they ran their family smallholding on land bought from Lady Wimborne just opposite the family brickyard.Reg and Alice had 8 children Vera, Macey, Ivy,Iris,Winifred,Betsy,William and Anthony.Reg Rogers small holding farm at the Mannings was on land bought from Lady Wimborne.Grandfather Two of his daughters were christened Bessie and Macey which were common travelling names. My middle name was Arnold who was one my uncles on my grans side f the family.As a small child I had the nickname of rabbits ears which was another Gypsy saying as someone whose listening to everything he shouldn't. Reginald died on 5th November 1969 and he and Alice are buried at St Clements church, Newtown, Parkstone, Poole.

 Reginald (known as Bill Rogers) (1926-2016)

Bill the eldest son of Reginald and Alice was known affectionatly as "The Storyteller" of Minnie the Mooch fame etc. He was born at the family home in Heather View Alderney and was a lorry haulage driver,clay and iron worker.His epitaph/tribute by the author /nephew Ray Wills was published in the Travellers Times magazine in 2016.

Sidney Rogers

At the end of the war cousin Sid Rogers bought up abandoned army trucks,creating Rogers Transport.Harold Rogers was the local builder.He lived on the Ringwood road Alderney Parkstone Poole. Charles known as Charlie ran piggeries at Wool lane old wareham road Parkstone Poole.

Stanleys

The Stanley's originated from the New Forest area and made a distinctive mark on the Parkstone area.They were recorded in Parish records as early as the 1600s.

Benjamin Stanley

Benjamin was the brother of Levi Stanley whose elders had emigrated and lived in Dayton USA. Benjamin had chose to settle down in an area in Kinson Dorset known to the Gypsies as New England at Turbary common. Benjamin had been disowned by their father and it was said that a curse was put on him and the future families for the next three generations to follow.

Samson Stanley snr

Samson was one of the very first Gypsies to move from heavenly bottom encampment in Parkstone Poole to move into a council bungalow. Sammy was a well liked Gypsy with a pleasant cheerful manner, he was at one time a rag n bone man and used to give school children rides on his grey mare and cart.Sammy Stanley Snr and sons (Sammy and Abe)attended Newtowns Albion pub(the snake).

Nelson Stanley operates his thriving Scrap metal business today on the Alder Hills at parkstone Poole. Despite his physical disability, losing a leg whilst attempting to retrieve a coin from his metal breaking crushing machine. Many Stanley's are still living locally in and around Kinson and have thriving businesses in Parkstone as well as in Hampshire.World boxing champions Freddie Mills,Abe Stanley and Ted Sherwood worked the boxing booths at Poole fairgrounds before becoming world boxing champions.

Sherwoods

The Sherwood family were recorded in the Census for Canford and Kinson from as early as 1841 onwards and were in Parish registers long before then.

William George James Sherwood married Eliza nee Downton.

Lily Eliza Sherwood the only daughter married George Thomas DAVIS in 1912.

Joseph Sherwood

 Joseph married Urania Burton the daughter of Henry and Priscilla Burton. She was born in 1855 at Sturminster Newton Dorset. Joseph and Urania lived in Kinson where they raised a family.

 Ted Sherwood - champion boxer.

Ted was born Edward George Sherwood in Fancy Road, on 13th September 1910 along with his twin sister Gladys Emma. Some of Ted's ancestors were travellers & tinkers. As a young lad Ted showed an aptitude for boxing, and soon began to take part in fairground boxing matches. He trained under Herbert Millett with nearly 130 bouts between 1929 and 1939.

 On 26th December 1930 Ted married Dora Thomas in

Branksome.In 1931 they had a daughter Ruby. Ted's occupation was given as Labourer.

Ted later took to drink but found salvation through religion, becoming an ardent member of the Pentecostal church in Poole, and one of their leading preachers. He often preached in the open air at Sea View in Poole and also from a soap box at Speakers Corner in Hyde Park, London. At this time he met the Reverend Dr. Ian Paisley Ted's wife Dora died in 1986, and Ted died in October 2000 in Poole.

Ian Paisley Minister of Northern Ireland, and Ted became firm friends. Paisley relates the following story about Ted, which can be found at http://www.earnestlycontending.com/ewministries/others/7reasonsbible.html ."A friend of mine, Ted Sherwood, an ex-welterweight champion boxer, once told me this story. Ted was saved from the depths of sin and, fired with the zeal of an unabated first love, was very anxious to win others to Christ. When he preached he went through all the movements of the boxing ring and to all criticisms of his peculiar mannerisms he would innocently reply, "Well, ain't I fighting the devil anyway?" One night Ted found himself amongst the throngs at Hyde Park. Disgusted at so many people listening to so much verbal trash, he decided he must attract as many of the crowd as possible away from the various meetings and preach to them the gospel which transformed his life. Tugging at his Bible-- Ted's Bible always seemed too large for his pocket-- he eventually got it out and set it on the ground. Taking off his coat he placed it over the Bible. Then he started to jump around the coat, shouting in consternation "It's alive! it's alive!" The crowd ran from the other meetings to see what was happening, and when Ted had a very large congregation around him he picked up his coat, lifted up his Bible and shouted "It's alive!" "What did you do then?" I questioned. "O told them how this Book found me dead in the graveyard of pollution and how it imparted new life to Teddy Sherwood the debauched, drunken and blaspheming boxer," he replied.

George Sherwood married Elenor Ric in 1740 at kinson parish now part of Poole.

William Sherwood is linked to the very large family tree of Sherwoods in the Poole area.

Sherwood family members Sidney Sherwood and his three sons Frederick,Alfred and Harry were tragically killed when an incendary bomb fell on their family home in Fancy road Newtown on 20th November 1940 during the second world war.

Sherwoods had a thriving coal yard bussiness on the ringwood road in Newtown.

Trents

Charles Trent scrapyard on Ringwood road, became the largest in the world with a large billboard proudly proclaimin this on the busy Ringwood road in the late 1940s/50s.

Bender Days

We all shared our benders there amongst the heathers deep

with granfer George and Mary sweet with jackals at our feet

there we shared our rabbit's stew and ate fagots in a pie

they smoked the herbs amongst the downs where country folk passed by

The greens were rich upon the moors where the foxes built their dens

where horses lay and cockerels crowed and rich folk hurried bye

the streams were rich with fishes then and springs upon the downs

where warblers sung afore the dawn and Mary Gear passed by

The days were hard and folks did cry of cold and lack of grub

where briar's stretched across the heaths of ladies of the crown n mud

though winds were harsh and nights were cold we shared our love and more

we sung our songs and shared our dreams each day upon the moors

The Gypsy folks and travellers no more do roam this land

where man has sold the heaths for yuln and built a promised land

of bricks and sand and glass with frames where idle men doth walk

where monies gained and fools are framed with fun and idle talk

Long gone are the days of wagons wheels vardos and benders frames

where rabbits ran and Gypsy son was singing in the rain

the tracks have gone and heathers grand across that fertile land

where dreams awoke and child first spoke at new dawn on the morn.

Ray Wills

The Turners

Turners are one the oldest travelling families in th UK.Turners were associated with Canford Lodge being involved in Freemasonary as well as possible roots in the Purbeck area. Many place names were associated with the family including Turners Pike, Turners Puddle and Turners Piddle etc.From the 14th century many Turners were MPs,Mayors and Sherriffs.

John Turner the famed artist

John painted throughout the county and was said to visit his family on the heathlands regularly.He painted pictures of the Gypsies including his "Gypsies at Sandbanks".He frequented the Poole area on his favourite spots was Sea View Parkstone.

John Turner

John was injured in the Great War and spent time in Dorchester Hospital, his brother was killed in the same 1914-18 conflict.John married Diana in 1949 at St Clements church Newtown Poole. St Clements was the Gypsy family church. Caroline Hughes and all her family had travelled down on horseback to attend Diana and John Turner's wedding. John Turners family were Romany people who had travelled the south and west country and lived on Canford Heath.

Diana Turner (nee Hughes) 1920-1999.

Diana was the third child born to John and Caroline Hughes in a horse drawn wagon. They were one of the largest Romany families in Britain.Diana's siblings were Mary, Annie, James, Thomas, Louisa, Caroline and Celia. They were all born in the caravan and would work on local farms, picking potatoes, peas and fruit, pulling sugar beet and hay making. Clothes washing was done from water taken from the stream that once ran all the way through the heath. Diana was also a fortune teller and attended the Great Dorset Steam Fayre.When Diana died in 1999 many Gypsies around the country visited the Canford Heath Travellers site to pay their respects.

Dianas mother Caroline Hughes was the 'Queen of the Gypsies' and was well known for her singing. Her voice was recorded in 1963 and 1968 when the family were living in a horse drawn caravan on the side of Old Wareham Road, Canford Heath. Her songs were published and can still be heard today from records held in the national archives.

Dan Turner

Dans father's family were Romany people who travelled around the South and West Country, lived on Canford Heath before there was a housing estate. Living in the caravan and in bender tents, they would eat from the land, rabbits, pheasants and chicken and plenty of vegetables cooked on an open fire in a two gallon pot. Clothes washing was done from water taken from the stream that once ran all the way through the area.For generations locals worked at establishing very successfull bussinesses, including hordes of brickyards,potteries and clay pits. Many Gypsies closely related to one another ran these enterprises.

Freddie Mills (June 26, 1919 -July 25th 1965).

 Freddie was born in Bournemouth in 1919. At the age of 17, he began a highly successful and colourful professional boxing career which made him the "darling" of the British fight scene. In 1942 at the height of World War II, he knocked out Len Harvey in 2 rounds to capture the British Commonwealth Light heavyweight Championship. He went on to win the European 175 pound title with a knockout over Pol Goffaux, and in 1948 defeated Gus Lesnevich to win the World Light heavyweight Boxing Championship. After losing his World Championship to Joey Maxim on January 24, 1950, he retired. Mills was extremely popular even in retirement and ran a highly successful nightclub. He also starred in a number of films and was a presenter on the early BBC TV music show, Six Five Special (1957). He died of gunshot wounds to the head on July 25, 1965 under a cloud of mystery. Although the official verdict was suicide, many people believe that it was due to him becoming involved in the London underworld of the notorious gangsters the Kray Twins.

Poole Fair

Sam and Esther Mckeowen ran a boxing booth at Poole fair where Freddie Mills, the famous boxer fought. Freddie was often seen standing outside the booth on a platform with other boxers, including Teddy Peckham, like Freddie, Teddy was a local boy who attended Heather lands school near Heavenly Bottom Gypsy campsite where Gypsy families lived in wagons.

The local public houses were another attraction to Gypsy families and of these there were very many in the area. Including The Albion pub which was affectionately known as the Snake and Pickaxe at Newtown and the Sea View hotel at Newtown. The Smugglers Arms in West Howe, The Bear Cross originally the brick makers arms ,The Shoulder of Mutton, The Rossmore Hotel ,The Woodman and The Dolphin at Kinson, which is now renamed Gulliver's all had many regular clientele.

The Sea View Inn Parkstone

The Inn stood on the high land above Kinson Potteries overlooking Poole Harbour. Kinson now is in no way associated with the sea, but 70 years ago the people from this side of the parish had many connections with the harbour and the sea.

Bear Cross

At the Bear Cross pub the landlords son Frank Lane built coffins for the local Gypsies.

The Shoulder of Mutton Inn.

Its name indicates that at one time meat also was sold there; a real carcass would have been hung out as a sign. The bar occupied the front room of one of the two adjoining cottages and today is little altered. There was stabling at the side. Augustus John the artist was a regular at both The Bear Cross and Shoulder of Mutton pubs while renting Lady Wimbornes Alderney Manor. At the Bere Cross,Pooles Jolly Sailor, Rossmore Hotel and Lord Nelson unofficial popular boxing matches took place between Gypsies and locals.

The Woodman Tavern Branksome was also a pub regularly frequented by Gypsies.

Robert Trottman

The St Andrews church's history in Kinson tells of many folk stories of smugglers with around 6 in all buried there including that of Robert Trottman the tea smuggler.

Local smugglers had included the legendary local smuggler Gulliver whose original surname was Gulifer,Harry Paye and Slippery Rogers.

Olde Canford

A few miles from Wimborne town
was Canford Manor school
where Lord and Lady Wimborne lived
just across the heath from Poole

Where Churchill came to visit
for they were his family
and the king of England also came
travelling in carriages of gold
it said that he threw coins to Newtown kid's
at least that is what I'm told
cause they were good as gold

It was at Canford Magna
it's name was written in the Doomsday book
the history books tell it
you just got to look

There were lodges on the heath that time
and rabbit by the score

then the years past
and Britain was at war

Granfer Rogers and his family
built brickyard's on the moor
the Luftwaffe bombed the heath that time
they mistook the brickyard for Holton heath
near Wareham's door
where ammunition was made
this caused much grief

There were foxes dens upon the hills
and chickens on the farms
but granfer had his six barrel
and lots of fancy new alarms

The Gypsys sites were scattered around
though some were diddy coy
there was lots of open country then
so good for girls and boys

Flowers grew wild and free at hand

with pine tree and the birch

heather stretched across the land

with poppies and sweet flowers

young girls they gathered baskets

young men they ferreted around the hills

Old men they smoked their pipes

Canford was beautiful then

before the cars and trikes.

Ray Wills

Other families were also stopping on all the many heath's and common lands and are all still well represented in Dorset and Hampshire. Most of them came via the New Forest and some of these were originally from Kent, Surrey, Sussex, Herts or Wales or show people from Hitchin in Hertfordshire. Many of the Traveller's from the New Forest settled in Bournemouth and the surrounding areas ,although some were in the area quite well before then as well ,so they probably went back and forth between the New Forest, Bournemouth and Purbeck for many years.

Many of these Traveler's who made Kinson their home, still returned every year to Alton, Medstead and Binstead for the hopping and strawberry-picking season. So very many of those old Gypsies families chose to stay out and camp on the many heath's that once covered a vast area of common lands of Canford. Many also married local village folk as well as Gypsy members and so the communities have combined to form what many of us believe to be a quite a unique community. Some were originally from Kent, Surrey and Sussex, whilst others had travelled from as far afield as Wales and Scotland.

Gypsy Lad

She married a Gypsy with big roving eyes

he gave her his heather and told her his lies

he was born on the common one hour afore morn

he told her he loved her then left her at dawn

He worked in the fairgrounds and ponies he rode

he was a one for the ladies and the gal down the road

he drove a big cart and he told you a yarn

he was noble and famous but his breeches were worn

He wore those big earrings and talked diddy coy

he loved all the ladies and gave em the eye

he mixed with the Coopers the Mabeys and Kings

though his name it was Castle he was the head of the ring

he could sale you a story and tell you a lie

say it was the real Truth then gave you that look in the eye

His family made flowers and kettles and tins

he was raised on old Canford just where the ole warbler sings

he lived in a caravan with high wooden roof

he walked with a limp and his language was uncouth

he swore and he told some terrible lies

though the gals loved his blarney and his lovely dark eyes

They hung all their washing on the bramble bush free

they had a dozen dogs and lots of New Forest ponies

his mother was Queenie and his father a King

he had him a fortune inside his gold wedding ring

his pals came from London for that's what he said

as he told her fortune then took her to bed

The bed it was bouncy and the springs they did squeak

he loved here there twice nightly each day of the week

she was a dreamer pretty and cool

some say a diamond and some say a fool

but he was only a Gypsy who grew up near Poole.

Ray Wills

Remembering the Canford Gypsies

Do you recall the Gypsies who lived on Canford Heath

there were lots of free wild horses and a mush who had no teeth

Vardo of all description and washing on the broom

crowds of folki laughing and the fuzzs yellow sweet perfume

Do you recall the singing of good queen Caroline

the Sherwood's and the Coopers, Johnsons in their prime

the dogs were all a yapping and the tin pan on the yog

you could barter for your living and buy a fortune for a bob

Each autumn at the fairground you could watch young Freddie fight

in springtime hear the warbler and goldfinch all in flight

there were stories in the Echo with photos on display

with their ancestors buried in St Clements not half a mile away

Talk was of the rozzers and the poor old diddyky

warning of the spells and the Gypsies eye

there were buckboards and chavvies barefoot on the ground

with rhododendrons and heather growing all around

Work was in the factories where Bill Knott sold his vans

the Albion old snake pub with Victor Clapcott the piano accordion man

Stanley's never bought a round but Sammy had his two feet on the ground

Granny King walked the roads oh how I remember her dark Roma tan

Phillips rode the highways and Rogers trucks were cool

you could see the Poole gas works view and the pool at Waterloo Arnolds played with horses on a chain and Sherwood's sold heather outside Woolworths high street Poole.

Do you recall the Gypsies who lived on Canford Heath

they were there many years afore we were young in teeth their camps were spread across the grass

their tales were told its true and John Augustus painted them

years afore me and you.

Ray Wills

Visiting my roots

I journeyed to New England was in the spring and morn
the Grass was growing green today and the chaffinch sang his tune
I talked to all the gaffers there and watched the zunners play
the cartwheels were a rolling still and the hare was in the hay
I strolled across to the bogs where vardo wheels sank deep
where reeds grew within the damp and Augustus drew the scenes
the hills across to lodge were high and the fuzz it grew so sharp
there were adders in the heather than and the Gypsies lit their lamps

Across from heavenly bottom the crew were stewing meat
there were sounds of Gypsy laughter from shawls down to bare feet
the cones were thick and brittle on top commons rich new downs
where rabbits ran from foxs and sounds of farmers guns

Then I journeyed over to Bourne bottom where folki rarely lied
where soldiers signed their papers and young mothers sat and cried
the heather it grew plentiful and the Dartford warbler chirped
whilst common gorgios laughed and the battles won their corpse

The vardos rolled along the tracks from Poole to Alderney

whilst Gypsy song and stories long told of better days yet to be

whilst clay was thick and sand was red and sparrows sang for free

I counted hopes amongst the dopes who gave their land for free

The wandering packs of travelling jacks who worked upon the soi

for pittance then was lost to whim and those soldiers lost at war

the blackbird sang his melody and the lizard squirmed so free

where Gypsy life and pikes own wife was making stew for tea

Amongst the gorse and yet unrehearsed the youth they sang her songs

whilst Caroline Hughes was lost in blues amongst the songs of poets on the vine n throng.

Ray Wills

Dorset Pastimes

Twas when was a young lad of Dorset breed

that I understood the lives they lead

I watched those rolling caravans

those heather-ed sprigs in outstretched hands

Old Darky Clapcott he could play the accordion cool

old Smokey he was nobody's fool

the hills were full of pine and cone

wherein the valley was my home

The brickyard chimney towered so high

where birds and clouds just hurried by

the dartford warblers sang each day

to take those morning blues away

Life was hard but we were free

we had our freedoms and our heritage history

where rabbits ran and fox chased game

where lords and ladies gained their fame

The Canford manor and the Magna road

the great ferns and Wallis downs

the fairground rides in old Poole town

the Pottery Arms and Shovel inn

where Reg got drunk just for his sins

The walks to market on Ringwood road

the pony trap man with his load

the peddlers and the village dope

wash your face with carbolic soap

Before Mountbatten opened the pub

where Bessie Rogers dated young John Dove

where lads and lassies fell in love

beneath the stars and moon so grand above.

Ray Wills

Dorset Gypsies

The Gypsies gathered on the downs from hill of lodge to olde Poole town

where blackbird's sang and rabbits ran amongst the gorse the fuzz and sun

the parish canford estates where lord and lady Guests held fetes

where Churchill came to stay and play across the chines and bourne of seas

they gathered in their homes of want with vardos high and benders squauint

where urchin children came to play and chavvies raced across the hay

where farmers toiled the land and rich were homes of state amongst the ditch

the traveling throng they rode the lanes from Upton oaks to lady Wimbornes frames

where St Andrews church did greet the new and old uns died amongst the dew

the lanes and turbary commons views with sea-view haunts right down to Wool

where Hardy strolled and Barnes did quote and Augustus John painted boats

where Turner etched and set the scenes across to Corfe where poets dreamed

where Egdon heath was home to birch and zunners played outside

St Mary' church

the Traveler's and Gypsies spread their homes across the gorse and heathered zones

from Canford lanes and Kinson Mead's they fed their family's amongst the weeds

then they were housed the gorja way on estates of brick Trinidad and West howe Mead's

where thousands were housed upon the greens of common lands not before seen

the estates of Rossmore, Turlin, Trinadad.Alderney,West Howe were homes to Travelers down to bourne sea

so when they say no Gypsies here we don't want their kind just cock your ear

cause Gypsy traveler's not dissapeared live amongst the crowds that populate our community no fear

the grass it grows course upon the downs where Gypsy life was spread around

Ray Wills

Kiers and Kackers

Keep well away from the Kiers and Kackers she said

with her eyes full of rage and her words full in face

don't you play with those scoundrels they lead you to hell

with their wanton low ways and the stink of the smell

For years I have pondered what words did it mean
why she were she so dark herself and she played on the green
where the fuzz it did spread and the ferns it was deep
with the birch trees close by where the warblers did sleep

Where the chimney top soared o'er brickyards and downs
close by the valley where the tribe bedded down
there neath the willow they spread and all their good days
singing the old songs whilst their zunners did play

I never did know why she gave me the eye
to beware of the kackers and their homes neath the sky
though their families moved on now I can barely recall
the days on the commons where rabbits did fall

Where the song thrush sang daily and the foxes gave chase
over the hills where the Gypsies did date
there were stories of artists who painted them bare
with brushes of oil and pastels of care

Though the sun it rose daily and the ponies ran free

where the common was wide then and stretched to Bourne's sea.

Ray Wills

Round Yon Yog

Frostbitten fingers wood on the fire

the snow n the ice n the blizzards for hire

fir cones and bracken and pots on the fire

blankets to share and the dogs in the briars

cartwheels a turning by day till the night

chaffinches singing a song to delight

Stories a told there as we sit around the fire

tales of the journeys and the good we aspired

stew pots and rabbits and blackberry pies

thorns of the berries and here's mud in your eye

Granfers and grandmas and little mush sleeps

clay pipes a smoking whilst little ones peep

benders that once spread across foreign soil

young men's hopes and old mens dreams told once more.

Ray Wills

The Gypsy tales

The Gypsies gathered on the down's from hill of lodge to old Poole town

where blackbird's sang and rabbits ran amongst the gorse the fuzz and sun

the parish Canford estates where Lord and Lady Guests held fetes

where Churchill came to stay and play across the Chines and Bourne of seas .

Ray Wills

That's the Gypsy life for me

Heather sprigs and pollen bee

silver birch and tall pine tree

wagon wheels rolling

fancy free

that's the Gypsy life for me

Yellow flowers of the furze

sandy trails

where sounds not heard

quiet havens beneath the sun

where deer and fox and rabbits run

Dogs in packs and fires a lit

horses ponies

bridals and bit

pegs of wood

and tins of pan

the dark dark tan

of the Gypsy man

Stews of rabbit

hedgehog pie

herbal potions

for the eye

floral sprays

kissed by the sun

bare foot children

free to run

Carts gaily painted by hand

dance and song

merry bands

with sparks that fly

into the open sky

miles of heathered countryside

On the move

by ordered law

no regard to rich or poor

vagabond diddy coy

common vested one and all

all branded by mans laws

Roll the wagon wheels

one more time

drink the freedom with the wine

when men were free to taste the vine

run the winding whispering windy trails

so let us dance just one more time

and listen to the Gypsy rhyme.

Ray Wills

Bournemouth

Lewis Dymoke Grosvenor Tregonwell (1758-1832).

Lewis Tregonwell was born in Anderson Dorset and for a
time he lived at Cranborne Lodge as the squire.As a small
child when about five years old he was taken one day by his
nurse to the roof of the south transept of the Abbey, where
repairs were then being carried out. Some attraction
appears to have diverted his nurse's attention and he took
full advantage of her lack of attention and climbed, which
alone fenced in the roof, to seize a wild rose growing out of
the wall. However he overbalanced himself, and fell right
over, falling some sixty feet. The nurse, hurried down the
turret steps, through the church into the churchyard, expect
ing the worse. Unexpectanly and thankfully to discover him
entirely unhurt, not even stunned, and busy picking daisies
!. The child was wearing at the time a very full dress made
of nankeen, and as there was a strong wind blowing, the
dress, becoming inflated, acted as a parachute, completely
breaking the force of the fall. Tregonwell became also a
Justice of the Peace and Deputy Lieutenant for the county
of Dorset.

Tregonwells second wife was Henrietta Portman. When
Henrietta's second child Grosvenor Tregonwell died after
accidentally been given a double dose of medicine, Henrietta
became depressed. They went on holiday at Mudeford for
her to recuperate and visited 'Bourne' and bought land and
built a house which he named The Mansion or Bourne Cliff
the first building of the future Bournemouth. Inspired by a
popular Regency notion that the turpentine scent of pines
had health-restoring powers, Tregonwell planted a number
of these stately conifers in the area. These trees, salt water
and a balmy climate led to the establish of Bournemouth as
a fashionable health resort.

After Portman Lodge was demolished in 1930 suspicions were raised that Tregonwell, was involved in some way with smuggling though these proved to be just specuation.

He died in 1832 and was buried in Anderson, but in 1843 his widow had his remains transferred to a vault in St Peters Churchyard at Bournemouth.

Few people in modern times will associate the grandiose area of Kings Park with Gypsies. Though in its early origins the area was inhabited by hundreds of Gypsies.

Lady Georgiana Fullerton

 She was the grand-daughter of the 5th Duchess of Devonshire. From very early she had been concerned with the sufferings of the sick and poor, at home, in London and in Europe.Her help was practical, scrubbing or sweeping floors, lighting fires and making beds. She financed the work she wrote novels, biographies and poetry. In Bournemouth, she founded St Joseph's Home in Madeira Road for poor Catholics from London suffering from tuberculosis. She was supported by the Duchess of Norfolk and Lady Kirwan. After her death in 1885 the home closed, but her husband funded the opening,in 1888, of another home in Branksome Wood Road inviting the Sisters of Mercy to run it. Among her many friends was Countess Pauline Von Hugel who established the Church of Corpus Christi in Boscombe.

The Talbot Sisters-Talbot Village -Bournemouth

In the 1840s, when Bournemouth was very much in its infancy, the wealthy Talbot family from Surrey used to come and stay at one of the new villas that had recently been built on the east cliff. The house was called Hinton Wood House, which later became the Hintonwood Hotel, since demolished and replaced by a tower block called Hintonwood.

Whilst staying in the area as children on school holiday the family's two daughters, Georgina and Mary (Marianne) Talbot, were touched by local poverty and unemployment they had seen with the plight of some of the poor in the locality and vowed to do something to help.There would have been poor agricultural workers in areas such as Holdenhurst, Throop and Kinson. Then when their father died and left them money they decided to move locally and to create the Talbot village community.The Talbot Sisters used the money to buy land upon which to build cottages with smallholdings, a number of farms, almshouses, a church and a school.

It is likely the large villas, and more specifically the wealthy families within them, would have attracted the less well off to possible employment opportunities such as domestic servants, cooks and gardeners, so perhaps that is how the Talbot Sisters came into contact with the poor.

Work to construct the village began in 1850,most built just over a decade.Tenants paid a rent and were expected to make a living working the land associated with their property.Most of Talbot Village was in the Kinson parish which became part of Bournemouth in 1931.They built the Talbot village consisting of St Mark's Church, the school, stables, allotments, farm and almshouses where the rules stipulated that only "persons of good character and sobriety be considered" and that no inmate was to "lay out offensive matter or hang clothes to dry in front of the almshouses."Nearly 30 years after Talbot Village housed its first arrivals. Its headmaster complained of "a large percentage of dullards, owing to low habits and the home influence of parents, a low standard of morality, poverty and lack of boots."There were no limits on religious allegiance but all housed there were required to honor the Ten Commandments.

Talbot was a model village proven to be a remarkable achievement.With its St Marks church, the school, the farm, allotments and provision of housing for its workforce. Although most of the original Farms have long since gone much of the original Village including the School, Church, Almshouses and Cottages remain. The wooded areas of the Village has been well kept and the Village is called 'The Green Lung of Bournemouth'.

Today the heart of Talbot Village remains as a conservation area, with many of it's buildings being grade 2 listed. Amongst pines and woodland, mostly hidden from the busy Wallisdown Rd by tall hedges.Lollipop Farmhouse, one of the village's former farms stands nearby at 74 Columbia Rd.It fell into disrepair and was fully restored in the late 1980s, and renamed Lollipop Cottage.The last of the village's working farms, Highmoor Farm, stands next to the Bournemouth University / Talbot Heath Estate development, on the opposite side of Wallisdown Rd to Talbot Village itself, and therefore lying within the Borough of Poole.

In 2011 the Talbot Village Trust decided that the farm was no longer viable and sold what remained of the farm's land to Poole Council for a housing development of 378 homes, 151 of which are affordable housing, including student accommodation.The Talbot Village Trust survives as a charity and continues the good work started by the Talbot Sisters all those years ago, giving at least £800,000 to good causes in the East Dorset area each year.

Talbots two sisters

Where smugglers did haunt and poachers did prey

from the heath lands of Canford to the shores of Shell Bay

their boot' they were worn and the children were poor

with lessons not learned and their manners absurd to the core

the gentry were rich then and their houses were grand

but the poor laboring men twere rest not assured

the benevolent sisters took up the cause

through the fine words of Owen and the cross of the lord

The village was crafted and the lines they were drawn

with cottage's fit for the weary and worn

with stable's and farmland so free to transcend

with the community rich in its peoples and blend

the primroses grew on the footpaths its true

with the church of St Marks close by the boundaries of Poole
Bournemouth n Poole

where the Kinson estate had stretched from Wimborne to Waterloo

still rich in its folklore and the Gypsies ole traveling crew

The Talbot community was true to the cause

with our lords ten commandments and its decency laws

though the poor men were rich in their community life

with the strength of the hand's and the skills of their knives'

the school it was set in the wood's of the land

where there's heath land's for grazing still free to ole Gypsy bands

close by the poor commons of turfs new England's fame

the sisters created a wealth amidst the stoned graveled lanes

Where sweet lodges were plentiful and men knew of their place

where the squires were rich and all of the lawbreakers hid of their face

in woodlands and heath lands where rabbits ran free the story of Talbot is pure history

on the Wallis Down's common's and in the rich lanes

where folks grew their crops and the fox ran again

the working men were free to gain the benefits of open land

the gaffers were dedicated and the land was free

where two sister's pledged their trust in thee.

Ray Wills

Flora Thompson (5 December 1876 – 21 May 1947)

Flora was the author of 'Lark's Rise to Candleford' the semi-autobiographical story of a child's country life. Flora spent fifteen of her newly-married years in Talbot Woods. The fact

319

that she lived at "Grayshott Cottage" (though a modern suburban house), Frederica Road, and that her husband was a Bournemouth Postmaster, has only recently come to light together with a photograph of her taken in 1926. As a child she gained an interest in writing attending the newly opened Winton public library in 1907.The first of its kind in the country and this proved to be a major event for Flora. "For the first time in my life," she said", I had access to a good public library and slipped in, like a duck slipping into water and read almost everything."Only then", she said in an article 1921, "did my real education begin". "The Public Library there was my Alma Mater". "I had no guide, and it was better so". "The discovery of each new writer, each set of new ideas, was the opening up of a new world."

Robert Louis Stevenson (13 November 1850 – 3 December 1894).

Stevenson was a sick man who came to Bournemouth for his health and for a time lived at his villa, Skerryvore in Westbourne, where there is a plaque. It was here where he wrote the children's classics of 'Kidnapped' and 'Treasure Island'. Inspired and influenced no doubt by the views of Poole harbour and Brownsea Island as his inspiration. Stevenson also wrote the story Strange Case of Dr Jekyll and Mr Hyde, naming one of the characters (Mr Poole) after the nearby town of Poole.

Stevenson s Days

Next to the bathroom at the top of the stairs

I remember as children we all said our prayers

the lines of the table's and verse oh so neat

the manners of gentlefolk we all learned to speak

There was food on the table though morsel's were meek

we were strong in our culture though our language was weak

we learnt from our masters and held back our tears

as we curtsied and frolicked throughout our play years

The poets were sound then with lines oh so sweet

there were hawkers and there were peddlers who all run down the streets

the air it was cold and the hares they did run

the farmland was plentiful by the roar of the gun

The fables and stories we were all told

our heroes were wise men and the hills made of gold

the church bells they rang there and the congregation grew

there was laughter abroad then and big boats sailed out from Poole.

Horse and jockey days

Where the horse and jockey pub now stands on the edge of old Red hill

there once was close a racecourse with horse's running still

the land was rich in history then and Gulliver was young

there were gal's who sold the flowers there and pennies for the young

The hill was rich in daffodil and the heather stretched to Poole

there were Stainer's cobbler's in Newton and Augustus painted cool

there were young men on the take as well and ferries sailed from Poole

the Gypsies lived upon the heath where the warblers sang their tunes

Where Knobby Watton smoked a pipe and gals swooned beneath the moon

the gaffers rode a stylish car and the fairground was in town

where water's lapped upon the land and lovers laid upon the ground

the sun came out to bless the gorse and the rabbits ran the down's

where Whites and Millers made men sweat for love of king and crown

The land was rich in clay and sand with gravel pits abroad

where brickyard's stretched upon the land and laborer's asked for more where poachers blessed the land with pride and Gypsies roamed to Poole

where Sankey Wards clay pits were found and potteries rich in stools

The work was hard and men were poor though ladies blessed their down

where children played upon the green and old gals pipes did smoke

the Ferris wheels were high and rich where darts did fly and score

whilst Gypsy lad and Gypsy gal laid upon the moors

The docks were green and plentiful and the grass was tall and sweet

where babies cried at birth awhile and Augustus paints the scenes

though the race course has gone and brickyards chimney towers

theres still the song's of warblers strong and poets words to read for hours.

Ray Wills

Lady Wimborne

Wallisdown Lodge once stood on Wallisdown Road - close to the Mountbatten Arms. This gave Lady Wimborne access from Canford Lodge to her lands from the public road. She was able to ride through these gates and be on her own heath land, with her various bridges (long since gone)thus she was able to ride to her Canford Magna home. Holdenhurst and Kinson had 55 villages and 21 serfs between them then. The locals were reliant on pigs for their livelihoods which were mainly pastured in the woodlands.

The landscape in the early 1800s was very similar to The New Forest of today with vast areas of heath lands. Kinson was then part of Canford Magna estate with the higher grounds known as Howe's and the main valley referred to as Bourne Valley. The area then provided turves which were used by the poor for winter fuel hence the name Turbary. The heath lands then were regarded as wastelands with no one owning it. But with everyone having free access to it. Initially there were some mud hut homes for some folks then later there were brightly colored Gypsy caravans at that time which belonged to the travelling didycoy. These Gypsies regularly would stop in the area on their route from The New Forest or to the Isle of Purbeck.These show up on the census throughout the 19th century as do tent dwellers whose homes were scattered across the local heathands and areas such as Sandford, Bere Regis Arne and Wareham.

Churches

Local churches popular with Gypsy families include St Andrews (Kinson village),St Marks (Talbot Village),St Clements (Newtown)Church of the Good Shepherd(Rossmore)and St Marys (West Moors).Canford Heath is now a nature reserve managed by the Borough of Poole with much of it encompassing the new Tower Park estate.

CHAPTER EIGHT

GREATER CANFORD

Canford Gypsies

When heathers stretched from Hamworthy to Waterloo

the Gypsies camped upon lodge hills to Poole

from old Wareham road to lane of Wool

Hanging their washing

on broom and furze bush branch

and playing their game's

of wish and chance

With pony rides

on bare backed frame's

from magna road

to the alders knee

born free and reins

Where Ringwood road met Wallisdown

a crowd of barefooted children

gathered around
then marched down to the Kinson school
to join in with the lessons too

At the foot of the Alder hills
I first met up with Jack and Jills
around the little rush filled pond
it was there we sat
with ducks and swans.

Where two Hamlin pipers
face each other and played their tune
at the big glass house
each day at noon

Nearby the Dorset Knob
of neither crust or door
we sat and ate from daisy floor
a picnic sack of this and that
Then we followed the Gypsies back
across their common path trod tracks
to Canford's many scattered camps

where all were welcomed

lords and tramps

As years went by they lost their common rights

for to sleep beneath the moon and star's at night

and to run or ride

across the sandy Canford tracks To light their fires

and chat till late

dance and sing and celebrate

the gift of God

the freedoms of man

and the wiry gifts of the diddy coy man

Now as I look across the. Canford scene

I'm amazed to think back to what once had been

for their tracks and trails are covered oer

by tarmac laid and the giant spill of housing maze

a complex tower park

and gone are the clan

who lit a spark

along with the gaily decorated caravans.

During the 18th and 19th centuries Dorset villagers still relied on the travelling hawkers and dealers who regularly visited their area. These Travelers' sold a wide variety of goods including fruit, cloth, china, earthenware pots, ribbons, baskets, to the local populace. Some of these Travelers were Gypsies, who also brought their many skills to the villagers, by mending chairs, burning charcoal, brick-making, making baskets and clothes pegs and, perhaps most importantly, mending pots and kettles, sharpening knives and scissors. Some of these chose to stay and make it their home.

Remembering the Canford Gypsies

Do you recall the Gypsies who lived on Canford Heath

there were lots of free wild horses and a mush who had no teeth

Vardo of all description and washing on the broom

crowds of folki laughing and the fuzzs yellow sweet perfumeDo you recall the singing of good queen Caroline

the Sherwood's and the Coopers, Johnsons in their prime

the dogs were all a yapping and the tin pan on the yog

you could barter for your living and buy a fortune for a bob

Each autumn at the fairground you could watch young Freddie fight

in springtime hear the warbler and goldfinch all in flights

there were stories in the Echo with photos on display

with their ancestors buried in St Clements not half a mile away

Talk was of the rozzers and the poor old diddyky

warning of the spells and the gypsies eye

there were buckboards and chavvies barefoot on the ground

with rhododendrons and heather growing all aroundWork was in the factories where Bill Knott sold his vans

the Albion old snake pub with Victor Clapcott the piano accordion man

Stanley's never bought a round but Sammy had his two feet on the ground

Granny King walked the roads oh how I remember her dark Roma tan

Phillips rode the highways and Rogers trucks were cool

you could see the Poole gas works view and the pool at Waterloo

Arnolds played with horses on a chain and Sherwood's sold heather outside Woolworths high street Poole

Do you recall the Gypsies who lived on Canford Heath

they were there many years afore we were young in teeth

their camps were spread across the grass

their tales were told its true and John Augustus painted them

years afore me and you.

Ray Wills

Gypsy Girl

She was just a Gypsy girl with her dark and dreamy eyes
she danced for Zena Martell, she was gifted and so wise

Her father was a Castle, her grandma was a King
she rode the carnival procession; they made her gypsy queen

She could out talk all the locals with her wanton gypsy ways
she dated all the playboys, but with her love she stayed

She made such lovely flowers from papers fine and neat
she talked the gypsy lingo; her lips were red and sweet

She had a way of walking, always caught your eye
her nature was so noble she rode the Ferris wheel
you could hear her on the sidewalks, her tongue was never still

She always talked to strangers, she had the common touch
with her Gypsy ways of talking she had the Gypsy luck.

Ray Wills

Poole

Poole gained its charter in 1250 it became a major seaport centuries later.By 1583 12 to 15 ships annually were visiting Newfoundland from Poole. For centuries large shoales of Dolphins were regularly seen in Poole harbour hence the Poole Dolphins emblem.

Ole Poole Town

They knocked down our homes in ole Poole town

old street light's washing gown's weathered storm's feathered beds duck n down

washboard blues tea chest refrains outside loos mothers pains

They made it rubble bricks n sticks deserted lanes old mens dicks

they took away our fun n games ropes n skips hopscotch lanes

gone are the flicks and alleyways the mother's calls and fathers ways

gone are the tears of yesterdays the Gypsy reels and the fish and kiddies play

the close knit families of yesterday the knocker up and the holidays

The ole rag n bone man on his cart the gas lit street's at night when it was dark the ball games played upon the walls mothers corsets fathers vests chalk and cheese Sunday best

they demolished happy days and years of grace with polished doorsteps smiley face

They took away our alleyways where our dreams were all displayed and made

moved us all to Rossmore place Turlin moor and wash your face- know your place

gone are the ways of ole Poole town the boys and gals the up' and downs.

Ray Wills

Children's Rhyme of the 18th Century.

"If Poole was a fish pool and the men of Poole fish"

"They'd be a pool for the evil and a fish for his dish"

Papa Benedetto

Papa Benedetto was an Italian Immigrant. He was an Organ Grinder who emigrated to The UK in 1952 and fought for the UK in the First World War. In the warm summer months of the year he would often be seen strolling down Arne Avenue Parkstone Poole. Carrying on his shoulder his hand operated Barrow Organ grinder. As soon as all the local kids saw him come down the road they would all sit on the path with their feet in the road to listen to him play. Once with his Dancing Monkey who would dance to whatever Papa played. After around 10 minutes Papa would stop playing and the children would drop pennies into his tin.

William Carter

In 1884 William the son of Jesse Carter virtual founder of the Poole potteries bought Kinson Pottery William was to be the father of Herbert Carter well known in Poole.

John Cabot

It was John Cabot who discovered Newfoundland in 1497 which transformed Poole, changing Poole's fortunes and those of its surroundings for the better for hundreds of years to come. It was not just a "Newfoundland" but it was also one of the biggest fishing pools ever discovered. The seas around the Newfoundland coastlines were teeming with cod, so much so, that ships had difficulty passing. From the late 1600s for almost two century's Poole experienced great prosperity. For with the recognition of Newfoundland as being British territory this made it possible for the development of the cod fisheries and with it the associated thriving Newfoundland trade.

Consequently Newfoundland and Poole had developed a special relationship over the years,with many Dorset men and woman making their home in Canada. So much so that it was probably the only place in the world where the Dorset dialect survived intact, due its remoteness from outside influences, long after the dialect had practically disappeared in England. So it was that the speech as spoken by the 18th century farm worker "zunner" in Dorset, was still to be heard all the way across the seas in Newfoundland . One lady in Newfoundland who descends from a Dorset man who left the then very small village of Kinson aged just 16 , recalled that" you can still hear the old style "Darzit" lingo there". Apparently they also have many of the old books and reference books there relating to Dorset as most of the population having come from Dorset.

By the start of the 19th century Poole was already a most prosperous town due mainly because of the salt cod trade from Newfoundland its manufactured goods, busy important shipbuilding industry and local thriving rope making business. At times Poole ship's sent nearly as many migrants to Newfoundland as its own total population with some of the first settlers in Newfoundland coming from Poole. Then just as a number of people from the Poole area settled permanently in Newfoundland. In the same way, many a fisherman who sailed from Poole brought themselves back a wife from the island. So that through these interchanges, even until the present time surnames on the electoral lists of Southern Newfoundland are identical with those in Poole and the surrounding district.

After the 1790s and the war with France had ended there was a gradual decline in the Newfoundland fishing trade.(Though the magnificent Georgian houses and public buildings, of that period can still be seen in Poole to the present day). The final defeat of Napoleon in 1814 however had drastically changed the fortunes of the Poole merchants.

The trade with Newfoundland had flourished all through the Napoleonic wars because Portugal, Italy and Spain relied upon the supplies of dried fish provided by the Poole merchants. Peace meant that the French and Americans could now fish the waters and there was a rapid decline in supplies available. As a result of which within just a few years many of the Poole merchants had ceased trading altogether and many faced financial rack and ruin.

Poole Park and ladies walking fields

In 1885 Lady Wimborne gave land in Poole council for parkland for the people of Poole. This was known as Ladies Walking Fields.In later years this land was used for the building of Poole Bus Station and Arndale shopping centre.

Poole Quay and the Gypsies

Poole in the early 1900's was a reasonably peaceful and law-abiding place and people could walk the streets safely even at night. Then on Saturday night the Gypsies from Newtown and Canford Heath visited the town to drink in the Quayside pubs the Jolly Sailor and Lord Nelson. Though often by late evening the drinkers became disorderly resulting in them being ordered outside. Often the Gypsies would challenge the dockers on the inside to come out and fight to see who the best man was. Local teenagers would see this as exciting and would enjoy watching the regular bare knuckle fights. Forming a large ring around the two men who would set about one another until or the other was knocked down or slipped.The opponent stood back and allowed him to get up and carry on if he wished to do so. With the crowds cheering them on, no-one interfered with the fighters and the crowd insisted on a fair fight. No doubt the fighters had probably had more beer than anyone else. As a result the fights did not last very long and they soon got dazed and too fuddled to stand on their feet properly and consequently there was no serious injuries.

The Gypsies and Dockers would not dream of trying to settle their differences by fighting except on a fair basis. There was never any suggestion of a gang beating or someone 'putting the boot in' or a glass being used as a weapon. At that time there no gangs smashing shop windows because they were bored. Usually the local Police turned a blind eye to these fights unless there was an unfairness. This was also the case at the Crown Hotel in market street Poole where there were regular bouts. Poole locals used to meet up with Poole Gypsies on a Saturday evening for the inevitable fight. A regular participant would hand a lady his teeth and shed stand by. With her handbag in one hand and his teeth in the other!

Black Bess

Black Bess was a tall thin young woman with very black hair hence her nickname.

Cockle Kate

'Cockle Kate' was a short and plump middle aged woman who probably got her name through hawking cockles and winkles etc from pub to pub. She had a very loud voice and a very vivid and varied vocabulary which she would demonstrate at the slightest provocation. She was regularly thrown out of a public house for her behaviour and then would stand outside and tell everone who passed exactly what she thought of the landlord his wife and family, along with a long detailed and vivid description of his ancestors from which it appeared that none of them had ever married. By the time she paused for breath, all work on the Quay has stopped and the dockers would egg her on for more. This would tempt her to describe in even more detail what sort of future she visualised for both the landlord and the dockers. The teacher of Kate's boy did not escape this treatment when her boy was deservedly punished at school, she would bang on the school door until the master came out and then set upon him leaving him scratched and bleeding. Bth Black Bess and Cockle Kate were well known to the local dockers and sailors who frequented Poole Quay in those days.

Granny Cousins -The knocker upper of Poole.

She was born in Morden village just outside of Poole though not registered at birth

She was reared in a laborers cottage her life was not of worth

It was afore the first great war when she took up her role of knocker upper around the quay

But she was nicknamed Granny Cousins by the workers of the pottery and vine

She worked the streets six days a week whether weather poor or fine

just to get them up in time

She was up well afore the day broke with her bonnet apron and shawl

you would see her shuffling down the streets in summers and in fall

You could hear her loud knocker upper calls

when the Lady's walking fields was called the rose walk

folks around here knew her well you should hear them talk

She joined the salvation army when she was retired

She was loved by the parish but died poor.

Ray Wills

Harry Paye

Harry Paye of Poole also known as Harry or Arripaye,was a privateer and smuggler. By the 15th century Poole had become a popular port of call for pilgrims, on their way to the shrine of St. James at Santiago. At that time there was great conflict between England, France and Spain with raids on coastal towns. Harry was responsible for leading the English reprisals. The Spanish and French were so angry that they sent a large fleet to attack Poole, which was unfortified. Following a great battle, the gallant men of Poole drove back the raiders using thick doors as shields. Yet, In spite of this the church and town cellars were burnt. As well as attacking Poole the raiders were after Harry Paye, but he was nowhere to be seen. They found his brother and they killed him and then they set Poole on fire. Two years later Paye got his revenge ,when he took 120 French vessels laden with iron, salt and lead and brought them back as a gift for the brave men of Poole. Paye died in 1419 and hes buried in the parish church at Faversham Kent.

Thomas Pitt

Thomas Pitt became best known as Diamond Pitt.Thomas owned a very successful trading company in Poole in cooperation with East India company of the far east as well as a great deal of local property. He became an MP and in later years as well as Governor of Fort St George at Madras. Later in 1702 he had the opportunity to buy the Great Diamond stone paying some £20,000 for it. He later had models made from the stone which he sent to all the major monarchs. Napoleons sword was in later years to bear the great stone.

The old Pick and Shovel accordion days

Victor Clapcott was a true accordion man

I heard him playing at the Pick and Shovel in old Poole town

was when my aunt Winnie Freemantle wore her Rogers wedding gown

you could buy a round then for less than half a crown

He could play that music like no one is heard since or before

we played postman's knock outside that old pub door

there was a cemetery just across the way

the pubs well gone now it's a Chinese restaurant nowadays

The streets were narrow and the quay was grand
we strolled on ladies walking field where the bus station now stands
they sold it off and the Canford Bourne heath too
gave us Baiter Point and the Arundel's view.
Ray Wills

The Oak Dales of Poole

The Kinson pottery stood near the old Wareham road
where the water tower was in sight just across from the Wold
the brambles did grow down to Oakdale and Poole
As children they played young chavvies and fools

The Turner's and Warren's did frequent the heaths
where Canford and sea view were up at the breech
there were vardos around and down the old lanes
where birdsong and chaffinch sang on the wane

The new inn-was open and the chapels at rest

where the beech trees once stood and the sparrows built their nest

the hurdy gurdy organ played in the old town today

whilst the children did dance and the grinder did play

The old song's have gone now and the Gypsies remain

though there housed in the terrace's in red brick and pane

no more do they wander yet some do remain

amongst the brass and the gorse where theres tinder and reins

Oh how they did turn to the dance and the song

when the accordions played and their stories went on

the brickyard's and viaduct's grew on the down's

where the gravel pits rich and the poets were strong

The Poole park was rich then so rich for the King

with its garden's of primrose and its fountains and streams

the dolphins they greeted one at each gate

where the lodges were rich and the sailors were mates

They say Churchill came here with his sketch pad and pen

his cigar's were well lit and their stories were famed

like the trails that were rich in rabbits and dens

where the fox once did frequent amongst poets and wrens.

Ray Wills

Poole fair always arrived in November.

Nights at the Poole fairground

I remember night's at the fairground

they said it was the biggest in the land

there were booth's in every corner

sounds of the rolling bands

the aisles were full of laughter

with sights for all to see

just a stone's throw away from Upton

stretched out by the sea

The Ferris wheel was turning

the swish-back ride's were fun

there were crowd's of happy children

in wonder everyone

The star's above were sparkling

the bumper rides were joy

there were Gypsy horses stalled there

with traveler's standing by

the wall of death was awesome

with bikes to catch your eye

Hear the thuds of the hard balls flying

at all those coconuts shies

this was the traditional fairground

some said it was the biggest in the land

with darts forever flying

goldfish bags to carry in your hand

The bearded lady danced there

the midget's gave a show

close to Poole old backwaters

where many breezes once did blow

Freddie Mills he boxed there

the Sherwood's were there too

with the Stanleys and the Crutchers

whilst Bill Rogers played the fool.

Ray Wills

The Gorse and the Brier

As a child I did play in the gorse and the Brier
I lit up the heath with a match made a fire
the fire engines came from Poole town that day
some came from Ferndown and a longs way away

Oh I collected the Coney's from top of lodge hills
with sacks and my go cart of rusty of wheels
I chased on the heath the Rabbits and hares
before I went in the nights to visit Poole fair

I knew all the Gypsies that ran on the sands
with lizards and adders and their diddy coy bands
there was birdsong and laughter and fern that went out to Poole
where the bog stretched across to meet Waterloo

The Gypsy queen told me that if I was real good
she would tell me my fortune with the clans brotherhood
I was raised on the Mannings where the goldfinch were in tune
where the gaffer was Rogers and the sun shone each noon

Though the pathways have gone now and its Industrial land

where the tower park stretches with houses so grand

though I can still hear the warblers as they sing in the briar's

whilst the pony's are staked out on the grasslands a while.

Ray Wills

During the eighteenth and nineteenth century Dorset villagers still relied heavily on the travelling hawkers and dealers who regularly visited their area. These Travellers sold a wide variety of goods: fruit, cloth, china, earthenware pots, ribbons, baskets, to the local population. Some of these Travellers were Gypsies, who also brought their skills to the villagers, mending chairs, burning charcoal, brick-making, making baskets and clothes pegs and, perhaps most importantly, mending pots and kettles, sharpening knives and scissors. In a world of limited horizons and make-do-and-mend, they were an interesting, if temporary, addition to village life. With some choosing to stay and make it their home.

Dorset Breed

Dorset blue viney and doorsteps to spread
crusty ole knobs and words quick to shed
country lanes twisting and rambling free
green open country with scenes by the sea

Thatched barn's and cottage's with chapels of rest
old country squires with stables so blessed
paddocks and harvests and brooks running free
countryside meadows lead to the sea
Church bells that ring out each Sunday morn
market stalls plenty and crop's full of corn
all pretty maidens waiting to dance
kisses on lips and young men's last chance

Willows and oaks with birch growing free
commons and woodlands with rivers to see
fishes to catch and cave's to explore
castles on hillsides and Hardy n more

Old country yokels and yarn for to spin
Gypsy tale memories and riddle dee whims
cross country ramble's and blackberry thorns

dock leaves and stingers and old faded porn

Crafted and weavers and dances on grass
bee stings and honey to bless you perchance
dog's in the farmyard and hens in their coop
farmers in bed and fox on the loose

Old crafts and new deals and artists and friends
poets and writers and old famous men
twisting and turning the roads and the bends
Turners great pictures and the poets quill pen

Fashioned and crafted and set free to share
the writer's and artists the fun of the fairs
the stickle back fishes and the newts in a jar
old un's to listen to and old tales to tell.
Ray Wills

Back Roads

I'm going to take the back roads

I'm going to string along

I'm going to take that journey

sing that old Gypsy song

I'm going to take my baggage and my Gypsy family

I'm rambling and I'm rolling on those ole roads cant you so

I'm going to take the back roads

on the beaten tracks

with the stars and moon to guide me

here's nothing do I lack

I'm going where the good lord takes me

hell guide me on my way

I'm going to take the back roads

I've seen the light of day.

Ray Wills

Campfire girl

She was just a campfire girl
raised in the back woods away from sandy shores
she counted stars at night and told your fortune free
she was a welcome sight under the old oak trees

Her mother was a Gypsy true with darts and flights she threw at
Poole
her father was a Gypsy man with love tattoos on arms and hands
they worked the fairgrounds and toiled the land
for income rich was to be their plan

Though said to say they were always moved on
from Canford hills to land of song
their wagons rolled across this land
with songs and tales that were so grand

The stories told were rich in hope
with kushti bok and strength of rope
the land was beautiful and green
where chaffinch blessed the trees so lean
where gorse and thistle blessed the downs
and farmers toiled and land was out of bounds

The rivers flowed and fish did leap

with salmon and perch to gain the deep

where blossoms decked the trees and boughs

where honeysuckles thrived amongst the cows

but the campfire girl she did blest the morn

where hedgerows thrived and rye and corn

where Gypsies danced around campfires

where locals talked of mush and kiers.

Ray Wills

Meg the Gypsy gal

Old Meg she was a Gypsy gal

she lived and loved upon the downs

where life was swell

where joys were too be found

she wore a dress of ember red

thou they do say she wore nowt when she was in bed

She worked each day for king and crown

all her dreams were upside down

her father was a tinker true

he sold cockles down in the bay of Poole

Her mother was a local dame
who grew in stature as well as fame
her children were all true diddy Coys
they were brought up to lie and give the eye

Her apples were like blackberry leaves she made such sweet rhubarb
pie
her gooseberry's were so green shed have you believe
she wrote a sonnet each and every day
she roamed the lanes down our way

They say her brothers were the purbeck hills
Her sisters were the Rockey sands where all the lovers each day hold
hands
her bosom was plentiful and her thighs so white and rare

It's said she took the lads for a ride to the local fair
they say she didn't care with roses and straw within her hairs

Old meg she was a Gypsy queen who folks say danced at Halloween
they say she was part of the local scene

her sisters often asked her where she'd been

but she declined to say.

Ray Wills

Old Country

I'm travelling back to the old country day's

with its vision's of hope and its old country way's

I took me a handbook and a harmonica to play

I'm riding those lane's and I'm ready to stray

With my light's in the wagon and my horse it is shod

I've stories to tell of the land and the sod

I'm singing the old song's that my grandmother taught

And I'm reading those scriptures that my Grandfather caught

Oh the journeys are hard and the road it is long

with my best gal beside me and you know I can't never go wrong

I'm heading for starlight and rainbow's to share

with my ducker and kinfolk I'm off to the fair

The heather growls thick and the bees they do buzz

mind you don't tear your dress dear as you stroll through the fuzz

the briars are thick and the weather is wild

you can watch the sun rise and nurse your wee child

Forever and ever I've dreamt of this day

when the fishes do jump and the zunners do play

where the grasshoppers leap and the stars twinkle each night

by the willow that bends and the adders that bite

Oh the tales that I'll tell and the fishes will dance

they'll be fairgrounds for miles and old tellers to chance

the breeders of horse's and barters to fare

with knuckle brave boxer's and ladies so bare

With the chaffinch and miners and brooms to delight

Gypsy fine vardos such heavenly sight's

food at the campfire a yog fit to see

travelling the lane's of this old country.

Ray Wills

Dorset Gypsies

The Gypsies gathered on the downs from hill of lodge to old Poole town

*where blackbirds sang and rabbits ran amongst the gorse the fuzz
and sun*

the parish Canford estates where Lord and Lady Guest held fetes

*where Churchill came to stay and play across the Chines and Bourne
of sea*

*They gathered in their homes of want with vardos high and benders
quaint*

*where urchin children came to play and chavvies raced across the
hay*

*where farmer's toiled the land and rich were home's of state
amongst the ditch*

the travelling throng they rode the lane's from Upton oaks

to Lady Wimbornes frames

*Where St Andrews church did greet the new and old uns died
amongst the dew*

the lane's and turbary common

commons views with sea-view haunts right down to Wool

*where Hardy strolled and Barnes did quote and Augustus John
painted boats*

*where Turner etched and set the scenes across to Corfe where poets
dreamed*

*Where Egdon Heath was home to birch and zunners played outside
St Marys church*

the Travellers and Gypsies spread their homes across the gorse and heathered zones

from Canford lanes and Kinson Meads they fed their familys amongst the weeds

then they were housed the gorja way on estates of brick on Trinidad and West Howe Meads

Where thousands were housed upon the greens of common lands not before seen

the estates of Rossmore, Turlin, Trinidad. Alderney, West Howe were homes to Travelers down to Bourne sea

So when they say no Gypsies here we don't want their kind just cock your ear cause Gypsy travellers not disappeared

They live amongst the crowds that populate our community no fear

the grass it grows course upon the downs

where Gypsy life was spread around natured o'er valley and dale

with scent of the flower and the rich golden smells.

Ray Wills

Mary Squires

Mary was famous following the Gypsy alibi trial. She was an elderly woman who was tried in the Old Bailey London in 1753. Accused for abduction, for prostitution, as a brothel matron and the case soon became national news. She claimed her innocence and a number of Dorset people appeared to vouch for her character and her innocence. The case was complicated by walk on parts for highwaymen and smugglers. Mary Squires counter-claimed that she was with the smugglers, in Abbotsbury and Chedington, at the time when the prosecution accused her of cavorting with highwaymen. Mary was sentenced to death, though this was changed to transportation. The Lord Mayor of London Sir Crisp Gascoyne, a notable humanitarian sensed an injustice in the case and left the Mansion House for a 300-mile journey to visit public houses from coastal Abbotsbury to Somerset to check out the accuracies of the charges. He came back with sufficient evidence to substantiate Mary Squires' story and secure her pardon. She was acquitted and took to the road to walk back home to Dorset.

Heather for your luck

Heather for your luck my love like days that used to be
just sprigs of heather wrapped in foil and flowers made by me
I saw them in the high street there on Poole town high street lanes
they sold them pretty sprigs my love just like way back when

The common's were their territory loaned from Ladies Guests
with Talbot sisters manor house and plentifully in game
the Gypsies toiled upon the land and maids curtsied to the squires
they hung their clothes on furze bush then and sat round open fire's

The cartwheel's rolled upon the lanes and the benders were on the heath

where little England swarmed with homes all little n so bleak

the birds did sing their melodies the warblers and the thrush

where birch was rich and gravel led ditch was home to rabbits wild

Gone are the days of ferreting with catapult in belt

where foxes chased the rabbit's fleet and labourers did sweat

the fields were rich in rye grass there and the sparrow sang at morn

where brickyards grew and greenfly flew upon the pleasant fawn

The local yokels sang their songs and the Gypsies turned and read their cards and Freddie Mabey swept the yard

where clay pits sweat was ever blessed and the gaffers clocked your day

whilst the poor man waged upon the land and the church bells chimed forlorn

the flowers grew upon the heath where Canfords lodge did stand

and soldiers lost their innocence in wars for glories grand

The tide did turn and the ships at Poole sailed out from harbour rich

where nelson and ship tasted lips of nectar sweet with brew

the Kinson life was full of strife and the stories told were true

of harvest's poor and men at war and Gypsies lives in Poole

Strange that the heather grows so rich on sandy soil and clay

where bee's do buzz amongst the fuzz and young gals went astray

the Gypsies told their stories then and were housed in west Howe lanes

where the co op grounds did stretch the downs where now the little kiddies played.

Ray Wills

Travelling Tales

Buckboards and saddles and cobs running free

vardos and benders with sweet histories

cornfields and cabins hillsides and beautiful leas

song thrush each morning springtime so free

Starlight at night time and lamps wicks all primed

zunners out chasing the bees from their hives

brook sides and meadows with cricket song sweet

rye grass and clover under bare feet

Cold night and slumber with ice on the downs

treetops with no leaves and the snow falling down

winters so harsh and yogs to delight

frosty bright mornings when God turns on his light

markets and stalls with bridles and bits all in sight

baskets she made and pegs worth a bite light

Floral wreaths hanging and crepe paper clowns

floral delights sold for a crown

mud on the wheels and rain on the downs

gathering fruit days and trips out to town

families treats and tales around the fire

a blanket to share and a tale from a liar

what could be better than a tale of a kier

Ray Wills

Romani rai

She was a Romany rai

a true didikai

she gave you the eye

she built all her castle's

beneath the blue sky

She never paid no rent

cause she lived in a tent

that's why they called her

sweet Romany rai

She had just bare feet

used the Romany speech

she could weave and tell yarns

would do folks no harm

She was swift in the tongue

for her the birds sang

she was a didikai babe

she took her truth to the grave

She danced at the dawn

was so good to be born

where cartwheels did turn

on the heaths sacred morn

She was a Romany rai

ate rabbit stew pie

gave chase to the mush

She was so dam kush-ti.

Ray Wills

Roger Ridout (1736 - 1811)

Roger earned his living as a miller, he was a bold smuggler who brought contraband from the coast, and stored it at the mill where he lived at Okeford Fitzpaine , a small village in Blandford Forum. There was an account of his activities, a local writer commented.(1895)[my] father stated that when a boy, in or about 1794, he had, when riding late at night seen the string of horses in the narrow road between Okeford Fitzpaine and Fiddleford with the kegs and other contraband goods on the horses. One or two men, armed, generally were in front and then ten or twelve horses connected by ropes or halters followed at a hard trot, and two or three men brought up the rear. This cavalcade did not stop for any person, and it was very difficult to get out of their way, as the roads, until the turnpikes were made in 1724, would only allow for one carriage, except in certain places.

The contraband goods were principally brought from Lulworth and the coast through White parish and Okeford Fitzpaine, through the paths in the woods to Fiddleford, and thus distributed. The author of this piece was the grandson of a Sturminster Newton JP who was reportedly bribed by Ridout.Ridout is reputed to have been employed by the Kinson smuggler Isaac Gulliver and he spent some time in Dorchester Gaol. Ridout died aged 75 and he is buried in Okeford Fitzpaine graveyard.

CHAPTER NINE

The Kinson Village and its Travelers

Kinson village is situated within the old parish of Great Canford and it pre-dates the Doomsday book where it was recorded as ChinesTu. After many name changes over the centuries it was eventually known as Kinson in the 1800s.

The Royal Oak.

At the centre of Kinson Until 1840 this inn was known as the Traveller's Rest, no doubt because it was a convenient halting place for travellers between nearby towns. Until the construction of the New Road, travellers coming from the north-west to the town entered over Longham Bridge and on through Kinson. Later the inn's name was changed to the Five Alls. The sign read:

I rule for all

I pray for all

I work for all

I fight for all

I plead for all.

It refers to five professions.

In 1863 the name changed yet again to the Royal Oak.

The Crutchers

Nancy Crutcher -known as Nancy Jeff

Nancy was well known by all the folk at the heavenly bottom Gypsy campsite and the Millhams lane house in Kinson where she made floral tributes and button holes for weddings and sold flowers in Bournemouth square. Many local people would go to Nancy and also her sister Gerty and earlier her mum Nancy when they needed flowers or wreaths made.Nancy lived at the big house in Millhams lane Kinson village with her husband Job Jeff and family from Bourne hill encampment.

Local Gypsy women like Nancy Crutcher (who grew up at Heavenly bottom) and Mary Mabey made exquisite floral wreaths,tributes button holes for weddings or fancy imitation flowers from coloured crepe.

Kinson village school were overwhelmed when hordes of Gypsy children from the encampments arrived there at the start of their new term.

Coles

The Coles were show people who worked with elephants at circuses and at fairs. A dark race said to originate from Spain. In the present age they operate very successfull fairgrounds businesses in the area.

There are a long line of members of the Coles from Kinson.

Fanny Cole (nee Longman)

Fanny lived in her cottage next door to the Dolphin public house in Kinson from where she ran her coal delivery business from her coal yard with her pony and cart. Shortly after the death of her husband in 1897 She bought the coal at Poole Quay and delivered coal all around the Kinson area.

Philip Mead

Philip Mead was a cricketer of renown. He played for Hampshire from 1905 to 1936, and for England in 19 Tests, scoring 55,060 runs in his career.

Cherrett

James Cherrett's had a beer shop and garden at East Howe in Kinson.Beer retailing and innkeeping were often coupled with other occupations, such as brickmaking, farming or a wheelwright's

St Andrews Church

The St Andrews 11th century church in Kinson village was the main church in those early days, the majority of wedding's funeral's and burial's took place there. Its ground's were much larger then than at present. Funeral processions were often stopped at the nearby Shoulder of Mutton pub on the Ringwood road for a tipple for the drivers.

Kinson smugglers once brought many a good keg of the finest French brandy from the shores of Poole to Kinson St Andrews church.

Isaac Gulliver or Gullifer (1745-1822)known as the Gentle Smuggler of Kinson/Wimborne. Isaac married Elizabeth Beale.

There are none so famous as the legendry local landowner Isaac Gulliver and his ship the Dolphin.With tales of numerous underground tunnels, contraband and moving tombs still being told. Isaac Gulliver was known as the gentle smuggler who never killed a man, and with his gang, ran 15 Tuggers bringing from the Continent to Poole Bay gin, silk, lace and tea. All of Gulliver's men wore the traditional smock of the Dorset farm hand. According to one description Gulliver of that time "kept forty or fifty men constantly employed who wore a kind of livery, powdered hair, and smock frocks, from which they attained the name 'White Wigs'. These men kept together, and would not allow a few officers to take what they were carrying".Issac Gulliver's men would carry the contraband up from The Chines in Poole Bay and then take it across Cranborne Chase to be distributed all over Southern England. Gulliver had several properties in the area although its believed that all of the contraband was stored in the tower of nearby St Andrew's Church (the marks of the ropes used to haul it up can still be seen in the soft sandstone walls of the tower)and in several stone graves in the churchyard constructed for this purpose and is said never saw a coffin.

Gulliver bought Manor Farm with land adjoining it and to the north of the present church in 1789.He lived there with his wife Elizabeth (Beale) and raised his daughter also Elizabeth, who married William Fryer. The wealthy Fryer family through their merchanting, Newfoundland fisheries (Gosse Fryer & Pack of Carbonear owned 40 ships from Poole) and banking interests (Fryers, Andrew & Co of Wimborne, Poole & Blandford Bank) were now descendants of Gulliver. They also owned large tracts of land from Parley up through West Moors to Verwood. They were said to be generous with grants of land permitting local development.

Elizabeth Gulliver -Elizabeth was the daughter of Isaac Gulliver. Elizabeth married William Fryer and both she and her husband William once made a small donation to Kinson School in its infancy. `She rests in the Fryer vault at St

Andrews churchyard. Once within the church itself it is now covered by an important and substantial monument, at the rear of Kinson church.

Other smugglers in the area included James Abrahams, Richard Frampton, Henry Tiller,Robert Trotman and Luke Budden all of whom were buried in St. Andrew`s churchyard at Kinson.

Robert Trotman, although not a local man, was shot on the shore near the Sandbanks road and was laid to rest in St Andrews cemetery Kinson in 1765.

On March 10,1861 Kinson smuggler, Richard Frampton, was buried at Kinson Church. He was aged 60. It is rumoured, no more kegs of brandy were brought to the church, the purple heather heaths were silent. The last pack horse had trotted home, no more gentleman of the night, would go riding by!

John Meade Falkner

 John Author of Moonfleet   (1898)which was set in 18th century Dorset and told the story of John Trenchard, a young boy who gets embroiled in the exploits of a smuggling gang.

Gullivers Days

Gulliver the pirate sailed in his Dolphins boat and pride

He Docked it in Poole Bay Chines when he was in his prime

Kinson was renowned for the famous splash at St Andrew's bridge

Where the green was rich in history of smuggling and that opened up the lid

The roads were wide and open where Gypsies trail's laid hid

amongst the Canford parish where treasure troves were hid

although the future king of Germany Kaiser was saved by Kinson lads

now looking back on it they say they must have been so mad

In the church grounds they buried old Trottman for stealing tea its true

He was wanted by the custom officer's from Bournemouth down to Poole

they say it's all a sorry state that Gulliver ran the show

with pub's and property stretching from Ferndown his wealth was sure to grow.

Ray Wills

Kaiser Wilhelm

In 1907 the German Kaiser's took a short stop at Kinson when he was aved by Kinson boys whilst staying at Highcliffe Castle. Whilst out motoring with a party of fellow countrymen his car became stuck in the muddy ford called Kinson Splash, a small tributary of the Stour which crossed Millhams Lane, the only bridge being for pedestrians. Some villagers heard cries for help and two boys Jesse Short and Bill Hicks ran to pull the Kaiser to safety. A piece of doggerel circulating the rounds afterwards ran thus:

Jesse Short and Bill Hicks

Did the work of quite six

When they pulled Kaiser Bill

Out of Longham ditch.

Bear Cross

Bere Cross may well have originally been called Bere Cross in earlier times.The Bear Cross pub was built in 1931-2, replacing a previous hostelry known as 'The Bear Cross Inn' or 'The Brick maker's Arms'.Bear most probably originated from the word Bere most common in this locality. The first landlord of the pub was George Ware.who was a brick maker by day, as were most locals. The plentiful clays of the area had given rise to a flourishing brick making industry by the mid 19th century. On Ware's death in 1883 the inn's license had passed to the Lane family, among them Frank Lane who worked as a carpenter by day building coffins for the Gypsy community at Alderney Common. His son Arthur Lane was born above The Bear Cross Inn in 1913, and could recall Augustus John who lived at Alderney Manor between 1911 and 1927 John would spend noisy evenings on the premises, plus similar evenings at The Shoulder of Mutton in West Howe.

Kinson as it were

The old school once stood upon the present village green

whilst cricket wickets fell nearby on the local scene

two master batsmen went to war in France

Reverend Sharpe oversaw it all perchance

Gulliver had property at West Moors and near brooks lane too

he was such a well respected gentleman and smuggler throughout Poole

had pubs at Longham and Kinson's Howes

where old burial grounds and farms abound

kids collected chestnuts from Pelham's each fall

where stream did flow under the old Millhams stone wall

A tulip tree was gifted from Newfoundland folk

it travelled from Michigan to Pelham's house village green's remote

a gentleman's handshake was agreed and swore

Pelhams to be used for common folks and poor

Kinson remained in Poole just prior to nineteen thirty two

twas all part of great heath-land's great Canfords domain near Poole

where chestnuts grew amongst twisting country lane's

Once the Kaiser fell into St Andrew's old bridge stream

saved by local boy's- oh what a scream

he'd just returned from visiting Lady Wimborne Churchill's aunt

at Canford lodge fine estate home of deer and stout

oh how this story got about.

Ray Wills

Mr. E. A. Elliott

Elliott discovered good brick clay when a well was sunk on his farm at Cudnell. A brickworks was started where the farmland met the crossroads, and hand-made bricks were made for two decades from around untill 1900. When the clay at Bear Cross ran out the brickworks was moved to the rise of land at West Howe, in Poole Lane. The clay here was a much better quality Ball Clay. In 1912 Elliotts drain pipes, terra cotta ware and roofing tiles were manufactured in addition to bricks. In 1922, Mr. N. T. Elliott entered the firm and by 1927 bricks were manufactured for domestic fireplaces and these, together with stoneware drain pipes, were made until the potteries closed in 1966.

The trade in clay from Kinson area continued for very many years. Pipe clay then stone ware pipes and with the increased demands for sanitary purposes flourished. As result a considerable number of the local working populace were employed in their manufacture and a substantial new market opened up in the Poole area. One of the most proficient for bricks etc was the Kinson clay works. Brick making soon became elevated to the level of an art with numerous brick works scattered over the countryside. Whilst the local potteries produced a wide range of items which were exported worldwide these were equal to or far superior in quality to anywhere in the world.

A long time ago in Kinson

A long time ago in Kinson village

they put them in the stocks on Kinson green

long time again when they danced around the May queen

they walked the cows to market along the Ringwood road

popped into the Bear Cross to rest their weary load

In the Shoulder of Mutton they took the funeral crew

twas a stretch to St Andrews church from the port of Poole

Gulliver resided in the great Pelham's house

he was a smuggler of tea you see

in cuckoo woods the bluebells did grow wild and free

there were cuckoos in the meadows then

in our early history

There were lodges across the wild terrain

over to lodge hills

Canford Magna manor

the Stour ran its course

with the meadow sweet flowers

we made daisy chains to pass away the hours

Natural water springs sprang up across the downs

rabbits at Wallisdown to Alderney

the Gypsies collected heather sprigs

to sale on streets at Poole

we collected our nanny goat

from the bogs of Waterloo

The blossoms were sweet

they decked the boughs

and folks talked like thee and thou

cows and ganders walked

the gravel and sandy tracks

and knobby watton wore a sack upon his back

Past history of Kinson village folk

which stretched from the village

to near the Antelope

the Snake pub was a favorite in old Newtown

young Nelson Stanley lost his leg

for the sake of a crown.

Ray Wills

Canford Dorset dates back to Saxon times covering thousands of acres of heatherlands of birch,pine,broom,furze,ferns and blackberry bramble from Wimborne to Poole Quay. A haven for wildlife of deer,fox,rabbit,lizards,adders and Dartford Warbler.A Charter of 1248, gave Turbary right to local people of the emerging town of Poole for cutting of peat for fuel, to graze cattle and hunt game.These rights ended with the Enclosure Act of 1822. Over the years New Forest and Purbeck Gypsies passed through, selling many wares,providing services, repairing furniture and sharpening knives/scissors.Local farmers,landowners and villagers relient on them as farm labourers and seasonal workers.The most popular custodians of Canford estate were Ivor Bertie Guest and Lady Cornelia Guest (The Aunt of future Prime Minister Winston Churchill) of Canford Manor.Becoming best known as philanthropists Lord and Lady Wimborne.Building over 100 'Lady Wimborne Cottages' for local people,donating land for a 'People's Park and Ladies Walking Fields and allowing Gypsies to live on Canford commons.

Many Gypsies made Canford their home creating numerous encampments, some of which had quirky names.Cuckoo Bottom,Heavenly bottom,sugar knob mountain,monkeys hump lane,cinders town,frying pan,wallywack,bribery island,the Bogs and Fox Holes. Others were named after the nearby road or commons,containing many flimsy benders and elaboratly furnished vardos.The artists Augustus John and John Turner were very popular with the local Gypsies who spent time painting them at these encampments.

Many great Gypsy characters frequented these encampments their names and stories becoming legendry.

At a young age Betsy Smith from Heavenly Bottom encampment was sent to Bournemouth by her mother to try and sell bunches of white daisies there. She was so good at it becoming the first of the famous Bournemouth flower girls. Legend has it that the local Gentry bought her flowers because she was so pretty.

Local Gypsy women like Nancy Crutcher (who grew up at Heavenly bottom) and Mary Mabey who lived in the crescent Newtown made exquisite floral wreaths,tributes button holes for weddings or fancy imitation flowers from coloured crepe.Nancy lived at the big house in Millhams lane Kinson village with her husband Job Jeff and family from Bourne hill encampment. Mary lived in Newtowns Terrace with relative show people the Kings and Castles.(Jean Castle became Pooles beauty Carnival Queen in the 1960s) prior to moving into nearby council housing.Groups of Gypsies were regularly seen selling flowers and lucky heather at their spot outside of Woolworths store on the streets of Poole.

Horace Cooper grandson of Louisa and one time rag and bone man in Wareham grew up at the Dip encampment Wallisdown.Kinson village school were overwhelmed when hordes of Gypsy children from the encampments arrived there at the start of their new term.

Sammy Stanley Snr, rag and bone man, gave local children rides on his grey mare and cart,becoming the first Gypsy to move from Heavenly bottom encampment into a council bungalow. In the early 60s Caroline Hughes (Gypsy Queen wife of John Hughes) parked in a lay by near the old Wareham road when discovered by US Folk singer Ewan Mc Coll.Ewan tape recorded the collection of Carolines songs. Which she had learnt as a child from her mothers lap and around the yog. Ewan took these back to the USA where they were sang by recording artistes worldwide.

For generations locals worked at hordes of brickyards,potteries and clay pits. Many Gypsies closely related to one another ran a variety of local bussinesses.The Whites became long-established shopkeepers /postmasters in the Kinson village.The Rogers family related to Stanleys,Scotts,Brixeys and Cherretts were brickmakers involved in building of both the Newtowns Weseleyn and Evangelical churches.Their many brickworks included those at Colehill Wimborne,Mannings Heath,Fancy road Newtown and the Dell Parkstone.

Charles Rogers used monies raised by his wife's (Emily Elizabeths nee Fancys pigs to start his first.Reg Rogers ran a small holding farm at the Mannings on land bought from Lady Wimborne.At the end of the war Sid Rogers bought up abandoned army trucks,creating Rogers Transport.Brixeys had a contractors/construction yard and Sherwoods a coal yard in Newtown.Mitchells and EF Phillips ran haulage concerns Fred Phillips had started with just a pony and cart on a sand and gravel pit at the Mannings Heath.Charles

Trent scrapyard on Ringwood road, became the largest in the world.

Bill Knotts first job was selling shoe laces and match boxes "up on hill" at Parkstone. Before establishing the worlds largest caravan empire Bluebirds in Newtown. Charles Stanley had a scrap yard Ashley road Parkstone and today Nelson Stanley runs Stanleys scrap yard at Alder Hills Branksome.Despite his physical disability.(Loss of a leg whilst retrieving a coin from his metal breaking crushing machine).

 Sammy Stanley Snr and sons (Sammy and Abe) attended Newtowns Albion pub(the snake).Bill Dibben a local rag and bone men was tragically killed outside the pub whilst crossing the newly built zebra crossing on its first day of use.

Local pubs popular with Gypsies -Bear Cross,Shoulder of Mutton,the Woodman,Rossmore Hotel,Smugglers Arms,Dolphin and Pooles Lord Nelson and Jolly Sailor.At the Bear Cross pub the landlords son Frank Lane built coffins for the local Gypsies. Augustus John a regular at both The Bear Cross and Shoulder of Mutton pubs while renting Lady Wimbornes Alderney Manor.

At the Bere Cross,Jolly Sailor and Lord Nelson unofficial popular boxing matches took place between Gypsies and locals.Freddie Mills,Abe Stanley and Ted Sherwood worked the boxing booths at Poole fairgrounds before becoming world boxing champions.International speedway star from Parkstone Brian (Nipper)Crutcher)arguably the best English speedway rider never to win the World Final, rode for Poole

Speedway at just 16.In later years managing his own motorist shop in Newtown.

Local churches popular with Gypsy families include St Andrews(Kinson village),St Marks (Talbot Village),St Clements (Newtown)Church of the Good Shepherd(Rossmore)and St Marys (West Moors).Canford Heath is now a nature reserve managed by the Borough of Poole with much of it encompassing the new Tower Park estate.

NEW ENGLAND

New England Gypsies

I journeyed to New England

within birch and heather down

I rode upon a pony there

where Gypsies bedded down

There was sackcloth on the floor there

clay beneath your feet

gravel on the sidewalk

the nicest folk's you'd meet

I trod upon the bracken

where the rhododendron grew

there were Dartford warblers singing

not far from Waterloo

The village children came there

to crown the Gypsy king

there were White's and Cooper's laughing

I heard a blackbird sing

Across from Wallis Down and Bear Cross

the Gypsy rovers danced

there was music in the air that night

when the Gypsy lady glanced

She said I was so gifted

I had the rose tattoo

I was a lucky fellow

from Alderney via Poole.

Ray Wills

Gypsies camped at "New England" encampment on Turbary Commons, fernheath West Howe from the early 1800s. (So Named by the New Forest Gypsies). The Gypsy travelling folk had a particular affection for Turbary common with its variety of foliage and landscape reminding them in many ways of the New Forest and so it was that they gave a section of what is now West Howe the name of New England. There was also a large encampment on Bankes common Turbary with some 15 gypsy families at one time camped there.

Turbary Rights

Those who had what were called " turbary " rights had a further resource in the cutting of turves for fuel. The turf was cut in less thick and solid junks than the peat of Ireland or Scotland. It was skinned off in thin strips by an instrument specially designed. In its manner of burning, too, it differed from the peat, smouldering in a dull, uninteresting way without any quips and antics of leaping flame, or steady joy of brightly glowing incandescence. Such as it is, however, it was, no doubt, a boon.

The Gypsies who lived on the "New England" encampments at Turbary Common West Howe gained employment on the farm at Talbot village.

Whilst particular gypsy families bought the land each family

379

took responsibility for specific strips of land for the encompments renting it out to all the local gypsy families as a safe place to stay. Having found out the land was going to be sold in the future for housing development local gypsies had two choices - to move on or buy it themselves, which they did.The gypsies there got water from the stream, until Turbary common got used by the councl for a landfill site. Although some family members can still recall when there was a well there with a hand pump.

These were William Doe,Mark Cooper (also known as Mark Hughes) and Henry Crutcher.

William Doe: took responsibility for the land at the South West part from the Fernheath Road area. Mark Cooper for the land next to William Doe, now South East side of Verney Road/Close. Henry Crutcher - North East side of Verney Close. Mark Cooper may well have also had the strip of land next to Henry Crutcher .The families who lived on New Engand over the years included the Pidgleys,Matthews,

Barnes,Coopers,Ayres,Does,Crutchers,Jeffs,Barneys,Lights,Warrens,Willets,Whites,Tillys,Brewers,Keets.Stanleys and Smiths.Their encampments included wooden bungalows built by the Romanies themselves. In later years after the war they were to be compulsary purchased by the local council and most of the common lands were built on to house the gypsy families becoming the largest council housing estate in the south of England and by 1975 there were over 2000 children per square mile living there known as West Howe.

Most of the following lived on or near New England

Barnes

John Barnes and Louisa Barnes (nee Willett)known as Queen of the Gypsies lived at New England. She died in 1935 and her funeral took place on September 25th 1935. Louisas husband John Barnes died in 1940 they are both buried in St Andrews cemetery Kinson.

Benjamin Stanley

Benjamin the brother of Levi had chose to stay behind in England and to settle down in an area which was known to the Gypsies as New England at Turbary common West Howe Kinson Bournemouth Dorset. Benjamin had been disowned by their father and it was said that a curse was put on him and the future families for the next three generations to follow.

Jeffs

Walter Henry Jeff married Cynthia Lee who died in 1013. He married Annie White at kinson st andrews church in 1917 He also used the name James Jeff. He is buried at st marks church walllsdown

Britannia Keet nee James (abt 1861-1925).

Just as you enter the Churchyard on your left at St Andrews Kinson is a Monument of an angel dedicated to Britannia Keet nee James.With a lovely verse written upon her lovely Angel memorial.Britannia married Keets who was also a local Gypsy his family originally from the new forest. She died in

1921 and is buried at St Andrews cemetery Kinson.

Phillips

The Phillips family it is believed for centuries via their forefathers had grazing Rights held under the Doomsday book.They grazed horses and kept pigs on Turbary common West Howe Kinson Bournemouth.

Annie White

Annies family came from the Bristol area about 1928 looking for work renting a Romany vardo of Mr Cooper on the New England /Turbary camp.

Probably taking them the best part of 2 years to reach Poole from Bristol.Annies step sister was born at Reading about 1925 and her step brother at Fordingbridge 1926 .

They lived at the New Eengland for a number of months. Then shortly after that they moved into a wooden shack 7 fernheath road very close to New England. Then later they moved to Acres road just down across the bit of common from New England. Annie said that "New England was a great place to live at that time but was spoiled when they developed the council estate after the war".

Annie White married Walter Dane Matthews the iligitmate son of Ellin or Nelly Matthews at Bournemouth in 1934. Walter had been brought up close to New England at the Bourne hill gypsy camp near Saunders homes of rest ringwood road West Howe till he was 16 yrs.The camp was owned by mr Hooper they paid 1 shilling a week rent. Then when mr Hooper died the land was sold and developed.

382

Walter Matthews

Walter then lived at a house close by in Heaton road off kinson road which his mother rented.

Annie the daughter of Michael White who died 18th 11th 1918 at vag Romany camp near Yeovil .Annies mother his wife was only married 3 years when he died he was her second husband.

Michael Whites parents,(Annies grandparents} were Richard White and Theodosia White nee Ayres.

Theodosia is buried at Wimborne minster.

Crutchers/Crouchers

Annabella Crutcher married Issac Light 1855.

Matilda Crutcher married Noah Cooper.

Does

John Doe

born 1832 in Wimborne Dorset.

He was A farm labourer

John married to Louisa and they had 12 children.

John Doe

This John married Mary who was born 1842 at Alton. In 1888 they were originally living in a tent in Stratfield Hants with children Frank aged 11 Job aged 8 and Harry aged 7.

Henry and Patience Doe

Lived in New England Poole in the parish of Kinson. They married and after 16 years had 8 children, 7 of whom are still alive. with children Alice, Patience, Henry, Liberty, Nelson & William. Alice & Patience were born in Basingstoke, Henry in Surrey and sons Liberty, Nelson & William in Bucks.

Johns daughter Patience married John COOPER on 5 August 1918.

Joby Cooper aged 27, single, born Bransgore?, daughter Edith aged 20, single, born Liphook?, daughter Nell, aged 18, single, born Petersfield?, daughter Rose, aged 16, single, born Sopley?.

Jeffs

Edith Jeff married John Warren

Warrens

John Warren married Edith Jeff. They later moved to live in Fancy road Parkstone.

Coopers

Georgina Cooper

Georgina was a well known character in West Howe, and was well remembered for riding her horse and cart while smoking a pipe and wearing her Trilby hat. Georgina Cooper seems to of had an eventful past with the law, and on many numerous occasion was charged for various offences, some of these were reported in the local newspapers at the time; The Wimborne Herald, December 3rd, 1908, reported a charge against John, Job and Georginia Cooper, Eli Hughes and David Wells, Gypsies, for camping on the highway at Lytchet.

John Cooper married Patience 15th august 1918.

Living in New England

I'm living in New England by the Fern heath valley spruce

where the heather and the brambles roam across the paths aloof

I'm walking down the same ole tracks where once the folki roamed

where the Dartford warbler still doth sing and the sand lizards have their home

I'm sat here reminiscing of how things used to be

when the travelers lived upon the heath not far from Alderney

where the peat they cut in turves so clean and the blackberry was rich

close by the birch and ferns where they paddled in the ditch

The Longham walk was rich and free and the stour was rushing oer

where the waterworks gave out its roar and the ponies bridled poor

where the rich man and the poor man said prayers down millhams lane where the old church still stands seems so far away

The gorse was thick and noble and the fuzz was rich in perfumed flower

where they lived upon the common then and sold heather n flowers

where their baskets were so awesome and the town it clock did chime

where Jeff's and Whites were settled in the land of gypsy rhyme.

Ray Wills

Charlie Williams

Charlie from the village

Charlie Williams lived in the Kinson village

just close to Cuckoo Woods

where the bluebells grew so thick and tall

close to where the stocks once stood

He lived with Bertha his loving wife

far from the Welsh hills tracks

where birdsong was once his childhood melodies

where nothing did he lack

There's the Little bungalow by the winding track

where I often came to call

where we chatted in the morning light

then at the evenings fall

Old Charlie was a Williams lad
far from his native land
where the valleys were of evergreen
the mines were steep tall and grand

Charlie could tell a yarn
when locals came to call
the children played there in the sun
whilst the wood pigeons gave their calls

He would sit and feed the robins there
you could see him every day
he feed them from his open hands
before he went away.
Ray Wills

For many years before the Kinson council houses were built the area was mainly heath land with few buildings. It was always very popular with the travelling Romany folk for many years who called the area "New England" and set up their large camps there. When the land was to be developed the Gypsy population were offered houses on the new estate at West Howe. Many of these Gypsy families eventually took up the offer. Some families did move on, but there are still hundreds of these families around today who proudly claim to be descendants of those early settlers. This West Howe estate unfortunately developed a false reputation as a troubled community.

At one time in the mid seventies when I was employed as adventure playground manager at fernheath on the co operative playing fields. The area had in excess of 2000 children per square mile and it was the biggest of its kind in the south of England.

Pelham's House

Kinson history includes references to Pelham's house in Millham's lane which was possibly a Hamlet surrounded by paling and the link during Napoleonic times between the local trading sea port of Poole and the great trade to Newfoundland in Canada. At one time in the 18th century the farm was owned by Isaac Gulliver, then later the house was bought by the Rolles-Fryers a family of wealthy Newfoundland Merchants. It is thought that it was they who had first brought the Tulip Tree from Michigan North America which now stands proudly tall and majestic on the front green lawn in the grounds of Pelham's.

Revd Percy Sharpe.

Percy was a local clergyman who encouraged regular cricket matches on the village green at Kinson. He was a keen cricketer and organized a local team of players two of them went on to play for England just prior to the start of the First War, but unfortunately they were both killed in action and never ever played for their country. Children were regularly invited into the grounds of Pelham's by the Reverend to collect chestnuts when they were in season he also organised annual Whitsuntide walks from the Tulip Tree.Pelhams stayed with Rev Sharp until 1930, when he sold it to the council on a handshake deemed to be used for the benefit of the people of Kinson and never built upon. In 1948 it was approved for Pelham's to be used as a community centre and in 1952 it was. The present Kinson village green was much larger then and covered the area now known as "Wicket road" off of Bramley road Kinson.

The Smugglers Wain

I went back to the Smugglers Wain

where Gypsies gathered and love remained

I saw the Kinson walk's and stories were told

of customs time's and hand's were cold

I went back to that time of olde

where field's were rich in green and tales were told

I chanced upon the smuggler's tracks

from Canford Magna to wally wack

Where Kinson folk did paint the scenes

where Augustus John did paint and poets dreamed

where rabbit's ran the tracks and local downs

of village greens and oer grassy mounds

Where grand cottages of Lady Wimborne stood

so tall and proud next to the wood's

where master Guest was gaffer king

where sparrows sang first song of spring

The white house of Pelham's graced the scene

down Millham's lane with tree's rich and mean

where stock's once stood upon the green

where witch's danced at Halloween

The vardos roamed the Canford lane's

through Poole tracks and Ferndown's horse's mane's

were rich in hair and supported ladies fair

in times of olde when fists were bare

The stream's and river of the Stour

where swan's did glide and bud's did flower

where bramble's stretched the lane's and water tower

where lad's did fish on line for many an hour

The merry men of Morris regale

danced their foolish antic show

next to the quay of Poole hi ho

where Johnny onion came to call

before the autumn wind's and fall

Those were the day of Poole's great fair

where Freddie Mill's and Stanley's boxed each night there

there beneath the canopy of star's and moonlight

where orchard's grew and Gypsies roamed

where Canford was their noble home.

Ray Wills

The Guest family

Kinson has a strong historical and philanthropist legacy of the Canford Guests/Bankes families and the Talbot sisters estates. The Canford estate of Lord and Lady Wimborne in particular in those early days encompassed miles of common lands some 83,0000 acres in all covering much of southern

England. It's fore bearers being that of the Guest Family, members of the upper class aristocracy, with strong links to the royal family and the Churchill dynasty.

One of the many bridges of Lady Wimborne which at one time spanned the nearby Ringwood road close to the Mountbatten Arms.It was one of a variety of carriage runways used by royalty to travel to the home of the Guest family.

The prince of Wales and future king of England we are told threw coin's from his carriage window's to the local barefoot Newtown children below, whilst visiting Lady Wimborne.The unique and attractive Lady Wimborne Cottage's,(Canford Estate Cottages) are prominent features throughout Dorset, around 108 of these distinctive model cottages were built then.

St Andrews

At St Andrew's church

down Millham's lane

the grass grew tall

it was a real bad pain

The stream it flowed beneath pathway neat

no one knew it was beneath their feet

the 11th century church it stands

with scented flowers well at hand

The river Stour runs nearby

the stinging nettles

the Blandford fly

The meadows rich

the Longham lanes

the church clock tower

the fancy window panes

The bell that chimes

out the hour

old Gulliver

the yellow scented meadow flower's

The modern hall

that John Moore built

the Purbeck stone

near the seaside silt

The Dartford warbler in the trees

the landscaped banks

with bumble bees

the car park that flood's each autumn rain

the renovation work

that took place down Millhams lane

The cemetery that stretched

one time across

the Millham road

before the cross

The congregation that sang his praise

the Kinson church

the history books

the revolving tomb

the little bridge

the hidden room

the family heritage

that dates afar

before the modern home

or car

The walks across to the Ferndown ridge

St Andrews church

look what they did.

Ray Wills

Many Travelers who made Kinson their home, still returned every year to Alton, Medstead,and Binstead for the hopping and strawberry and pea-picking. Another stopping-place was Horton Heath, near Cranborne and, of course, West Moors Common, which then came under the Parish of Hampreston.

One cannot ignore the influence of the influx of Travelling and Gypsy communities to the Kinson Parish at that time when they used this terrain on their numerous journeys and routes from the New Forest, through the Somerset, Wessex and Purbeck area. Many of these folks from the travelling communities lived in tents or benders in the early days ,then later in caravans or Vardos. Often these were skilled artisan's, horse trader's, builder's, flower sellers, craftsmen, tinkers, fortune and story tellers , show people and farm laborer's. Many of them often worked for local farmer's on the estates, fruit picking,hop picking.Many others went potato gathering etc, or in trading or bartering their many skills, such as sharpening knives and making pegs, selling floral presentation's or wreath's.

Irish navvie Travellers

A great many Irish Travelers had also flooded into the area earlier with the growth of the railways and roads. Most were Navies and did laboring on the building of the new railways, roads and viaducts. These newcomers looked remarkably very different from the locals, with their long gartered high socks,neckercheifs and their caps. In more recent times these Gypsies and Travelers settled in this area on common lands courtesy of the Guest and Talbot families. Moving into and settling in the surrounding neighborhoods taking advantage of the work available from emerging railways and the need for viaducts, brickyards and claypit's.They used their numerous skills in these developing industries along with the demand for house building, sand and gravel pits and clay pottery industries. All helped no doubt to a great extent by the nearby thriving shipping port of Poole for trading worldwide. Most members of these travelling communities in those days lived in tents or benders then later on in caravans or Vardos.

Over the years a great many Gypsy travelling families settled in the local area and a lot of family names became part of its rich heritage. Then in more recent times due to various government Land Acts and reforms a great many of these were housed in areas such as West Howe, Rossmore, Alderney, Trinidad, Branksome, etc.The West Howe estate in particular was the largest housing estate in the south at one time with in excess of 2000 children per square mile. This was built specifically to house the local Gypsies. In recent centuries travelers had settled in the area on local common lands courtesy of the Guest and Talbot families.

 Many of these traveler families built thriving businesses locally in the haulage, sand and gravel, potteries, coal merchants, brickworks and scrap metal industries that emerged out of the local initiatives. Some of these which had originated from humble beginnings as pony and cart or pig sties initiatives, used as a source of income to fund the ultimate industry and these thrived and grew in size and demand to become extremely wealthy local enterprises. Some of which are still with us here today. These travelling Gypsy travelling families remain rooted in the local communities with the names well known and respected along with the show people, such as the Whites and artisans such as the Coopers.

In the Kinson village there were a prominent group of families, notably the Whites, Crutchers, Coopers and Jeff's. Whilst in the wider Kinson parish you had very many more Gypsy travelling families including those of the Arnolds, Ayres, Barnes, Barneys, Brixeys, Castles, Cherretts, Coles, Crockers, Crutchers, Does, Domineys, Fishers, James, Jeff's, Kings, Lamb, Lights, Lovell's, Mabeys, Mitchells, Nippards, Penfolds, Phillips, Ridgeley's, Scotts, Sherwood's, Smalls, Smiths, Stacey's, Stanley's, Squires, Trent's, Tuckers, Whites, Williams, Woods, etc. There were very many more, some of these folks were flower gatherers, others were basket makers, brick makers, broom makers, show people. Whilst many worked with horses or were dealers in scrap metal and rag and bone.

Back to West Howe

I journeyed back to West Howe many years ago

when winter time was hard with cold wind freezing snows

I gathered all my memories and stored them in a trunk

composed a poetry book of rhymes to tell one of those times

he ladies rode their bike's to work through Poole lanes dips and dales

there were Gypsies on the heath lands there and heather for your
luck as well

the co op grounds were rich in rye grass and the tree's were young
and prime

the Canford warbler sang his song and the adders were all fine

The coppice was rich in green and the dew was on the ground

the Cole fairs were rich in didykoy and the big show was in town

long before the houses built for Gypsy families

long before the common land was sold for ladies spree's

The goldfinch chirped on fuzz bush thick and the broom was rich
with flower

Arnold's grazed their ponies there amongst the gorse and close by
the river Stour

the Smugglers Arms was tall and proud and the gaffers took their
pride

in Workmans laboring skills and the young men took their brides

The land was rich in gravel, clay and the Frank Phillips sand was *free*

there were many church bells ringing proud on Sundays by the lea

the village children danced their reels and the schoolmaster was strict

they say that councilor George Spicer saved the trees and Sankey Ward took the bricks

There were many folki around this day can all recall those day's with pride

when Turbary and Kinson were rich in trees and wide

where rabbits ran upon the coppice and the zunners went to play

at scrumping fruit from Alderney hospital and rabbitting with ferret's along the way

The knuckle boxer's showed their skills like Freddie Mills too-shay

where Bear Cross stood with brotherhood of Guest's and family May

the Crutchers and the Dibbens with Sherwoods and the Whites

played darts with fine flights and sported game whilst Jeff's gave chase along the race

with names handed down with pride and Abe put up a fight

Of Gypsy clan and tattooed man with Giorgio's in disguise

The dolphin and Pelhams house were then as to today that's a surprise

when St Andrew stood so prime and good to while the days away the stocks and green now paint the scene where folly true was scorned

whilst village school took kids from Poole and slates were hard and worn

The twists and turns of kids now born will tell a tale or two

but none can trace the master race of when West Howe was born for true

the pavilions gone and bowls along and there's only Oakmead school

where children meet with deep regrets and play by the golden rule.

Ray Wills

Dibbens

Roy (Nobby) Dibben had 15 children mostly girls they lived in batchelor crescent west Howe Kinson.

Bere Cross Hotel

The old inn at Bear Cross was originally a thatched cottage a little behind the site of the present hotel. It was strategically placed at the crossing of the two main roads, just gravel tracks with grass verges and overhung by trees. A large sign on the wall proclaimed its purpose. Supplies were brought in from Poole and on special occasions, when extra beer was needed, a donkey cart had to be dispatched in haste for further supplies. The new Bear Cross Hotel was built in 1931 in front of the old inn which was then pulled down.Two cottages at the back of the inn were all that remained of a little community beyond Kinson for many years; these, too, have now gone.The name of Bear Cross appears to mark the crossing of two roads near a dip in the land known as Bear Bottom. 'Bear' in this case probably being a corruption of the Dorset place-name, Bere.

Artists and Writers

Other writers and artists who frequented the area at that time included the famous artist John Turner who painted scenes of the Purbeck and Corfe Castle from Sea view in Parkstone.

CHAPTER TEN

Kinson and Beyond

Kinson Days

Looking back on my childhood days now it is amazing that so very many of my school friends and family and friends had traveller Gypsy origins. In Newtown, Alderney, Canford area this was pretty obvious, yet even when I moved to live in Wareham it seems that there they were similar as with the Patemans, Whites, Lovell's, Hughes, Ayres, etc. It's now remarkable to me that local people in this area of England have so much hostility towards the traveller when in fact a great many of them have travelling origins, one just has to look at the local names in southern England to see this is so true.

Their names included -
Coopers,Stanleys,Phillips,Rogers,Scotts,Coles,Dominey,Fisher,Mitchell,Trents,Sherwoods,Dibbens,Crutchers,Whites,Jeffs,Jones,Johnsons,Ayres,Mays,Kemp,Squires etc.

And yet local folks are up in arms when travellers visit the area each summer. There's an outcry about the litter they leave, yet folks make no sound when the tourists who visit the local towns leave the streets, town centres and beaches full of waste. With the council's budget this amounts to millions of pounds annually to clear, along with the dog fouling of the parks and nature walks of the local commons, not to mention the towns pavements. Along with the fly tipping which has become a major problem locally as well as the drunken hooliganism which abounds in our town centre's at weekends. Yet for a few weeks of the year there an outcry by the press populace and councillors when a handful of travellers visit the towns.

The traveller campfire or Yog has always had a central point within the Gypsy traveller life. We have this instinct in us to build a fire and to sit around it late into the night it became sacred to our identity. Nowadays with the development of indoor kitchens and family barbecues this is being lost.Ive always had this inert need to build a fire and sit around it since early childhood its part of my makeup I guess and probably one of the things which attracted me to the philosophy of children's adventure playgrounds. A place where children could light fires under supervision and on every adventure playground I established or worked on in the inner cities and new towns of the UK (some 16 or more sites).These fires or bar b q areas were central. These were meetings places to cook, share food, stories, sing songs and confide ones fears and hopes.Similiarly with the Scout campfires and the established children's school camps such as at Carey Wareham in Dorset. These freedoms are essential to our well being and much is lost in the present childhood with their demise. My freedom loving ways were noted when I was employed in Skelmersdale for the Development Corporation and Banardos where the senior Development officer Mr Pritchard made allowances for my radical social activist ways by saying he's a Gypsy, lol.

Newtown

Bourne Bottom Parkstone encampment known affectiotely as Heavenly Bottom.

The Fancys

By the mid 1880s many members of the Fancys families were living in Poole,Greater Canford,Wimborne Minster, Hampreston ,Osmington and Longfleet. In the 19th century they lived in Arne Wareham since 16th century and were brick makers at Sandford Wareham.Whilst many of their descendents lived on the Gypsy encampment at Bourne Bottom and Heavenly Bottom Parkstone Poole.

David Fancy -Brick maker(13th Jan 1793-6th Nov 1876)

He was Born at Wareham.He was the son of James Fancy and Sarah nee Christopher. David married Elizabeth Skinner in 1815 they had 5 children before her death in 1824.David remarried to Sarah Crocker in 1831 . Their Children included William,Susan, Thomas, Gideon and Ellen. (Gideon's daughter Emily Elizabeth Fancy was the authors Ray Wills great grandmother).She married Charles Rogers.

By the mid 1880s there were Fancys living in Poole,Greater Canford,Wimborne Minster, Hampreston,Osmington and Longfleet. Whilst many of their descendents lived on the Gypsy encampments at Bourne Bottom and Heavenly Bottom Parkstone Poole.

Fancy road tales

Down fancy road on Canford heath before Tower Park was born

the finch's chirped upon the heath and the pigs looked battle worn

the bombs had fallen from the skies and the brickyards all were red

there was little in the way of food so folks ate herbs instead

Old granfer lived on Manning's heath and Joker told his yarn

there were chickens running in the pens and horses in the barn

the Lady Wimborne bridge it spanned the Ringwood road from Bear

Cross to Poole

whilst the German air force bombed the land and bombs sank in boggy Waterloo

Old Stainer cobblers was bombed

and the air force Canadians n yanks in the gardens were hit

the folks all remember then when lamps were seldom lit

the rationing of food was declared and rabbits were a must

folks rode their bikes to work at Wallisdown and the laundry out at town

The work was hard and the land was wild when the Gypsies were around

they all lived upon the heath caravan's sites scattered around Newtown

the stories they still tell today when the snake was the local pub

though times were hard the people were kind with warm hearts full of love

and the wiser ways of the Gypsy man.

At Sugar Knob

At sugar knob mountain by monkeys hump lanes

the children kept goats on long iron chains

in cinders town near frying pan the children danced

when rabbits ran

The Gypsies came to wallywack above high moor

folks had never seen their likes before

their caravans were decked with lace

with polished glass to see your face

There were so many Gypsy camps

folks said they traveled from over France

Hemley bottom was home of Kings

Sherwood's and White's remembering

At bribery island folks did vote

to keep their home's n keep the quotes

Lady Guest did rent them out

to local lad's with digger shag and baccy snout

The upper class Gypsies lived in Wolsey road

the spinning tops were busy that side of the roads

the rag men came with their heavy loads

at least thats the stories what we've been told.

Eventually Gypsy families were gradually encouraged to settle down in the local community with most of their children eventually attending local schools at Branksome heath, Kinson and Rossmore. Thus many of my school friends came from Gypsy stock. There are still folk lore stories in the area of Kinson when hordes of barefoot local Gypsy children from local campsites turned up barefooted at Kinson village school on the first day of the new term.

Augustus John (1878 – 1961)

One cannot talk about local Gypsy travelers without mentioning Augustus John the artist who was Britain's leading portrait painter in the 1920s and a defender of New Forest Gypsy rights.John spent much of his life painting and etching the local Gypsies and was regarded with much respect by both the Gypsy community and the wider art world. He developed a nomadic lifestyle and for a while he lived in a caravan and camped with and amongst the Gypsies.

In the early years of the 20th Century John would make his reputation as an artist moving on the edges of a number of influential schools & salons of the time, exhibiting with the New English Art Club and the Camden School Critics compared his works with that of Matisse and Gaugin.Tragedy struck the John clan in 1907 when shortly after the birth of her 5th child Ida died. With two other children by Dorelia, John struggled with Ida's family over who should take responsiblity for the children.

He moved to Alderney Manor in 1909 with a lady companion Dorelia McNeill, by whom he also had children. Michael Holroyd's biography of Augustus Alderney Manor is described as "a strangely fortified bungalow larger than most houses, built by an eccentric Frenchman. Alderney Manor occupied 60 acres of Woodland near Ringwood Road and included a walled garden, cottage and stables". It was rented to him by Winston Churchill's Liberal aunt Lady Wimborne. Who was said to be "pleased to have a clever artist as a tenant." all for the rent of £50 a year. The site was almost opposite to where Alderney Hospital is now situated. The family lived a very Bohemian existence often mixing with the gypsies who inspired his famous paintings "The Mumpers" ,"Lyric Fantasy", "Washing Day" and drawings and paintings of his children. At this time in 1888 the population of Newtown was said to be "about 1,800 people, all poor".

The John family and friends arrived in a colourful caravan of carts & wagons with children singing as they came down the driveway. They soon turned it into the very picture of a bohemian commune the coach house converted into Johns studio. Johns many visitors oftens staying for days, months, even years. Others stayed in the blue & yellow Gypsy caravans dotted around the grounds and when numbers swelled for weekend parties, they added gypsy tents or alfresco in the orchard. The children between private tutors for the girls and school for the boys, ran wild over the heathland and through the woods & bathed naked in the pond. Over the years they acquired all the trappings of a back to the land community; cows, a breeding herd of saddleback pigs, various donkeys, New Forest ponies, carthorses, miscellaneous cats & dogs, 12 hives of bees that stung everyone, a dovecote from which all the doves flew away and a 'biteful' monkey.

At the outbreak of the First World War John was perhaps the best-known artist in Britain. His friendship with Lord Beaverbrook enabled him to obtain a commission in the Canadian Army and he was given free rein to paint what he liked on the Western Front, but is only known to have completed one painting. He was also allowed to keep his facial hair and therefore became the only officer in the Allied forces, except for King George V, to have a beard. After two months in France, Lord Beaverbrook had to intervene to save John from a court-martial after he was arrested for taking part in a brawl.

At Alderney Manor he led a very eccentric life as well as holding regular noisy parties with all his friends from the art and literary circles who came down from London on a regular basis. Figures such as Thomas Hardy, George Bernard Shaw, T E Lawrence, James Joyce, Dylan Thomas, W B Yeats, David Lloyd George, Ramsay MacDonald and Winston Churchill who had their portraits painted by John.The years at Alderney Manor were the peak of John's artistic career. Everyone who was anyone seemingly wanted to have their portrait painted by the erstwhile King of Bohemia.

Thomas Hardy on seeing his portrait painted by John in 1923 remarked "I don't know if that's how I look, but that's how I feel." As well a portraits of friends, like Ottoline Morrell and W.B.Yeats, he painted Lloyd George, Ramsay MacDonald & Winston Churchill. A controversial portrait of Lord

Leverhulme, the founder of Port Sunlight, was returned to John minus its head, the soap millionaire having been offended by the artist's depiction of him. The resultant outcry at this insult to John's artistic integrity reverberated worldwide.

At intervals John would leave for his studio in London or for a continental tour in search of Gypsy camps or new lovers.Johns affairs were almost too numerous to mention being renowned for a reputation with the ladies and his romantic ways although he himself was rather a frightening figure with his long dark hair and beard. Though the claim that he had fathered some 100 illegitimate offspring was no doubt an exaggeration.

At one time he painted nude a young local girl Mary who lived close to me on Manning's Heath road in Alderney. This event caused quite a scandal at that time within the local church going community. Augustus also painted our families first home the delightful Heather View which grandad Reg Rogers also had rented from Lady Wimborne prior to having his cousin Harold build our home The Mannings.. John was a controversial figure, both for his unconventional lifestyle (he lived for a while in a commune and was known as 'The King of Bohemia and King of the Gypsies.

Johns children attended Danecourt School in Parkstone which only had eleven pupils until the appearance of the Johns offsprings. At Alderney they were said to be completely undisciplined, ".they would shin up trees in bare feet, run with a pack of red setters, plunge into the frog-laden pond, and, to the distress of the parson, dash naked about the place getting dry". The family left Alderney in

March 1927 when the Manor was pulled down, and a new housing estate built. The consecrated ground, being occupied by St Barnabas church. Augustus John moved to Fryern Court, at Fordingbridge, where he died on 31st October 1961.

Augustus John and the Gypsies

They say that John Augustus was fascinated by Gypsies

that's why he drew them every day

some in their fine and dandy clothes

some naked in the hay

He was a Gypsy roving guy

with his paint brush and his pen

he lived upon the Canford common lands

with his vardo set in clay n dens

He painted our house heather view

with its roses around the door

its red and white bricks of the land

where Crusoe came to call

They say that whistler was a friend of his

along with Lloyd George

he sketched the chavvys with charcoal then

guess he knew

Rogers Sid

The famous London art museum

stores his scenes to see

some are of the common Gypsy folki

others lost at sea

His wife was Ida and his sister Gwen

plus all his lover maids

they lived within the manor road

near to Wally cave

The art studio was made of glass

though his farm like his life was mean

he kept a lot of pigs you see

plus goats that he would wean

His looks were dark and ugly then

with his long coat and his beard

some folks said he was eccentric

others thought him weird

The art world thought him master stroke

with his flair of all things bright

he painted girls bare in the naked light

but I guess he was alright.

Ray Wills

Alice Elizabeth Gillington (1863-1934)

Alice was a pioneer collector of songs from English Gypsies and also an active campaigner for Gypsy rights. She and her brother, John Gillington lived in two caravans, the Brown Caravan and the Yellow Caravan and followed the Gypsy way of life throughout their lives. They stayed together, but they did not always camp with the Gypsies. "We could easily find camping ground where the Gypsies do, but my brother doesn't care to be out in the open for various reasons, one of them being the cut-throat ruffians that infest the Forest roads. We have a gun, but no dog." Throughout her writings, she mentions many Gypsies. She also talked of meeting up with many Gypsy families including Betsy Page (sometimes called Betsy Bowers) Tom Pateman, Walter and Eliza White along with the Wheelers, Sherreds, James, and Willetts. Alice died of a stroke at 27 Balmoral Road, Poole, Dorset, on 22nd of May 1934 though her address was 'The Caravans in Lilliput, Parkstone, Poole, Dorset'.

The old clay cutters

There were gangs of clay cutters on Mitchells site

cutting clay by day and night

the work was tiresome and the hours long
but they we're mean and they were strong

On Alder hills they dug the quarry
their kids to feed and waif's they had married
the Talbot land was rich in clay
with a good days work for a poor man's pay

The brickyard's stretched across the land
from Wareham road to Turbary's sand's
Old Meg the Gypsy lived in her cottage on the heath
where tinker's blessed the turves's so deep
to cut their turves' was to survive
in winter time when love was wild

The warblers sang their songs for free
whilst the adders and lizards squirmed beneath birch trees
the common land was fit to roam
with Gypsy vendors with high curved domes

The sacks were plentiful on the ground
where fir cones dropped and beggars scrounged

the Talbot sister heard their pleas

the working men and poor widows teas

So they built a village to be proud

like its Winton soil the land was loud

the White's and Rogers created bricks

with chimneys tall and windows thick

the common man used land so free

to build their homes in Alderney.

Ray Wills

For many years Gypsies had Lady Wimborne's permission to live on the heath of Canford until it all came to an end when Poole council bought some of the land in 1954 and sold it to developers with the proviso that the housing plots would have restricted prices for private sale to resolve the problem of a shortage of housing in the borough.

Many local traveler families built or else helped to build thriving businesses locally in the haulage, sand, gravel, brick ,potteries, clay and building industries. A great number of these new initiatives sprang up locally, including potteries, coal merchants, brickworks and scrap metal industries. Many of them often often originating from very humble beginnings or funded by their family pony and cart or pig sties initiatives. Such was case with my great grandmothers Elizabeth Fancy's project, where she started with one pig and culminating in the Rogers family brickworks.

 These projects and humble starts were used as a source of income to fund the family industry and often these thrived and grew in size and demand to become extremely wealthy local enterprises. Some of which are still in existence today and many of these Gypsy travelling families remain rooted in the local communities with the names well known locally and respected. Alongside the show people such as the Whites, Coles and the artisan's such as the Coopers.

Newtown also was the home of the largest scrap metal yard in the world the large billboard displayed it in the 1950s at Trent's family yard viewed then on the nearby Ringwood road.

 Local residents of the area know the higher ground of upper Parkstone affectionately as (up on hill) with its many shops, clubs and friendly societies and of course its monkey house ,so named due to a musical organ grinder who frequented that spot on the Ashley road with his monkey. Then many of the local landmarks could be seen from train carriage windows in Poole including the Limmer and Trinidad Water Tower and the chimneys of the Omnium brickyards at Manning's Heath and Dorset Brick Company (DBC) clay pits of Sankey Ward at Broom road Alderney.

The Crutcher's are another family with traveler roots, one of its members Brian became famous for his speedway riding at Poole Pirates. At that time many young people were fascinated with motorbikes and the local heaths were often used as tracks for these keen youths to practice their daring skills until the eventual housing of which is now known as

Tower park. The heath land's then considered by many as wasteland's and were gradually built on and the local Gypsies were housed, or moved on. In time official site's for Gypsies were set up locally. The main one being based next to our farm at Manning's Heath Road. In time the Gypsy fraternity adapted well to their new brick built homes though still retaining the delightful artistry of interior furnishings and their cultures and identity. A great deal of the land at Canford was actually very boggy and required lorry loads of rubble courtesy of E.F. Phillips to infill before the housing foundations were in place.

At that time 1960 there was a question and uproar in the House of Lords in parliament when it was announced that Lord Wimborne had made millions of pounds of profit overnight from the sale of the land to Poole Council.

As a child I well remember catching the wee Rossmore bus from Trinidad House to up on hill to attend the Saturday children matinees at the Regal cinema on Ashley road or playing on the disused quarry's at Alderney or the corner of Trinidad and Ringwood road with my many cousins and local travelling friends.

Local churches

The church of The Good Shepherd in Rossmore was built by local preacher Sankey Ward in 1931. Sankey owned many clay pits in the area and built many houses in the locality. St Clements church was the main local church in Newtown with a rich local family tradition many of our Rogers relatives were church Wardens there for many years. Along with the Wesleyan/Methodist church where the family contributed towards its cost of building and the more modern evangelical church on the Ringwood road, both were contributed to and built by local Rogers families/ builder's.

Before the houses

From Bourne valley bottoms along the dirt track
the caravans rumbled to lodge hills and back
through hedges laden with bramble and gorse
lovely chestnuts to nibble with our little horse
there at Coy Meadow's we drank from the streams
little fresh springs and wonders to dream

There were Gypsies at Beales in town today
We'll tell you your fortune then be on our way
the village kids saw us and give us the eye
our caravan homes smoked right up to the skies

With rabbits to ferret and hedgehogs to eat
songs around the campfire and family to meet
the wheels rolled daily and the stars shone at night

there were folks in their glory and clothes to delight

There was food on the table and rugs on the floors
the candles were lit and designs on our doors
the music we played there with accordion Joe's
the songs that we sang were older than dough

There were times which were hard then and folks who did stray
but we were far wiser than many today
the grass grew so course and the daisies were spread
like creation was labeled for the good and the dead

The Queen of the Gypsies was dark and so rare
she had braided long hair and spent days at Poole fair
The wagons were rich and the lamps they were gold
the children danced naked upon their tip toes

The chaffinches sung at the break of the day
as we ambled along with our stories to say
now there's just tarmac and Tower Park ridge
where once there was magic with old uncle Sid

They lived on the heath's then when the land it was free

before Lord Guest of Wimborne sold it for houses for thee.

Ray Wills

Lord Robert Baden Powell(1796–1860).

It was at Brownsea Island where he based his very first Scout camp in 1907. Thereby founding and establishing 'The Scout Association. The wife of Baden-Powell was herself a local Poole lady; her maiden name was Olivia Soames. She originally lived with her family at Grey Riggs in Parkstone. (Poole).Baden-Powell and Olivia were married in 1908 at St Peter's church in Poole which was the largest church in the town.

First boy scouts

Ten Dorset boys from Bourne and Poole

took a trip to Brown sea Isle with the first scouts crew

three half a crowns they paid each one

to spend a time there and have some fun

Lord Baden Powell he took those local boys

to teach them scouting with all its joys

the skills of craft and camping too

were held at Brown sea isle just next to Poole

That first camp is now history
with generations of scouts at jamborees
the campfires lit and the songs were sung
those far off days when we were young
Its worldwide fame and Girl Guide's too
were born at Brown sea next to Poole
with chant's of boy's and ventures blessed
they planted the seed -you know the rest.
Ray Wills

Louie Foot
Louie Foot rode an old Ford T
she was a real coolest lady you ever did see
she gave lift's to the clan through Rossmore steep hills n lanes
services through Alder hills to upon hill n back again

421

Ted Sherwood was the boxing king

He was a true preacher diddy coy

He won so many Lonsdale belts

First won coconuts at Poole fair shies n said he gave foes a black eye

Mr's Bonham Christie she was a sad recluse

on Brownsea Island shore's

she had a wicked gun they said

she fired it all twelve bore's

Lord and Lady Wimborne lived at Canford School

The amity was a flea pit in the old town of Poole

Poole had two white hearts plus a pub with no name

whilst the grasshopper's danced opposite Bournemouth's fast lane

Our trouser's were short then and our legs were so sore

Though the gentry were rich landowner's and we were so poor

Poole had a promenade amidst of the quay

where the sailor's all danced their night's on the spree.

Ray Wills

On Longham way

I strolled through Millham's Mead to Longham's Way

I spied rabbits in the fields at play

I spied fisherman and boys at water upon the Stour

so hard at play today wouldn't have it any other way

The fields were emerald green and the thorns and bracken were so thick and course

saw the swans in flight and the scattered n chained up Gypsy horse

the day was hot just like English summers so long ago

but the season's now seem to come and go fleetingly

The squirrel's they played beneath the great oak bough's

whilst the reed's did sway and the nettle's caste their spell today

the butterfly red admirals soared just like wisps of play

I glimpsed a heron then he flew away it was just like any other day on Longham way.

Ray Wills

Wimborne

Stan Collier

Stan Collier worked on Priddle farm

When hours were long and men grow strong

in higher Barnsley's woods and leas

where he milked the cows for you and me

That cottage close to wooded lanes
that twist and turned to wind yon frames
where zunner boys did run the lanes
fishing and playing childhoods games

The dogs did bark and mice did hide
the rivers twisted through countryside
where cars rare rode the country lane
where church bells rings to horses manes

Here dogs gave chase in packs of ten
to hunt the fox to please squires men
where Priddles farm was rich in lore
where Stan Collier worked and planted all

Where cocks did crow and boys did boast
of girls they chased and loved the most
where Wimborne bridge did ride the Stour
as a child I holidayed there for many an hour

Where market town each Thursday noon

we gathered to seek fun and silver spoons

where heifers sold and pigs did snort

where farmers sold and home did brought

their spoils of days not long ago

when farmers put on a wondrous country show

Ray Wills

Romany genes

She had Romany genes

she was born in the briar's

one of sixteen children

everyone would admire

Her mother was faithful and her father was true

they lived on the hillside in ole Waterloo

she travelled the fairgrounds and ran with the pack

she was chased by the boys but there was no going back

Her life it was hard but her love it was true

she courted her sweetheart in ole Waterloo

her father was Nelson and her muter was Jane

they roamed all the commons and strolled through the lanes

they ran with the pack like gypsy folks do

and they lived by their wits in ole Waterloo

Her boyfriend was handsome and he courted her true

gave of his love and his humanity too

they ran in the lanes and they rolled in the green

where the rabbits did scamper and the fox never seen

They married in church one Sunday at noon

the vicar was laughing and they danced to their tune

the Gypsy folk sang the harmonica played

in the village of memories where children were made.

Ray Wills

Dominic Reeves

Dominic Reeve was a prolific writer of tales of the Gypsy life. Dominics wife Beshlie was also an artist and author herself. Dominic also wrote about the Gypsies he stayed with at the Higher Camp, gypsy encampment which was just past the

Mountbatten Arms, along the Ringwood road Alderney Poole. This was in 1950s just before they built a Council estate at nearby West Howe Bournemouth and made the Traveler's move into houses there. Dominic also parked up in a lane on the outskirts of Dorchester in the late 1950s.

In his book Beneath the blue sky Dominic gave a very illustrated account of a visit to Parkstones Canford Heath Old Wareham road area.Mentioning the site as being "a part of a vast estate laying in barren and unenticing land near Poole"."A favorite of old fashioned travellers many still with horses and wagons". Dominic mentions meeting an old man named Righteous who was nearing 82 who was a Romani of some 21 siblimgs.Later Dominic visited a small pub in the backstrets of Poole which was well used by Travellers.Entertained by a step dancer name of Little Eli. (This maybe the Angel or the Yaucht).

Dominic Reeves

Dominic came to Kinson downs where Gypsies bedded and young girls were heaven bound

the wheels did turn there and times were tough on the common land of peat and bluff

he rode the trails of bracken down where birds did sing o'er rabbit's mounds

where folks worked hard when hour's were long amidst the days of swallow song

Where Mountbatten Arms doth stand today afore the Shoulder of Mutton along the way

where birch did grow amidst heathers sweet with adder n lizard's at your feet

near Alderney where John did paint naked ladies so frequent

where Sankey Ward built house's for the rich and lady Wimborne s lodge was close to pitch

The writer stored his memories of Gypsy life beneath sky and trees

where crafts were rich in lore and pen where kids grew tall and fern did bend

the local people in Kinson free were rich in style and histories

the Longham bridge over the river Stour to Ferndowns haunts and village squires

The war had took the youth its true with tales of valor from Waterloo

the commons rich in gravel clay and stone but to the Gypsy it was home

where grass was mean and trails were sand and fortunes told to open hands

where families came from New Forest glades to build their homes and get it made

Dominic wrote and his wife did paint the Gypsy story oh so quaint till they were all housed on West Howe land with brick's of Rogers builders band

the chimneys grew tall upon the land and pigs were sold in markets grand

the gaffers paid you on the land and the rich grew richer you understand

Those days of Gypsy life so free were recorded there in histories

with Dominic's books of fame and lore he painted it as it was after the war

the Gypsy families are still abroad you can hear them sing with one accord

their heather sprigs are sold today in Poole high street just like it was yesterday.

Ray Wills

Heather view

How I remember days at our house heather view

with views across to Poole and Waterloo

where Marion Archer and I did play

upon the swing above the hay

The cottage stood upon the hill
with rambling   roses twisting around the window sills
the bricks were as if painted red and white
with the door of green and the stable light

The furze was sharp and the broom was rich
where ponies grazed and willows pitched
the gravel road was rich in time
where Augustus John painted the house so fine

The common lands stretched to magna road
with foxes lairs and newts and toads
the rabbits played upon the downs
where Gypsy folk were bender bedded down
The Archers lived at heather view
where Sankey Ward clay pit was chimney new
where clay was rich and sand was prime
where horses grazed most of the time
The E F Phillips lorries drove by each day
where kid's would chase and run and play

the daisy banks were green and rich

with buttercups along the ditch

The common hedge's were thick with dew

where golden spiders crafted webs so true

where lizards squirmed and adders chased

amongst the heathers rich in bloom and face

The days were long and sunny too

with views across to town of Poole

where train did chuff and spout did steam

from lights of town and birch tree leans

Those day's have gone and where we played

replaced by speed of moneys made

where factories stand and office space

lost their place to mans disgrace.

Ray Wills

CHAPTER ELEVEN

The Purbeck and Wessex Trail

'If one wanted to show a foreigner England, perhaps the wisest course would be to take him to the final section of the Purbeck Hills and stand him on their summit…. Then system after system of our island would roll together under his feet"

431

E M Forster.

The Purbeck Isle

The Purbeck and surrounding area of Hardy's Wessex is famous for its Portland stone, the Jurassic coastline and its great writers and poets such as Thomas Hardy, Enid Blyton and William Barnes. It is full of history and close by is the town of Dorchester with its link to the birth of the Unions with the Tolpuddle Martyrs and Judge Jeffries known as the hanging judge. The delightful Purbeck hills can be viewed across the sea from Bournemouth and Poole.Purbeck includes the historical towns of Wareham, Swanage and Corfe along with enchanting villages of thatch and stone, such as at Winfrith, Wool, Creech,Stoborough, etc, crafted out of Portland Stone and the imaginative Coves and bays such as Lulworth, Durdle Door and Kimmeridge.Its attractiveness lies in its scenic beauty and its narrow twisting lanes and views with a surprise awaiting you around each bend for every traveller places which the artist Turner painted regularly.

Wareham

The town had numerous characters after the war years notably the House family, old man House and his son Freddie as well as Mrs Roff who lived in their cottage at Eat Walls. Then there was Cedric Hughes who may well have gypsy bloodwho lived by the river and frequented all the local pubs. He was a great story teller he also was the local bell ringer at St Mary's church for many years. There was also the notorious Michael Joseph who as a youth crashed his motor bike and as a result lost a leg, he developed a notorious reputation with the young ladies considering himself a Don Juan and gained national news as beingthe News of the World front page "The one legged Romeo".

 In the 1950s/60s Wareham was also home to the future Tory MP David Mellor and the successful soccer star (England under 21 and Ipswich Town and Bournemouth goalkeeper)David Best. Local boy Millser Greens father Farmer Green was another great character who still spoke in the Olde Dorset dialect and was to be seen and heard each Thursday market day in the gatherings of farmers on Wareham Quay pub.

The Wareham name took the maternal link as George and James are both recorded as being Mr Small's offspring. At that time Shroton was well known for its fair and its common land which would have attracted travelling Gypsy families.The Wareham name was often used throughout Dorset by travellers who no dount had their origins in Wareham itself which may well have been a Gypsy site of some importance in the 15th century.

The Shrove Tuesday Football Ceremony of the Purbeck Marblers.

This event Shrove Tuesday is still celebrated each year and was the day that the new apprentices were accepted into the Ancient Order of Purbeck Marblers and Stone Cutters and after the annual meeting the new freemen had to kick a football through the village of Corfe Castle, some say with a glass of beer which others tried to spill.

The heath lands then were regarded as wastelands with no one owning them. But with everyone having free access to them. Initially there were some mud hut homes for some folks then later there were brightly colored Gypsy caravans at that time which belonged to the travelling didycoy. These Gypsies regularly would stop in the area on their route from The New Forest to the Isle of Purbeck. These show up on the census throughout the 19th century as do tent dwellers whose homes were scattered across the local heath lands and areas such as Sandford, Bere Regis and Wareham.

Having lived in Poole and Bournemouth for many years and discovering my Gypsy family origins with the numerous Gypsy traveler names in the locality. It was a surprise therefore to discover so many similar names in the Wareham Purbeck area when I lived there in my later childhood and youth. Names such as Whites, Ayres, Hughes, Lovell's, Young, Pateman and Burdon's. No doubt these were the same families who came from the New Forest and due to their traveling life had found their way to the delightful Purbeck which was obviously a regular route at that time, as was Somerset.

During the 18th and 19th centuries the villagers of Dorset relied heavily on the travelling hawkers and dealers who regularly visited their area selling a wide range of goods: fruit, cloth, china, earthenware pots, ribbons, baskets. Many of these were Gypsies, who were skilful in repairing chairs, burning charcoal, brick-making, making baskets and clothes pegs and mending pots and kettles, sharpening knives and scissors. Some chose to stay and make Dorset their home.

Purbeck Gypsies Early history

The earliest record of Gypsies in Dorset was found in the Parish Register of Lyme Regis 14th February 1559 when Joan, the daughter of an Egyptian, was baptised also in that same year a group of Gypsies were prosecuted in Dorchester but they were released on a technicality when they proved they had entered England from Scotland.

During the Civil War twelve travelling men were rounded up in Uplyme, they were paid to leave the area. Many Gypsies settled in the Purbeck area. Later during the eighteenth and nineteenth century Dorset villagers relied upon the travelling hawkers and dealers who visited their area. These sold a wide variety of goods: to the local population these Gypsies, mending chairs, burning charcoal, brick-making, making baskets and clothes pegs and, perhaps most importantly, mending pots and kettles, sharpening knives and scissors. Some chose to stay and make it their home.

Burden

Burden is a renowned Romany name especially in the Wool area.

Samuel Cherrett was born 1865 in Wareham. He was the father of 10 children including Dorothy and Maurice. Samuel died 1929 in Poole.

Purbeck stone

Old London was built of Purbeck stone

Sir Christopher Wren was well in tone

435

with Westminster abbey and old Big Ben
they took those stones and carved them then

From Purbeck tide with surfing foams
they cut those famous Portland stones
from Purbeck hills and countryside
made monuments to greet a king and royal bride

The work was hard and hour's were long
with only sweat and warbler's song
with noble brow's and knightly gaze
they shaped those stones to be amazed

Now those stones stand so proud and tall
amongst royal hearts and regales halls
the Purbeck hills still call to man
where seagulls nest above the sands.

Older route to the Purbeck

We took the old route to the Purbeck my Gypsy friend's and I there was goodies in the vardo's and new age caravan's so high

we took the Wareham old road again through olde England's olde domain

we travelled o'er Egdon heath through Wool and Wareham's lanes

There were sights to see each morning scenes of Corfes great hill's

twists and turn's of Purbeck stone winding river's mill

pictures of old thatched cottages Creech great Grange n more

Kimmeridge bay in the morning's light and fish upon the shore

The road it gave great pleasure as we looked o'er Swanage bay

with fairgrounds on the hillsides kids and lambs at play

the wheels they did keep turning and the songs we sung were old

like the Romani Gypsy language that once our fathers told

There were tanks upon the crossroads where Lawrence once made home

where Hardy walked and wrote his tales and William Barnes he once called home

the birds they chirped at daybreak and the deer in Warehams woods

the Sanford lanes were full of Rhodes and the chaffinch chirped so good

The band were full of stories the old uns told a rhyme

of the golden age of Gypsy when travelling was in its prime

the trees were full of blossom there with berries on each bush

it was a lovely journey we all said it was kush-ti

The Worgret track was bumpy as we crossed the bridge again

there were farmers making furrow' and chickens in their pens

the rabbits ran through meadows and the blackbird sang it's song

memories of Purbeck seemed to go on and on

The gaffer's all remember when we cut turf's upon the heath

where old Meg had her cottage there and as a chavvy I once cut my teeth

the lanes have all been covered with tarmac and rich man's gain

but the Gypsy roads are remembered as we go to Wool again.

Ray Wills

The marble stone of the Purbeck Isle at Portland was used for many churches nationally as well as by Sir Christopher Wren for St Paul's n Westminster for rebuilding of the city of London following the great fire of London.

Nicky Hann.

She was a farmer's daughter from Lytchett Matravers an

attractive 'rebel from the sixties summer of love,' who played and sung in the familiar Joni Mitchell style. She wrote the song Purbeck Hills' which was released in 1963 and soon became an anthem throughout the Purbeck area. With a chorus of "Lovely, lovely Purbeck Hills, green and forever wild, I believe you'll always be here to keep and warm my child".

Percy Westerman (1876□1959)

 Percy was a British writer of boys adventure stories was quite an eccentric man. Author of over 170 books, which emphasized traditional virtues of patriotism and discipline. He lived in Wareham on a houseboat called The Barge on the river Frome. With his three closest friends his dogs after leaving his job with the admiralty at Portsmouth. Here he wrote most of his books. His writing career began with a sixpence bet made with his wife that he could write a better story than the one he was reading to his son, who was ill with chickenpox. His first book for boys, 'A Lad of Grit', was published in 1908.

Baden-Powell's Scouting movement, founded in the same year, was strongly influenced by many of his books. In the 1930's he was voted the most popular author of stories for boys. He was the founder of the Redcliffe Yacht Club. His books sold over one and a half million copies. At the age of 70 he was forced by a fall to leave his houseboat for dry land but he continued writing. He died at the age of 82.

The Fancy's

The Fancy family originated in the Purbeck area at Turners Puddle in the 1600s. Christopher Fancy was born there in 1612 then by the 1700s many Fancys lived at East Stoke, Moreton and Melchester Regis then later living in Hampreston, West Parley, Pimperne, Portland and Arne at Wareham. By the mid 1880s Fancys were also living in Poole,Greater Canford,Wimborne Minster,Hampreston ,Osmington and Longfleet. They were brick makers at Sandford Wareham and many of their descendents like Gideon Fancy and family lived on the Gypsy encampment at Bourne Bottom and Heavenly Bottom Parkstone Poole. Gideon Fancy was the father of my great grandmother Elizabeth Fancy who married Charles Rogers my great grandfather.

David Fancy(13th Jan 1793-6th Nov 1876).

David was a brick maker

David was Born at Arne in Wareham where later he married Sarah Fancy.They had 5 children, William, Susan, Thomas, Gideon and Ellen.

James Fancy married Sarah Christopher

David Fancy

David the son of James and Sarah married Elizabeth Skinner in 1815, they had 5 children before her death in 1824. David remarried in 1831 to Sarah Crocker, they had a further 5 children.

Gideon Fancy

Gideon married Elizabeth they were parents of Emily Elizabeth Fancy.Who was the authors Ray Wills WHERE THE RIVER BENDS great grandmother. She lived at Bourne bottom campsite in Poole with her father Gideon Fancy and his wife Elizabeth.There were very many other Gypsies camped there apart from the Fancy's.

Daisy Fancy

Daisy lived in Wareham in the 1800s and later years moved to live on the Parkstone Poole encampment.

Franklin

Eli Franklin was the President of the National Romany Right s Association.

The Black Bear Hotel-Wareham

As a child I lived in the black bear hotel

where celebrity's came from near and far

there were film stars of screen and stage

the Beverley's and pop stars of that golden age

they came to Wareham on the Frome

where the Purbeck hills were our true home

The grockels came to walk and stare

along with poets and artiste fair

the banter of the market stalls

the fish you caught and the names they called

The church that stood upon the hill

the walls of grass and the meadows fields

the cows that gathered in Stoborough lane

the pound where I courted Mary Jane

The school where Stuckey gave us boys the cane

the quay with monkey Susie inside a cage

with her big tin collecting box upon a chain

The press and media came to stay

in black bear rooms for high class pay

the little shops that sold quaint pots

the sandpits and the best walls smocks

The tourist haunts of Lawrence Shaw

the anglebury cafe and the kids so poor

the Lady St Mary bells that chimed

the verse I wrote and the poems that rhymed.

Ray Wills

Carey /Wareham

Carey schools camp

Dorset had by the 1960s established its own unique children's holiday campsite in the woodlands of Carey Wareham this was established by the Dorset County Councils Education Department and provided a base for parties of up to 120 school children to attend each fortnight throughout the season from spring till autumn as well as for youth groups and others. From its delightful setting children were able to take part in overnight camping expeditions throughout the Purbeck as well as orienteering and they gained certificates in camping and youth endurance with the Duke of Edinburgh Awards. I was fortunate to work there for a few seasons as Assistant Warden.

Carey boy scouts

I once was a boy scout

at Carey schools camp

we put up our tents

and sang our camp songs

Around campfire's of logs

beneath pine trees so tall

and listened to sounds of the wood pigeons call

We walked through the Purbeck

and took in Corfe in one day

we carried our rucksacks

a full pack all the way

Then we had breakfast at the foot of the hill

beneath the castle of Bankes

and I remember it still

We rode out to Brownsea

the home of our clan

and had a nice red complexion

and a lovely dark tan

We did all the action's and sang all the songs

that's how we all grew up so healthy and strong.

Creech Grange Arch is Denis Bonds 1740 folly, where pillars and arches look down through a gap cut into the Great Wood to Creech Grange below.

A great many travelling family names are still prevalent in the Wareham area, names such as the Patemans,Ayres,Whites,Lovells,Hughes,Stanleys and Coles. Gypsy campsites were also scattered on the Egdon heath at Sandford, Bere Regis, Arne, Corfe and Lundigo for many years.

Lulworth

Visit to Lulworth

Carousel ladies with wishing well hats
cricket players with willow wood bats
trumpet players in the village band
they all had me to make promises
I couldn't keep
they all rode to market
in a green jeep

The Durdle Door surf
it was mighty a roar
the sand it was fine
and the love was amour

The crabs they were tiny
they bit many toes

and the rugged rocks

they tore at your clothes

The baskets were laden

with lobsters a crying

though there many a che

happily frying

The Lulworth Lord Weld

he was in his castle terrain

the tanks were firing upon the range

the castle drew grockels by the score

the trust it was financially fine and secure

Though the village was dead now

had sold off its hopes

at the last war times

poor old Johnny

said it twas a crime and eloped

Whilst the car park prices

were too dear by far

so don't come to Lulworth my dears

if you get there by car

Ray Wills

The Weld Family of Lulworth.

The Welds are one of the oldest in England, dating from before the Conquest. Reginald was descended in the direct male line from Edrick surnamed the Wild, or Sylvaticus, who was nephew to Edric, Duke of Mercia, husband of Edina daughter of King Ethelred. One member of the family was Sheriff of London in 1353. The most notable members of the House of Weld since its immigration into Dorset are : Humphrey, Governor of Portland Castle, who bought Lulworth in 1641, and completed the building of the castle; Charles Weld Blundell, is now tenant of Lulworth Castle. Lulworth Castle was designed by Inigo Jones, and for more than three hundred years has " stood four-square to every wind that blew" .

Geologists tell us that the rocks of Durdle Door are 140 million years old, and that it was formed by the action of the waves finding cracks in the vertical limestone beds and creating caves, which eventually collapsed together to form the arch.

Dorchester

Thomas Hardy (June 1840 -11 January 1928)

Hardy is one of England's most famous writers. Hardy lived

in Dorchester at Max Gate and is best known for his books based on the people and surroundings of Wessex including the classics of Tess of the D'Urbervilles and Far From The Maddening Crowds. Hardy was a an ardent anti-vivisectionist, his wife Emma hosted anti-vivisection meetings at Max Gate and in 1909 he wrote: the practice of vivisection, which might have been defended while the belief ruled that men and animals are essentially different, has been left without any logical argument in its favour. He also protested against the blinding of caged birds for sport and supported a campaign by veterans of World War 1 to have the practice outlawed, which it was in 1920.

William Barnes (22 February 1801 □ 7 October 1886)

William Barnes was born at Rushay in the parish of Bagber in Dorset. The son of a farmer. Former solicitor's clerk Barnes is best known for his poems using the Dorset dialect. Barnes was a Poet,Teacher,Revd and Visionary. He was also a great friend of Thomas Hardy and also Lord Mayor of Dorchester.

One March morning in 1818, a Magnet coach pulled up with a great dash and clatter of steaming horses , outside the Kings Arms in Dorchester. A portly lady with two young girls got down. The younger miss had blue eyes and wavy brown hair, and was wearing a sky blue □spencer or jacket. By chance a lawyers clerk was passing at that moment. When he saw the girl he muttered to himself: That shall be my wife.That was Julia Miles, daughter of James Camford Miles, an excise officer recently appointed to Dorset.

The youth looking on was seventeen year-old William

Barnes. Some years later he noted: In 1827 I took Chantry House at Mere, and on a happy day happy as the first of a most happy wedded life I brought into it my most love worthy and ever-beloved wife, Julia Miles, and then took boarders. His solitary exile had lasted four years and seven months. They had been courting for nine years.

Judge Jeffrey's

Judge Jeffries of Dorchester Dorset was known as the Hanging Judge holding his Bloody Assize in Dorchester where he tried 312 people and sentenced nearly 200 to be hanged. Here thirteen men were executed and the heads of some were impaled on spikes and church railings, left there for several years as a warning of the penalty for treason. Jeffries ordered gallows to be erected in many other Dorset towns and villages to execute men thought to be Monmouth supporters. Whilst those in Wareham were put to death on gallows on the towns surrounding grassed earthen Walls.

Judge Jeffries

Judge Jeffries was the hanging judge

he lived in Dorset town

with miles of open country

all belonging to the crown

With market day on Thursday

on Sundays there were hangings with everyone for free

*for all the little children and family to seeJudge Jeffries was the
hanging judge*

he worked on gallows hill

Bere Regis to Dorchester they remember him still

*with miles of open country and nearby castle on the hillThere were
kings and queens of England*

who sat upon their thrones

where aristocracy was rampant

where common folks were poor

and wise men lived alone.

ROMA DAY

It was Roma day in Dorchester town

*where Hardy penned and Barnes wrote his rare sweet dialect poetry
down*

where the music from accordion played

when Gypsies danced and dreams were madeThe storytellers told their tales of the Dorset towns rich country dales

Where farmers wives and dairy maids all gathered around in the Dorset green rich country glades

they told their tales of years gone by when Caroline Hughes was but a child and shy

when the market town was rich in life where yokels bartered dawn to night

where Vardos rolled and Gypsies danced across the hills like true romance.

Ray Wills

Wool

Parsons

Joseph Parsons a Gypsy's child was recorded in Wool on the 26th of February 1792.

Burtons

Ugaria Burton was baptised at Wool 1800.

Woolbridge Manor House

Woolbridge Manor stands on the left bank of the Frome near

Woolbridge.The present house was built by Sir John Turberville, who was sheriff of Dorset in 1652. The original ancient house was garrisoned in 1644, and the present one was likely erected by Sir John when peace was restored.

Turners and Turbervilles

Tur berville said to have links with the Turners Gypsies a very old family in Dorset.Hence the local place names like Turners Puddle and Turners Piddle.In the 14th century the Tur ber villes were MPs,Mayors and Sherriffs. Many Turbervilles were freemasons with links to Canford Lodge in Poole.There is a possiblity that the artist Turner was related and he was a regular visitor to Dorset and painted numerous pictures of Gypsies on the heaths of Canford and at Sandbanks.

The Gypsy Family Trees of Francis & Mary Clayton and John & Mary Booth: from about 1750 to about 1900 from the South Midlands of England to the North East and North West have the Turbervilles in their family tree.There are very strong links of Turbervilles with the Bere Regis area. Though it is believed the names origin is french and was first recorded after 1066 when the Normans invaded Britain.

Though the name Tur ber ville earliest personal references were to the poet George in 1540 and Nicholas Tur ber ville at Bere Regis in 1577.

The Tale of the Turberville Ghost

Two friends, both of whom were D'Urbervilles, some two centuries ago were driving in a large lumbering coach from Bere Regis to Wool. They quarrelled and at once got out and, as was the custom of the time, fought. One was killed. Ever since, the ghost of a coach has rumbled along the road from Bere to Wool at night ; the noise it makes on its journey can be heard by any one, but the vehicle can only be seen by those who have Durberville blood in their veins. The last person who saw it was, Mr. Windle' tells us, a gentleman who did not know the legend, but was connected with the D'Urbervilles family.

Bindon Abbey-A story goes that the twelve bells of Bindon Abbey were stolen by night, and are now in the churches of Wool, Combe, and Fordington. Tradition has it that 5 of Fordingtons 8 bells were obtained that night.

T.E Lawrence (1888 1935)

When Lawrence resigned from the army he wrote "Seven Pillars of Wisdom". He enlisted in the RAF in 1922 under the name J. M. Ross. but changed it to Shaw (no doubt under the influence of his close friend Bernard Shaw)when his real identity was discovered by the media, after leaving the RAF and joining the Royal Tank Corps. Lawrence lived a recluse life in his cottage at Clouds hill at Bovington Dorset.

He enjoyed his hobby of riding his motor bikes. He supposedly crashed his Superior motor bike whilst avoiding two local boys on pushbikes who suddenly appeared in front of him on the wide road leading down to the army camp at Bovington. He died it is said as a result of his injuries sustained from this accident. There are many controversial conspiracies about Lawrence and his so called accident. He was buried locally nearby at the quiet remote church cemetery at Moreton village. His life and adventures have become popularized most famously in the film starring Peter O Toole as Lawrence of Arabia (1962).

Lawrence

Across the field's of tragedy

inspired by his fame

the reckless spirit it lives on

inspired by his name Across the desert homeland's

the Arabs ride again

the white dress into battle

his like well never see again

He ride's upon his camel

his motorbike remains

his flag the union jack

though his caravan remains

His words only a tower

his death a bitter twist

his reign was set in granite

his words were truly writ

His armour it was courage

his valour it was true

he fought for Truth and justice

long after Waterloo

His stories they are endless
his claim to fame was won
riding with his brother's
beneath the setting sun
His army life was settled
upon the hill of cloud's
he was buried out in Moreton
his funeral was proud
His rank and style was freedom
he rode the hurricane
his fame was Lawrence of Arabia
though he took the name of Shaw
he rode the sands of battle
long before the Iraqi gulf war's

Long before they killed him
with lies and treachery
he fell off his bike that day
at least thats what they say
his like will never be seen again
yet his spirit still remains.

Ray Wills

The Batman

Once I was a batman

at the officers request

I ironed all their uniforms

so they looked their very best

I polished up their brasses

made their beds and cleaned their rooms

I lit up all the fires

put on their favourite tunes

I brought them tea in bed

then nursed them when their drunk

I organized their day

though I was just a punk

I polished all their shoe

brought their papers too

but I was just so innocent then

before I read the news

I worked inside the mess

at their request in the officers best home

I was young n naive then
just one kid on his own

Then later I got educated
I saw the miners strikes
I saw the poverty in Biafra
thats things I did not like

I read upon George Orwell
heard Lennon and Zimmerman
they taught me peace and demonstrated
just how to understand

That war was just a consequence
of some big brother plan
then I left home to wander
learned to be a man.
Ray Wills

True Love Stories n Tales

We looked in the embers and he told us those tales
twere many a long year n I remember it well
the fire cracked and spat then and the kettle whistled through
whilst the yog it was burning red and the moon it shone too
he told me of times the good and the bad
the life on the roads then and the people so sad
he talked and his story though was painfully true
as the chavvies all listened to the wise one they knew
their vardos were tall now and the drapes they were red
with the cushions of wool and the warmth of their beds
he smoked of his pipe and he spat in the fire
whilst the logs they did hiss n burn and the young men desired
the women were frisky I heard him to say
when the times they were hard and the men earned their pay
the cobs they were wild then but their coats they did shine
the locks of their hairs and their manes they were strong
like the men folk who rode them on the banks of the drom
he told is of gaffers and gorgas so fine
and of men who lived only for a bottle of wine
of pasture so rich and of woodlands so free

where the hares and the rabbits ran over the leas

he told us of the deers and the pheasants and the grouse in the dell

the lord of the manor and the surround high walls as well

the homes they were stately and the master was rich

he owned all the land there in the country and ditch

whilst the homes of the traveller was built in the mud

consisting of benders and bracken and yet was full of true love.

Ray Wills

Dorset Man

When Barnes was in Dorchester reside

Purbecks were true countryside

the Egdon heath was a desolate place

where the peasant folks

they knew their place

Where geese and gander hissed all day

and little zunners ran and played

where grass was green

and banks were high

where rivers and streams set the scene

across the durzet countryside

From Wool bridge manor to Lulworths door

across Egdon heath to studland shore

the grass was tall and manners fine

where toffs and lords drank berry wine

In Wareham town on Thursday morn

they came to collect the corn

the corn exchange twas packed with farmers too

the market place sold lambs from Wool

The trees were high and rivers Frome banks were wide

where Samways kissed his future bride

the Swanage crew were set to shore

and Weymouth beach was waiting for

lords and ladies kings and queens

pastors clergy and foreign deans

Poole harbor was the place to be

famed for its cargo's out to sea

Hardy wrote of these times

romantic notions and tales of woe

people places from Poole to lundigo

Tolpuddle men met in secret haunts

to form the union of free men

from ranks of time and history

Purbeck was born from out of the sea

An island set in Purbeck Portland stone

with lanes and hills and dips and dales

country folk sights and smells sea side foam

heather-ed hills and grassy walls

listen to the thrush that calls

The surfing seas

the silvery sands

the poetic words

of the durzet man.

Ray Wills

Winfrith

Winfrith Village life

I went down to the village where the school yard it still stands
where children play in summertime and lover's all hold hand's
I ambled down to poets lane and butts close nearby
where roses grew around the thatch and stranger's all passed by

The post office was so quaint with a doorbell that chimed
there was a village postman on his bike and a poet quoting rhymes
the village church stood on a hill and a well was set in stone
lots of flowers on the footpaths and lots of quaint cute homes

The pigeons close was shelter there for sparrows all in line
with thrushes singing in the bush next to a ladies washing line
the old school lane it beckoned me with its quaint rustic stone
where local yokels stopped to chat all on their own way home

The water lane was rich in grass with roses around each bend
where lovers stopped to kiss at night and old men would pretend
the carpenters wee cottage was rustic and with charm
there were lots of dandelions on the banks and Gypsies selling alms'

On giddy green the children played hopscotch and beggar's fool

nearby the cob web cottage proud where Nelson met his Waterloo

the badgers brook was rich in life with poets passing through

just close to Wareham town and just a walk away from Wool

The rambling roses beckoned me and the banks were full of flowers

every minute spent there was rich in countless hours

the sun smiled on the village scene and the church bell rang at noon

when life was rich in village charm and it ended oh too soon.

Ray Wills

Dorset rambles

I went fishing in Dorset and climbed the Purbeck hills

swam in the sea off of Studland and travelled so footloose

we camped in Carey on the Corfe downs

Sketched the ruins of history and then went to old Poole Town

Nowhere else can you find a place where each bends not the same

winding lanes of Purbeck stone and leafy heather' lanes

where a castle sits on hillside there and boats are in the bay

where good folks come from London town and lands so far away

Dorset has its beauty where the artist paint's the scene

Hardy wrote his tales of love and Enid Blyton her childish dreams

the hills are set in clay where stone of Londons made

God's in his glory there and the meadows are rich in glades

The Portland Bill awaits you and the Durdle door it stands

where Lulworth bay is awesome and lovers all hold hands

the commons have their glory in Canford village scenes

one man writes its poetry and Barnes doth pen his dreams

The Wareham walls surround the town where kings were off time's gained

whilst Cromwell rode his armies and Bankes and Weld did reign

all the ramblings of a poet cannot hide its wealth

where forests rich in fauna hide the deer and olden branch

Ray Wills

Swanage.

John Webber (1771-1852)

John was a stonemason quarrier.Married to Joanna nee Bower. They had four children Jane, Thomas, Priscilla and Moses. Members of the family included Job and Patience Webber

Swanage

The hills of Swanage stand steep and proud

with Purbeck stoned dwellings

quaint little lodge homes

tall scenic remnants of a bye gone age

far off the highway

the home of the sage

Twisted roads weary with hedgerows in tow

sandy beaches' that stretch

seagulls and crows

little thatched cottages

quaint hotel retreats

tidy shop front's with gifts well in reach

Sandy beach avenues with freedom to run

summer kissed meadows

a place in the sun

high in the distance

the castle on the hill

bramble highways

view's that could kill

Long country walks

cute little lanes

a place to retire to

or come back again.

Ray Wills

Enid Blyton (1897 □1968)

Author of children's books of the Secret Seven and the Famous Five series. As a child Enid spent many happy summer vacations in Swanage where she no doubt gained a great deal of her inspiration and ideas for her future stories for children from the Purbeck surroundings of Corfe and Egdon heaths. Gypsies are mentioned in a number of her books like "The Animal Lovers" where they are seen as thieves and untrustworthy people. Apart from one Gypsy Zacky Boswell the storyteller who the children befriend and he tells them stories and educates them all about the animals of the commons of Enid Blyton's Dorset

Blytons Days

I recall the secret seven and the famous five

those Enid Blyton stories kept me alive

tales of caves and treasure troves

maps and walks above Lulworth cove

The sandy shores of Sandbanks downs

the Studland beach and the dunes so white

the rocky cliffs of Dorset towns

the hilly walks o'er Purbeck mounds

The secret tunnels that we took

the castle gates at Corfe the ways we took

the rambling countryside and towns

the bikes and dogs, the kings and crowns

the Englishness of Swanage beach

the view of Wessex just out of reach

the grassy meadows where we played

the Punch and Judy show's on our summer holidays.

Ray Wills

Worth Matravers- Swanage

The Square and the Compass Pub
The pub is situated high up on the Purbeck Hills'.

The Square and Compass

On top of the Purbeck where the stone was cold and mean
the travellers and hikers walked the paths of Dorset scenes
where yeomen once were local and the landed Gentry dwelled
where sheep and hills were rich in rhyme and the poets write there
still

In the olde stoned pub relic where fire sparked so free
where hearth is home to wanderers and folks who are free like me
where Augustus John the artist pictures were hung upon the wall
next to the old Stone museum where dinosaurs once roared

The masons etched their histories and the hills were rich in dew
where the wind blew cold on winter days deep within the hues
the dogs they sat down close to the fire and the drinkers toasted zen
whilst olden Dorset folki breathed life into its flames

The sign it swung outside the pub where chickens all ran free where stone tables laid their stories yet to see

the atmosphere was rich in trust and the poet viewed the scenes

upon the Purbeck hillsides there so close to Halloween

The square and compass told it's tales upon the hilly downs

where lovers met and couples kissed their steps left far behind

the cockerel crowed and gave chase to the farmers wench

upon the Purbeck hillsides where Hardy his stories did vent.

Ray Wills

Lyme Regis

Petitions to both Houses of Parliament for the abolition of Negro Slavery were lying in the town for signature. In fact two petitions were sent one from Lyme generally, and another from the ladies of Lyme Regis. □The female inhabitants of Charmouth also sent one. William Pinney, MP for Lyme from1832, came from the Pinney family of West Dorset who had been involved with the West Indies, sugar production and slavery from the 17th century. The family received more than thirty thousand pounds in compensation when slavery was abolished in 1834. The freed slaves did not receive any compensation at all.

An early account of a Gypsy baptism states that in1558 Joan the daughter of an Egyptian was baptised at Lyme Regis Church.

Beatrix Potter

Children's author spent a holiday in Lyme in 1904, and used some views of Lyme for her story, Little Pig Robinson.

John Fowles (1926-2005)

John Fowles lived from 1968 at Lyme Regis, where he set the background for his famous novel "The French Lieutenant's Woman" . He was greatly influenced by Thomas Hardy, seeing his heroine as a latter-day Tess of the d'Urbervilles. The film of the book, which was shot in 1981 and starring Jeremy Irons and Meryl Streep, reminds viewers of Jane Austen and "Persuasion", as both feature scenes on Lyme's famous harbour wall, The Cobb.

Mesach Wills

Mesach was a raor grinder and was born in Wareham 1908.He married Louisa Fletcher, Louisa was the daughter of Selbea/Sylvia Stanley, herself the daughter of Peter Stanley, known locally as 'The Gypsy King,' and William Fletcher.
Mesach was also related to the Cherretts.

Stanleys

Peter Stanley King of the Gypsies (1732-1802)Peter married Sarah and they lived at Wareham. The parish register of Puddletown confirms that he was aged 75. However his church burial headstone states him as being five years younger. It was quite a common practice for Gypsies to add a few years on to their ages at death. In memory of Peter Stanley, King of the Gypsies, who died 23rd November 1802, aged 70 years.'puddletown_church.

Sarah Stanley (1721-1821)

Sarah was an important person in the community known and respected as the Dowager Queen of the Counties of Wiltshire, Hampshire and Dorset.Peter and Sarah had 9 children seven of the nine survived to adulthood -Selbea, William, Sabra, Aaron, Peter, Paul and Henry. They were a Gypsy family who were renowned in Puddletown (formerly known as Piddletown) Dorset and the surrounding area.The family spent most of their lives travelling around Dorset, Wiltshire and Hampshire.Sarah was buried at St Marys church Puddletown cemetary in 1821 Her funeral was attended by many people.Her death noted in newspapers with a large number in attendance She was refered to as the vagrant MajestyQueen.

Arron Stanley

Arron of the New Forest *known as King of the Gypsies.He was the* son of Peter born 1729 known as king of the gypsies lived in Corfe Castle he was a razor grinder and tinker.*He was issued with a removal order on 10th May 1792,claimed to be 62 or 63. On 2nd March 1801, also in the parish of Corfe Castle, was the settlement hearing of Aaron Stanley, who also was a razor grinder and tinker, and his father, Peter, is also referred to in the documents.*

Another Peter Stanley was born 1771'he was a Razor Grinder and Tinker.He married Mary Drake in Church Knowle in 1792.

Henry Stanley born 1778 at Winterbourne Kingston. Henry the son of Peter and Sarah. Henry married second wife Sarah Mills in 1832 and had other children by her, living at Fordington near Dorchester

In 1803, the Hampshire Chronicle of 28th February gave an account of Henry Stanleys role in a race taking place in Dorset in the early spring: Starting from the town-pump in Dorchester he ran to the town-pump in Weymouth for two guineas; the distance is about eight miles and a quarter, and the time allowed was an hour and two minutes, but he performed it with the greatest ease one minute and a half within the time.The person who made the bet was a young spendthrift of the neighbourhood, who, fearing he should not be able to see fair play himself, hired a horse for his favourite Cyprian to accompany the light-footed prince, but she not having attended Astley's Lectures on Horsemanship, and finding it impossible long to retain her seat in the usual way, immediately crossed the saddle, and in that state entered Weymouth, at full speed, by the side of her infatuated adorer, to the no small gratification of a numerous assemblage of spectators. As was commonplace amongst the Gypsy community they occasionally found themselves on the wrong side of the law, in particular Henry who managed to acquire a one year spell in the old Dorchester prison for assault.

John Stanley

John married Sarah Fancy on the 29th Apr 1802 at Arne Wareham.

Owen Stanley

Owen married Harriet Worden.

William Stanley, Born 1859 Wareham, Dorset.

William married Mary nee Bellam.Their children were

Henry,Charlotte,Mary Ann, Charles, Caroline, Robert, Emma, Selina and Susannah

The Powys brothers

Writers John Cowper Powys, T.F. Powys and Llewellyn Powys feature Dorset heavily in some of their work. John wrote several Wessex-based novels including Weymouth Sands (1934) and Maiden Castle (1936). novels and short stories were set in Dorset and Llewellyn Powys's Dorset essays are regarded by some as the best ever written about the county.John lived for a while in Dorchester which became the inspiration for the setting of his novel Maiden Castle.

Vivian Collin Brooks (1922-2003)

The Author so loved the name of a Dorset village near Weymouth that she used its title "Osmington Mills" as her pen-name.

Weymouth sands

Us kid's all went to Weymouth to build castles in the sand

with our pockets full of shillings in days when life was grand

We took our sandwiches and honey wrapped up in paper towels

we counted all our blessings then and waved at all the cows

the journey was delightful with pastures all the way

sheep and ponies in the paddock's and what a holiday

The sun was out and shinning the clouds were cotton wool

my brother brought his lizard pet and I brought my comics too

The town was full of people there were deck chairs by the sand

you could smell the sea spray in the breeze and hear the big brass band

We saw the fairgrounds carousel and bought a currant bun

there were lots of ice cream vendor's there and a fat man on a drum

the sand was so inviting and the sea was warm and clean

there were tourist's in the shop's nearby it was a delightful scene

I saw the punch and Judy show set up there on the sands

There was lots of candy floss and pop with gals in summer gowns

Weymouth sure looked beautiful such a busy little town

There were open top buses flying by with children cheering too

my brother built a sand castle and my sister played the fool

The boats were sailing in the bay and the cliffs looked quite a sight

I was playing in the sea and the crabs on my toes ouch they had a bite .

Ray Wills

William Wordsworth (1770-1850)

Wordsworth spent two years from 1795 to 1797 living at Racedown

474

Lodge, in the far west of the county of Dorset. It could be said that he discovered himself as a poet during these years, gaining the self-confidence to write, and developed a working relationship with Coleridge that led to their joint work on "Lyrical Ballads".

The Gypsy and the Hobo

Music playing in the woodlands glades

castanets and violas piano accordion French maids

redheaded rascal with tall hat and tie

fancy dress bosom and to die for thighs

musical interludes and children at play

donkeys serenades at the end of the day

moonlight and stars twinkling free

Glastonbury nights on the Wessex country

rambling tales told by storytellers bold

campfires a blazing to keep out the cold

hedgehogs and rabbits scurrying by

kisses and promises in the gypsy sworn eyes

frostbitten mornings dew and the frost

blades of rye grass birch branch and logs

tin kettle whistles and birds in the trees

goldfinch and chaffinch nestled so free

hands held and promises gifts of the night
rover in conflict trailblazing sites
woodlands and heartlands vardos to see
the splendor of Gypsies humble neath leas
cracks and handshakes given to contracts
gentlemens agreements love in the sacks
wagons and cobs in very good steads
songs of the moonshine down by the reeds
comforting words and hugs in the night
kisses and promises then put out the lights
weddings to celebrate and fairs yet to see
chavvies in prayers walks to the sea
stories once told of days long ago
when England was young and farmers did sow
gentleman's talk and hobos last call
a kiss for the Gypsy a night on the fall.

Ray Wills

The Whites

Major White

The Portland stone Quarryman in the early 1900s was a travelling Gypsy who happened to be in the town of Branksome at a point in time. He was one of the many Whites who were quarrymen. It is said that the Whites lived in Portland for over one hundred years working on the quarry's.The late Alan Chalkie Whites father Bob at Wareham always was keen to say that his family ancestors originated from Kinson village Bournemouth.

Annabelle White

My great aunt was born in Wareham town

best fairground people shows anywhere's around

they came from Surrey and travelled free

in vardos tall and families to seeThe Whites were Gypsy family

with Kings and Castles and old Mabeys

they sat around yogs and told their tales

beneath old oak leas and they ate their grog.

Ray Wills

CHAPTER TWELVE

Gypsy Gatherings

Round the yog

Frostbitten fingers and wood on the fire

the snow and the ice and the blizzard's- kept warm attire

fir cones and bracken and pots on the fire

blanket's to share and the dogs in the briars

Cartwheels a turning by day till the night

chaffinchs singing a song to delight

stories a told there as we sit around the fire

tales of the journeys and the good we aspired

stewpots and rabbits and blackberry pies

Thorn's of the berries and here's mud in your eye

Granfer's and Granma's and little mush sleeps

clay pipes a smoking whilst little ones peep

benders that once spread across foreign soil

young mens hopes and old mens dreams told once more.

Ray Wills

Like most nomadic groups, Gypsies traveled around looking for work, following set routes with particular regular stopping places which have been established over hundreds of years. Many of these traditional stopping places were established long before land ownership changed and any land laws were in place. Many such places were established by feudal land owners way back in the Middle Ages, when Gypsies would provide agricultural or manual labor services in return for lodgings and food. Nowadays most Gypsies travel within these same areas which were originally established generations ago. Their familiarity and presence in an area can often be traced back over centuries . Many Of these traditional stopping places were taken over by local councils or by settled individuals decades ago and have subsequently changed hands on very many occasions, however Gypsies have long historical connections to such places and do not always willingly give them up. Most families are identifiable by their traditional wintering base, where they will stop travelling for the winter, this place will be technically where a family is from.

Gypsies have always loved the freedom of the road to travel this has always been in their blood. So much of their history and traditions have evolved from their travelling way of life. This lifestyle has enriched their world and is the background to their historical meetups.The yearly routes they take often brings them into conflict with the wider community. They have always traded their skills,bartered,taking part in fairs or in their regular family excursions and to collect fruit from the fields.

These yearly shows, festivals, fairs and fruit picking events are paramount in the Gypsy traveller communities life.Heres was where they would meet up exchange news and gossip with old friends and family members. Deals and exchanges are made here and the young people meet up with cousins and hopefully find a sweetheart. These are traditional events with a very long history many going back to the mid ages when there were festivals, fun days and shows throughout the land with markets and holy days in abundance. These events have a distinctive culture and lifestyle of their own, which goes back many centuries and it is recorded that their origin's go back to pagan custom's when seasonal gatherings were held for trade and festivity. In Roman times, fairs were high days holy days or holidays on which there was an intermission of labour and pleadings.

By the 7th century, a regular fair was being held at Saint-Denis under the French Merovingian kings. In later centuries across Europe, on any special Christian religious occasion, particularly the anniversary dedication of a church, tradesmen would bring and sell their wares, even in the churchyards. Such fairs then continued annually, usually on the feast day of the patron saint to whom the church was dedicated. In England, these early fairs were called a wake, or a vigilia, and many formed the basis for later chartered fairs. These fairs began to develop in the early Norman period, reaching their heyday in the 13th century.

From the 12th century, many English towns had gained the right from the Crown to hold an annual fair, usually serving a regional or local customer base and lasting for two or three days. By the Middle Ages almost 5,000 of these fair's were granted royal charter's and attracted merchants, nomadic entertainer's, juggler's, musician's and tumbler's. These were most probably the ancestors of today□s show and fairground people.A charter fair in England is a street fair or market which was established by Royal Charter.

Originally, most charter fairs started as street markets but since the 19th century the trading aspect has been superseded by entertainment; many charter fairs are now for funfairs run by travelling showmen. The travelling tradition is very important as it has allowed Gypsies and Traveller's to move around the country to take up employment opportunities and to meet with family members regularly. As well as to attend all these special occasions, markets, fairs, christening's, wedding's, illness and funeral's. It entails a entirely fresh way of looking at the world, a different way of perceiving things and a completely different attitude towards accommodation, work and life in general. The former days of Barnet September Fair, Birmingham Onion Fair, the October merry-makings at Hull and the Nottingham Goose Fair have unfortunately long since disappeared.

The following are examples of a variety of these functions, events and occasions, where the Gypsy travelling community have made their impact in the UK.A great many of which are still regular family haunts of the Gypsy community.

The Stourbridge fair

This fair was one of many authorised by King John I of England by royal charter in 1199, provided for the building of this leper chapel in Cambridge, and it became the largest medieval fair in Europe.

Origins of the Gypsy Showmen, Circus performers and entertainers.

Byzantine historian Nicephorus Gregoras (ca. 1290/91-1360) writes in Roman History about the performances of acrobats in Constantinople, 1321, under the rule of Andronicus II (1282-1328) " Recently, that is, during the first decade of the fourteenth century, we saw, in Constantinople, a group of nomadic people numbering about twenty, talented in certain parts of juggling. They originally came from Egypt, but then, as if they followed a circular path from east to north, they travelled over Chaldea, Arabia, Persia, Media and Assyria. Then, turning toward the west, they wandered through Iberia to the Caucasus, Colchis and Armenia and, from there, farther through lands populated by all the tribes which are found in the area reaching as far as Byzantium, and in each land and city (which they visited) they presented their artistry. And the artistry they presented was amazing and full of magic. Yet it had nothing to do with magic, but rather it was the result of skill, inventiveness, and long practice."

"Let us speak at least briefly about some of their pieces: They placed two or three ships masts straight up on the ground. On both sides ropes were fastened so that the masts would not lean to one side. Then they pulled a rope from the top of one of the masts to the other. They also wound a rope around the masts from top to bottom so that they created spiral steps to climb up.

One of the men, after he had climbed to the top with the help of these steps, stood on his head on the top of the mast; he put his head on the tip and stretched his legs toward the ground, then he alternately spread his legs and put them together. Then with a short jump he grabbed the rope hard with one hand and remained hanging and, from this position, he circled and whirled around the rope several times, spinning his legs in rapid succession up toward the sky and down toward the ground like a wheel. Then, instead of using his hand, he grabbed the rope with his calf and hung upside down. And again he turned and swirled around in the same way.

Then he stood straight up in the middle of the rope, took hold of a bow and arrows and shot at a distant target. From that position he shot with the greatest precision, as no man could manage even if he were standing on the ground. Afterwards, with closed eyes and with a child on his shoulder, he walked through the air along the rope from one mast to the other. And that was what one of them did."

"Another performed on a horse. He whipped him into a trot and, while the horse ran, the man stood straight up on it, now on the saddle, now on the horse's mane, now on its back, and he kept changing feet as if he were flying like a bird. Then he got off while the horse was running, grabbed it by the tail and after the next jump he was suddenly back in the saddle. And, while performing this stunt, he did not forget to keep urging the horse on. Those were stunts that that acrobat showed.""Another placed on his head a two-foot pole, on the top of which he put a vessel full of a liquid; then he walked all around for a long time while balancing the vessel. Then another placed on his head a pole that was at least three fathoms long. Around it was wound a rope creating a sort of steps. A boy took hold of it with his legs and arms and alternating them he climbed up to the top of the pole and then down. And that man who was carrying the pole on his head did not stop walking all around. Another one had a glass ball that he threw high into the air, and, when it fell, he caught it, sometimes with his fingertips, sometimes with his elbows, then with something else, and then again with something else."

"I am not going to describe the various dances and other showpieces that they performed. Every one of them could perform not only his own piece, but all the others besides. And they could do not only these tricks, but numerous other ones. Since those performances were risky, they lived dangerously; often someone fell and died. When they left their homeland, they were more than forty, but hardly twenty arrived in Byzantium. We ourselves saw one fall from a pole and kill himself. Collecting money from the spectators, they travelled around the whole world both to earn money and also to perform their art. After leaving Byzantium, they travelled through Thrace and Macedonia and arrived in Gadir (Cádiz) in Spain. And they made the whole world a stage for their theatre."These were as described obviously the very first circus showmen long before the rational circuses evolved and became so popular throughout the world.

Under the stars

Last night I slept under the stars

in my vardo rich wagon and my faithful entourage

my eyes they were heavy but my heart it was free

as I slept beneath the woodlands beneath the stars and the treesMy journeys were long over tumbledown tracks

over hillsides and valleys with my hopes on my back

I sang of the old days when my people were free

from the haunts of the masters and the taxes and feesI dreamt of the pastures where my folks grew and bred

when all we possessed were bread and the rest

in our tumbledown wagons and benders to rest

on the heathers and commons in a world we loved bestSo play on the fiddle and toot on the flute

sing of the good times and the lanes and the routes

the bird song at morning and the stars there each night

the promise of morning afore the first light.

Ray Wills

Campfire Nights

We sat around the yog my good friends and I

we told those old stories and we told them old lies

there were good times and bad and we went on the spree

in the summers and long winters in the hills past the leas

Oh the days they were long then and the nights they were cold

put some logs on the fire friend my bones getting old

pass me the pan and the kettle and tins

put the pot on the yog boy and pass me the gin

Oh the trails they were mean and the weather was cruel

in the time of the yearnings when the mornings were cool

there was food on the table and mats on the floors

when the chavvies were crawling right out of the door

You can look at the stars and tell me you know

the pathways to take by the red embers glow

you can taste of the stew boys and take the gals arm

then you can dance in the moonlight and use up your charm

Tell her your stories and laugh in the firesides hot glow

whisper sweet nothings tell her you love her just so

whilst we can whisper our prayers till the stars start to fade

487

then wel take off to bed for the chavvies to make

Oh the winters were harsh then and the snow it was deep

we lived on the rabbits hedgehogs and beet

we sang around the yog there till late was the night

went off to get some much needed sleep

then we said our goodbye and left fore the new morning light.

Ray Wills

St Boswells Fair

This fair is held annually on July 18, the Saint's Day of Boisil in the Gregorian calendar, and the Gypsy fair dates back to the early 17th century. Once this was a sheep fair, then it steadily grew to include cattle and horses and by the early 1900s, there could be as many as 1,000 horse's for sale. While the men sold the horse's their women went door-to-door selling clothes peg's, paper flower's and haberdashery. Here there would be all manner of stall's and sideshow's, coconut shies, shooting galleries, boxing booth's, and Gypsy fortune tellers. The fair was so popular amongst ordinary Borderers in 1820 that Ettrick Shepherd, famous poet, James Hogg, turned down an invitation to the coronation of King George IV, to attend this fair.

Appleby Fair

Appleby Horse Fair

If you are going to Appleby fair in the British summertime

remember me to one who lives there she was once a good friend of mine

if you are going in the breezy weather or when the perfume's on the heather

God bless the Gypsy folki there and say a prayer for Rosie Queen of leather

Oh the horses were grand you understand with colt's and cobs for to wonder

the grass was green and the streams were wide with wonder's on the side of the ford

oh the children danced and the folks did sing and the weather it was awesome

with the sun so bright until the night

But the sights were grand you understand

with livestock and fair trappings with vardos serene and old men's dream's

to send your hopes a packing

With rides and barns and tales to send

the crowds were high in numbers

with talk and rides to satisfy

at Appleby in the summer.

Ray Wills

This most popular fair is held annually at Westmorland, Cumbria. It has taken place every June since the reign of James II, who granted a Royal charter in 1685 allowing a horse fair "near to the River Eden". Since then, Gypsies, Traveller's journey there each year from all over the UK. Some thirty thousand people visit the fair each year and it is one of the oldest horse fairs in Britain. The fair is held outside the town on an area formerly known as Gallows Hill (named after the public hanging's that were once carried out there), however now it's known as Fair Hill. At Appleby today the Gypsies arrive a week before the fair and eventually form a city of their own crowning the hill behind the town. Hundreds of horses change hands at prices that can range from fifty to several thousand pounds. There is other trading, in trailers, wagons, flat-carts, harness, clothing, footwear, bedding, cushions, china, glass and jeweller - all the trappings of Gypsy culture.

The importance of the horse in Gypsy life

The horse is almost a trademark of the Gypsy life and culture with horses often painted or carved on the sides of their wagons, carts and lorries. There may well be paintings of Gypsies inside their vans too to take up the theme. Horse-dealing has long been a gypsy sideline or a major occupation for many gypsy folk in Britain. In earlier times a reliable trade could be looked for from farmers and other private individuals, coaching and freighting businesses, for work down the coal pits or in the Army. Although there may no longer be a demand for working horses, the recreational market for hunts and riding schools has increased to replace them. A living can still be made by a Gypsy with generations of experience and working knowledge of horses behind him, particularly so if he has too has veterinary skills and blacksmith trade.

Despite moving to motor transport, Gypsies still continue to retain this special relationship with horses. With their children taught to ride at an early age, and a pony may be taken on the road alongside the trailer. Such reliable horses were never sold under any normal circumstances and they became solid and respected members of the Gypsy family. The Gypsies have always had a high regard for their horses and the eating of horseflesh was banned, for to them the horse is a sacred animal and has always been a symbol of good luck and prosperity.

Although dogs are a vitally important part of the Gypsy household. A good one can be relied upon to stock the pot with hares and rabbits, but it is also essential for guarding the home while everyone is out working. A dog can be trained to catch or retrieve game and carry it straight to the trailer: some are able to locate hedgehogs, which can be uncovered and cooked.

The lurcher is probably the favourite Gypsy breed which is a cross between a greyhound and a collie, with a hint of deerhound, wolfhound, Alsatian, Doberman or poodle. They are called lurches from their behaviour when coursing a hare, which dodges and doubles back: a good lurcher will anticipate this behaviour and turn with it. Gypsy dogs are bred for fierceness, and will not hesitate to bite any intruder. Though amongst the Gypsy family they are gentle, friendly and reliable. Gypsies have never seen the point in keeping an animal that doesn't work for its living. Dogs are kept outside the trailer, and should not be stroked or touched before entering it and they are not allowed to lick the face of a sick person. Gypsies would not even drink from the same dish that a dog had used and cats were also considered unclean.

Stow Fair

Held at Stow-on-the-Wold on the nearest Thursday to May 12th and October 24th,sometimes it could be the Thursday before or after the charter day. The main source of wealth in the Cotswold was wool and by holding two fair's a year in Stow it allowed people in the surrounding hill's to bring their sheep to be sold. The fair's were a public holiday and people would travel in to Stow to see what goods the Italian, French and Flemish trader's had to sell. A variety of produce was sold here including date's and fig's, olive oil, sugar and almond's, ginger, pepper and clove's along with stalls of carpet's, tapestries and soap, damask, taffeta and lace.

There would be juggler's, tumbler's, and musician's playing fiddles and flute's. The town grew to provide the accommodation, food and stabling for the growing numbers and it was able to offer the services of blacksmith's and wheelwright's. Gypsies gather from all corners of England for this meeting and hundreds of horse's are paraded and sold, all in one day.

As sheep farming declined in the Cotswold's the character of the fair slowly changed and it became a horse fair popular with farmer's, huntsmen, professional horse dealer's and Gypsies. In recent years the fun fair no longer visits the town and the horse sale's moved to Andover's ford, about 6 miles to the east of Cheltenham. Now, there is one of the biggest Gypsy horse fairs in England. Many Gypsies arrive there in traditional horse drawn caravan's, it has become popular with photographer's, artist's, and the public who don't want to miss the atmosphere of such a colorful event, the charter granted over 500 years ago, still decide the dates of the fair's.

Cambridge Fair

This Fair is some 800 years old dating back to a charter of the middle ages. It's held at Midsummer Common, Cambridge. Lee Gap Fair-West Ardsley on August 24th and later on 17th September. Originally held for three weeks and three day's around St Bartholomew, but now it is held on just two days. It is always held on these dates unless the day happens to be a Sunday and then it is held the following day instead.

Horse-fairs have always figured large in the Gypsies' year. A hundred years ago, there was said to be over a dozen in England, many of them mediaeval trading fairs which had become incorporated into Gypsy culture. Families flock here from all over the country during the weeks leading up to its opening, and camp nearby to be ready for the day.

Kenilworth Horse Fair

Kenilworth fair is held at Thick thorn, in Kenilworth each year. This popular fair has been operating there for a number of years with three events held there and with the main event being held on private land.

Water Orton Horse Fair & Market

This is held in October each year with refreshments, entertainments and trade stands, family fun where all are welcome to attend.

Weyhill Fair

Weyhill Fair itself was a particularly famous fair, dating back to at least the 1300s and is referenced in several historical texts. William Langland mentions it in Piers Plowman, "to Weyhill and Winchester I went to the fair," and a letter from Queen Elizabeth I, then Princess Elizabeth, to Henry Cecil in 1554 refers to the fair, remarking that it is already 400 years' old.

The principal fair at Weyhill, a little village west of Andover, took place during October, although there were also fairs there during April and July. In October the sale of animals, hops, cheeses and leather vied for attention with fancy goods, exotic sideshows and boxing booths, swings and roundabouts. Weyhill Fair itself was a particularly famous fair, dating back to at least the 1300s and is referenced in several historical texts. William Langland mentions it in Piers Plowman, "to Weyhill and Winchester I went to the fair," and a letter from Queen Elizabeth I, then Princess Elizabeth, to Henry Cecil in 1554 refers to the fair, remarking that it is already 400 years' old. The principal fair at Weyhill, a little village west of Andover, took place during October, although there were also fairs there during April and July. In October the sale of animals, hops, cheeses and leather vied for attention with fancy goods, exotic sideshows and boxing booths, swings and roundabouts.

In the October of 1870 the Salisbury and Winchester Journal

made reference to the fair's historical importance, reminding readers that "This long-established and well-known fair . . . which commences on the 10th of October was, till the reign of Queen Elizabeth, no more than a revel," adding that "in the year 1599 Her Majesty granted a charter to the bailiff and corporation of Andover in which she conferred on them the right of holding this fair." For good measure the paper includes a quotation taken from the Magna Britannica, published in 1720, which states that "this fair is reckoned as large as anyone in England for many commodities, and for sheep indisputably the biggest."

Newspapers also carried several advertisements around the time of the fair in which local produce was promoted and ease of transport advertised. The Reading Mercury of 4th October 1884 announced that "On Friday October 10th a special train will run to Weyhill, leaving Reading at 4.25 am," and a malster in Devon promoted his goods by declaring "that he has returned from Weyhill Hop Fair and, having made extensive purchases direct from the growers, he is able to offer the best article on very advantageous terms."

Weyhill's hop fair was held on 12th October and all the hops from Farnham and Alton were taken there in wagons and carts. Its location, so close to hopping centres where many Gypsies obtained casual work, was enticing, so it is hardly surprising that the fair attracted many Gypsies and Travellers, providing them with a source of income. They ran boxing booths, made sweets and cakes, sold baskets and made merry and it was also an opportunity for Gypsy horse dealers to strike a bargain, as well as a chance to meet up with family and friends.

The Reading Mercury of 4th October 1884 announced that "On Friday October 10th a special train will run to Weyhill, leaving Reading at 4.25 am," and a master in Devon promoted his goods by declaring "that he has returned from Weyhill Hop Fair and, having made extensive purchases direct from the growers, he is able to offer the best article on very advantageous terms."For good measure the paper includes a quotation taken from the Magna Britannica, published in 1720, which states that "this fair is reckoned as large as anyone in England for many commodities, and for sheep indisputably the biggest."Newspapers also carried several advertisements around the time of the fair in which local produce was promoted and ease of transport advertised.

Hop Farm Gypsy Arts Festival

Held yearly in September and set within some 400 acres of the Kent countryside. This is still one of the South East's most popular event venues, the spectacular Oats village providing the perfect setting for a great family day out. Providing live music, dancing, storytelling, open fire cooking demonstrations, tastings and Gypsy Traveler craft's. Plus music, art workshop's, and Gypsy Traveler film screening's. All of the events and activities are free. However there is the normal admission charge to enter the Hop Farm.

Vardo days
I once had a vardo and its wheels they did roll and spin

I rode it to Ringwood and the Dorset great show in the spring

my father boxed at the fairgrounds to the lord Queensbury's rules

oh the days they were long then when we lived down near Poole

I once had a wife she was dark and so wise

she sang to the bird's and had sparkling green eyes

she would tell folks their fortunes so Gorgas beware

don't pick all the heathers from Poole basket's fairs

We worked in the meadows and down at the quay

for many long hours we drank beer by the sea

the light's they did shine there and the star's they did glow

when we danced in the night whilst the old maid's did sew

Though those days have long gone and our masters have too

I remember the days long ago when we camped near Sea View

there were cones on the hillsides and boats in the bay

the constitutional hill was so steep and our lives were so gay

Our homes they were rich then with satin and lace

with tattoos and artwork all over the place

our lamps they were gold and our talk it was free

when we lived by our wits and we told folks that we were true
Romani. - Ray Wills

Basildon Gypsy Parties

Held yearly in June, where there are many gathering of families and where weddings take place and are said to date back to 1770 when it was even then an ancient custom. Up to 5,000 people are said to have attended in 1881 alone when 200 gallons of 'Gypsy broth' were sold!.Then the encampment had been enclosed and there was an admission charge. In later years it was managed by local residents who dressed up as Gypsies and formed 'tribes and they advertised it as a 'Gypsy Carnival. It appears that after 1897 the old tradition had ended, from local accounts it was assumed that the 'real Gypsies' were no longer attending. However old local Gypsy Travelers did confirm that 'real' Gypsies still attended these 'parties' yearly alongside these locals dressed up as Gypsies.

Fun Fairgrounds

Many of the local show people such as the Whites, Kings,Castles, Ayres and Coles are associated with these fairs which operate throughout the UK.

The Gypsy Fairground

I went to the Gypsy fairground where I first meet Gypsy Jo

We went upon the Ferris wheel seems so long ago

Her father was a tailor and her mother was a queen

She took me on the spinning wheel she was my swinging scene

One time I'll remember when the vardos reached the sky

The grass was green and thick then with dew with rabbits running bye

There were bird' upon the branches where the willow spreads it's fall

With their Gypsy children dancing long before their falls

The piano accordion was playing from the hands of Victor Clapcott the Gypsy tattoo man

The Gypsy gal was dancing there her tambourine in her hand

The fire was a glowing and the sparks they flew so high

There were pastures a plenty and a haystack with a river running by

The folki they were blessed there with children by the score

With pack's of dogs a chasing tails and tales of long gone wars

The music that they played then was rich in words and tone

When I kissed her beneath the raging sun and loved her more and more

The foxes were on the hilltops hidden from our view

There was heather and rich gorse a stretching from Alderney to Poole

The sands of time have rolled along and the tides of surf will sap

The beaches ,where they all carried the shawls and loving mats

There were tinkers then and travelers and old Johnny onion was in tow

The fairgrounds offered substance then and the harvests were on show

The darts did fly upon the cards and the bumper cars did spin

There was candy floss and coconut shy and sweets for uncle Jim

The days are gone when we cut rye grass and sliced the wood and cane

When flowers were made on Canford hills

I wish we could go back again.

Ray Wills

Gypsy Fairground Days

It's a hard road to travel with folks to meet on the way

with a horse and a foot in the stirrup and a look caste away

where there is moonlight a shining and theres stars all aglow

with the rumbling wheels of their wagons on the Romany roads

So I'm off on the highway by the heather and dales

where the sun it comes up and the music is swell

theres dog's here a barking and boys at the fair

with gals to surprise you with flowers in their hair

Oh the fairground wheels a spinning and the darts are in flight

with the roulette wheels churning by day and by night

the booth's are all open and the rides are all free

on the first day at Blackpool down by the sea

The tellers of fortune have drawn all the pack

with their eyes on the client and their son in the sack

the night draws the seekers of wisdom and sights

with the songs of the crooners and the lights oh so bright

The music is awesome and the melodies spin

like the dreamers of old when the harvest begins

the accordion plays a sweet melody like the Parisian nights with their words lost at sea

The Gypsy rides in with his lingo and tan
like a thief in the night with his whispering band
the highways and bye ways have cursed the lament
whilst history has lost all its sacredness spent

All the roads they had traveled and the sights they had seen
like a lost generation without their 'May Queen
for its take to the hills and get off the land
only their footprints are left now of this regal band

Yet you blindly look each morning at dawn
where the heaven's were open and your ways were forlorn.
Ray Wills

Fairs and Memories

So many fond memories come flooding back

like the buckboard rides with uncle Jack

like the country walks with cousin Jane

the bat and ball games down our lanes

The children of the families who lived next door so close to me

the township choir the church bell rings

the boys in starch and the girls in spring boy could they sing

The crowds that gathered on the green

the may day dance and the witches broom's at Halloween

the fancy ways of Mrs. brown

with her bosom wide and her dress top down

The boys who gathered on the leas

the marble games when we scuffed our knees

the constant scramble for chestnut's falls

the long bike rides and the tree so tall

The Sunday chapel sermon with pastor Greene

the church bells rang within and the country scenes

the fun we had at the local fair

with the pretty girls who sported beehive hair

The cross-eyed tramp and the village fool
the train ride out to visit Waterloo
the parade ground chants and the bugle calls
the army life for anothers cause

Those days are past and their moments gone
but the memories they linger in the poets songs
the harbor lights and the battle cries
the run out games and the big surprise

Down country lanes and village tracks
where boys kissed girls beneath the sacks
where fathers eye was born anew
afore each new birth of baby new

The tumbledown and roustabouts
the Ferris wheels and the big top shouts
the cannon fired and the artistes bared
their skills of life at the shows we loved and the country fairs
when boys were boy's and we always dared.

Ray Wills

Fairgrounds

I went to see the Gypsy in the fortune telling van

they were broadcasting the bearded lady and the tattooed man

the coconut shys were busy and the waltzer was in spin

the bumping car's were riding well and the kid's were in a whim

There were pugilist Gypsy boxers and a vardo caravan

the big wheel was in motion and the music played its tune

there was a small of diesel oil in that air and the dart's were all a flying zoom

The guns were aimed and firing at the yellow ducks passing bye

with candy floss in our hands and toffee apples you can stop and buy

the one armed bandits were singing and the penny slot machines

the speed ways wall of death was just about to begin

The Gypsy gal's sold flowers and heather in the baskets every night

there were Gypsy gals a dancing there and lovers smooching holding tight

the goldfish jars were all in line and the net to set them free

the nights were full of wonders at Poole fair by the sea.

Ray Wills

505

Gypsy

I travelled those fairgrounds and all those great shows
to find me some Gypsies that I ne'er did know
I searched for those Kings with dark skin and more
with words that twer course and hides saddle sore

met with some tinkers and hawkers by trade
I met up with a teller of fortune and slaves
I mixed with the bests the Shaw's and the pride
of England's traveling circus with dark roving eyes

I glimpsed their fair world of satin and lace
with drapes that did flow and smiles upon their face
their ponies were wild and the dogs they did bark
they lit up their candles and lamps in the dark

Their tales they were long and they gave me a thrill
their stories were old and they spun that great wheel
their vardos were tall and their stew it was rich
they traveled this land through heathers and ditch

I was born with the look of a traveling man

they called me a Gypsy wherever I am

my folks they were destined to warrant a wish

as they stumbled through life with the sign of the fish

The wheels they did roll and the pen it was wet

with fables and songs that flowed from their nets

their hair it was dark and their skin it was tan

their eyes looked you over and into the man

I never found Kings or Queens of my clan

I guess ill remain just a traveling man

with eyes that light up when I hear the wheels spin

when the fairgrounds organs playing when the Gypsy gal sings.

Ray Wills

Dorset Steam Fair

Held each year at Tarrant Hinton north of Blandford Forum

Dorset The steam fair attracts almost a quarter of a million people each year and it still is one of the world's largest gatherings of steam engines. Situated as it is within some 6000 acres of rolling grassy hills. it is one the biggest outdoor events in Europe. It includes many road locomotives, steam engines, traction engines, steam lorries, steam rollers and fun fair,exhibits and very many other great variety of attractions and fun for all the family.

Ye olde Dorset Steam Fair

Ye old steam fair is here each year

upon the downs with fun and beer

the oil it smells and the tracks are mud

where cars are parked upon the meadows green

the carousels play and delight the scene

the crowds flock here again this year

To buy the goods or storm the gears

theres Gypsy folk and travellers tales

with smoky air and diesel smells

there's big machines to roll and ride

across the Dorset countryside

508

Where zunners run and play and stare

at all the folks within the fair

with marquee tents and music rock

stalls to sale and gears to lock

Amusements rich in fields of green

bikers parades and beauty scenes

crowds of folks flock here each year

to mingle and to enjoy the spirit here

where hills are steep and views are grand

the steam fair spreads across this land.

Ray Wills

Blackpool South Shore Sands

"Those were the days of Sarah Boswell and her nephews Kenza and Oscar; Johnny and Wasti Gray; Elijah Heron and his son Poley; Bendigo and Morjiana Purum; the Robinsons; Dolferus Petulengro and Noarus Tâno."Blackpool South Shore Sands historically is one of the most famous venues of Gypsies anywhere in the UK. Revd George Hall-"It has been said that if an architect, a caterer, and a poet were commissioned to construct out of our existing south and east coast resorts a place which, in its appeal to the million, might compare with Blackpool, they would utterly fail, a saying not to be questioned for a moment". "Yet the sight which thrilled me most, as I beheld it years ago, was not the cluster of gilded pleasure- palaces in the town, but the gay Gypsy squatting on the sand-dunes at the extremity of the South Shore". Living-vans of green and gold with their flapping canvas covers ; domed tents whose blankets of red and grey had faded at the touch of sun and wind ; boarded porches and outgrowths of a fantastic character, the work of Romany carpenters ; unabashed advertisements announcing Gypsy queens patronized by duchesses and lords ; bevies of black- eyed, wheedling witches eager to pounce upon the stroller into Gypsydom ; and troops of fine children, shock-headed and jolly all these I be held in the Gypsy which is now no more. " Life enjoyed to the last " might well have been its epitaph.

On the south shore at Blackpool seaside resort there were Gypsy caravan's and traditional fortune teller's for many years. This enterprising Gypsy parade was always extremely busy attracting all the Lancashire holiday-maker's from all areas of the UK. With shooting-galleries, merry-go-round's, switchback ride's, water chute's, and other side shows, and Gypsy horse sales.

Their caravan's were visited regularly by famous celebrities and here the Petulengro Roma family worked the cards in their booths for generations. Lords and ladies and celebrities from all over the world would gypsy fortune tellers such as Gypsy Rose Lee. The south shore was well known as the headquarters of Gypsy families such as the Boswell's, Petulengros,Young's ,Heron's and Lee's. The Romani's of the Northern Counties would gather here telling the fortunes of the visitors many of whom came in their hundreds and thousands.

Revd George Hall- commented Tom Lee, an English Gypsy, broke up a loaf of bread and strewed the crumbs around his tent when his son Bendigo was born, for some of the old-time Gypsies hold the notion that bread possesses a protective magic against evil influences. Then seated one day in the tent of Bendigo Lee on the South Shore at Blackpool, I questioned him about his father's practice. " In the days when I was born," he replied, "there were people that could do hurt by looking at you, and I suppose my dadus (father) sprinkled the crumbs lest any evil person going by should cast harm upon me." A distinct survival of the belief in the evil eye.

The wandering peddlers, entertainers, acrobats, stilt walkers, and the men with their three-card or thimble-rigging tricks. The showmen, a quite distinct group, gather around the area near Tattenham Corner fairground. Up to 1971 the Dip Fair was the focal point of the Downs with its swing boat, merry-go-rounds and switchbacks fighting for space with the circus and sideshow attractions. Every year there was a new wonder to see - Barnum freaks and elephant headed boys, or Globe of Death rides - one named Cyclone Tim went so far as to ride the wall accompanied by a lion.

Royal Ascot

Gypsies have been regular visitors to Royal Ascot week since 1711 as a meeting place, along with the nearby Derby Epsom Races. Originally held on common land , where many scattered Gypsy families meet up at this popular major event each year. Here Gypsies are seen selling flower's and lucky heather. Gypsies are also well known throughout the world as successful horse trader's and trainer's, the Romany Gypsies were an important part of the racing fraternity and took their place alongside the owner's, tipster's and the betting public. The Gypsy cob horse is a recognized breed and which is exported all over the world.

The Royal Family also has a long connection to Gypsies. Prominent at these races in days gone by was Matthias Cooper, a Gypsy to whom the late King Edward, when Prince of Wales, would toss a golden sovereign. Matthias was a well-known Gypsy who wore a white hat, yellow waistcoat, black cut-away coat, and white trousers. It was from him that Charles G. Leland obtained most of the materials that he used for his work entitled The English Gypsies and their Language. Following his death his sons, Anselo and Wacker, continued to attend the Epsom races for many years.

Sir Alfred Munnings wrote: 'Never have I quite felt the alluring, infectious joy of the races, the tradition of Epsom, as I did in that first year after the war, 1919'. Munning's was a professional painter of horses and their jockeys with a fondness for Gypsies- they struck him as a picturesque, swarthy crowd, especially the women, with black ringlets and heavy ear-rings visible under their large black ostrich-plumed hats. With a certain irony, they called him 'Mr Money', but were happy for him to admire the artwork of their carved and gilded wagons, and to follow the camps until he had finished his portrait work.

Munnings first introduced his fellow-artist Laura Knight to

Epsom Races. Laura Knight made a good impression on the Gypsy models that she met at the Derby, and was allowed to follow them around the country to complete her paintings. In later years she wrote: 'I became friendly with an adorable, but frail, old gypsy woman, called Mrs Smith. She it was, who, while posing for me at a race meeting, said: "You like painting Romanies - why not come to our camp?" I never had a better model than Granny Smith, a true Romany. Although an old woman, her hair was still a jetty black, plaited close to her small head; her form was dainty and she was proud of her well-shaped hands and feet. The beauty of her features was not badly marred, even by a broken nose. "How did it happen?" I asked. "Me 'husband - twice", she replied. In one of the largish canvases I painted of her on her wagon step, she sits wearing her best hat, trimmed with ostrich plumes. Long gold ear-rings dangle from her ears; rows of coloured beads encircle her neck and hang over her gaily patterned shawl.'

The potter Charles Vyse working with his wife Nell from the Chelsea Studios in Cheyne Walk, Vyse produced beautifully sculpted statuettes of people he had met on the Downs. Each year they travelled down to Epsom to study the short runs, only a hundred of each design, and were popular in the USA in the 1920s and Gypsies who formed the base for their figures. These were produced in 1930s.

Gypsy Rose Lee

I wrote the following poem as a record of my visit as a

young man to South Shore Blackpool crossing her palm with silver and having my fortune reading at the tent of the great Gypsy fortune teller to the stars. Gypsy Rose lee was pop star Billy Fury's favourite psychic consultant
Rosa lee knew and foretold for all the great celebrities of the 1950s and 1960s including: Diana Dors, Alma Cogan and Eli Kazen.

Cinderella Rose Lee

Cinderella the Gypsy lived upon the great south shore

where Blackpools golden mile stretched and was well worth waiting for

they called her Rose lee for she was a seer and true

she told you lots of fortune tales there on the beach at old Blackpool

Her booth it was well lit up with the stars picture's on her door of artiste's by the score

close by the donkeys serenades upon the Blackpool shore

She wore a scarf of gaiety and her lamp it was well lit

her cards spread on the table just across from where you sit

her eyes they looked right into you and read your mind and soul

she was dark and so very beautiful and her ear rings she did fare show

Her dress it was long and dignified just like a lady of good taste

for her skin was dark and mystical and her beauty was in her face

Of all the Gypsy ladies her words were true to form

she told you how it was from the day that she was born

Her booth no longer sits there on Blackpoll's golden mile

where famous lads and lassies came to call to see her golden smile.

Ray Wills

My reading that summer day was amazing I was told by "the fortune teller to the stars" that "there would be lots of troubles in my family but that I was clever too and not get inolved".I was told that "I had the sign of the rose tattoo and that later in life I would travel thousands of miles overseas to the USA to live with an American lady, (my previous wife). All of which became fact.

Long gone are that Gypsies gathered on the sand-dunes at the South Shore along with their gaily colored vans of green and gold of flapping canvas covers ; domed tents and blankets of red and grey. Along with their stylish and

grandiose artwork, the skilled work of Romany carpenters ;
loud advertisements announcing Gypsy Queens patronized
by Duchesses, Lords and stars of stage and the
entertainment world. Those were the days of Old Sarah
Boswell and her nephews Kenza and Oscar ; Johnny and
Wasti Gray ; Elijah Heron and his son Poley ; Bendigo and
Morjiana Purum ; the vivacious Robinsons ; Dolferus
Petulengro and Noarus Tano".

Gypsy fortunes

Those Gypsies ladies with their heads hung down

the tarot readings and the words that show no frown

the I ching coins jingle and the roulette spins

they'll tell your fortune from the mood you're in

They'll read the lines there in your hand

they'll look inside the heart of man

their intuition and their dark dark eyes

the romance is burning in the lore and wise

The headdress ladies with their astral plains

they'll thumb the stones and grant you love or pain

their caravans all laden with sheeky satin sheets

their lamps all lit from their body heat

The signs and wonders and the stars at night
the horoscopes and cards that flow just right
they take your silver and your chance of luck
they hoodwink many for the common buck

The music plays like Egypts theme
Indian Sanskrits and melodic reams
the nights of starlight and the days of chanc
just take the heather sprigs sir and stir romance

The Queen of Gypsies thumbed the orient pack
she'll spread those cards and then hit the sack
the night time fancies have all flown away
in the Gypsies world of chance and play.
Ray Wills

Fruit picking
Another tradition for Gypsies is fruit picking with regular

family excursion's each year. One of these was held in Evesham in the area known as the black country of Worcestshire. At nearby Redditch each year I would travel there with the Cook family and others which was a short distance from the beautiful Malvern Hill's for fruit picking sessions in the mid 1960s. This was seen as a regular yearly fun family occasion which I attended with large families piling onto the backs of lorries for the family excursion.

Harvesting in the black country

In the black country travels through the wind and the rain

the Gypsy crew travelled through the countryside lane's

the Cooks and the Dawsons from old Redditch town

on their wagons and trailers and horses and reins

to pick of the harvests from the fields of the plains

gathering the fruits of their labours down those old country lanes

by Malvern hills mansions and villages plain

they gathered and weighed the best once again

Their children were chavvies and the mushs all gave sprite

they picked and they gathered from mornings till nights

they weighed them and traded for their labours to see

In the heathers of Evesham they travelled so free

oh for the joys of the summer a gathering by the leas.

Ray Wills

Heavenly Travellers

He's promised a place in heaven for me

says the travelling man and I want to see

the heavens so rich there and the freedom to be

a believer of life and true liberty

The good lord he travelled the trails of the land

preaching the word so they'd understand

he brought them the message and the truth for to see

the blessings of God and the grace yet to be

The Gypsies and nomads the Roma of kings

the vardos,the benders and the stories they would sing

as they sat around the yog and they told of the times

when the travellers were free and they lived by the branch of the vine.

Ray Wills

Under the stars

Last night I slept under the stars

in my vardo rich wagon and my faithful entourage

my eyes they were heavy but my heart it was free

as I slept neath the woodlands neath the stars and the trees

my journeys were long over tumbledown tracks

over hillsides and valleys with my hopes on my back

I sang of the old days when my people were free

from the haunts of the masters and the taxes and fees

I dreamt of the pastures where my folks grew n bred

when all we possessed were bread and the rest

in our tumbledown wagons and benders to rest

on the heathers and commons in a world we loved best

so play on the fiddle and toot on the flute

sing of the good times and the lanes and the routes

the bird song at morning and the stars there each night

the promise of morning afore the first light.

Ray Wills

Today many Gypsies are afraid to reveal their Gypsy roots and presence openly in society because of the unfair stigma attached to their identity and the various unsympathetic laws against them. Nowadays most Romani travel within the same areas that were established generations ago. Most people can trace their presence in an area back over a hundred or two hundred years. Many traditional stopping places were taken over by local government or by settled individuals decades ago and have subsequently changed hands numerous times, however Romani have long historical connections to such places and do not always willingly give them up. Most families are identifiable by their traditional wintering base, where they will stop travelling for the winter, this place will be technically where a family is 'from'. A significant part of our national heritage has passed into the hands of the Travellers.

Sources and Resources-Bibliograhy

The Gypsies- Charles Leland 1882

Gypsies: A Persecuted Race - William A. Duna (1985) Duna

Studios

Gypsies: from India/from the Indus to the Mediterranean-Donald Kenrick

Gypsy history - sci.anthropology-STEPHANIE G. FOLSE (sfolse@du.edu)

A History of the Gypsies^ Walter Simson

"Gypsies, Tinkers and Travellers",Sharon Melch

Gypsies of New Forest-Henry E Gibbins (1909)

Gypsy Americans by Evan Heimlich

Gypsies Tinkers and Travelers. -Sharon Melch

"Gypsies, Their Life, Lore, and Legends -Printed in Great Britain by Latimer Trend & Co Ltd Plymouth Konrad Bercovici

Gypsy experience of Holocaust -Eve Rosenhaft, a historian at the Liverpool University's School of Modern Languages

"Gypsies," by B. Gilliat-Smith (The Caian, vol. xvi. No. 3). e thorns tagged your toes

Gypsy Magic for the Family's Soul -Allie Theiss (2006)

The Gypsies - Sir Angus Fraser

"Gypsies of Britain - Brian Vesey Fitzgerald) Pompeu Fabra University

Gypsy Folk Tales- Francis Hindes Groome, [1899], at sacred-texts.com

Gypsies of the Heath - 'Romany Rawnie' aka Betty Gillington

522

published by Elkin Mathews 1916

Gypsy Advocate-James Crabb (1832)

Gypsy Storytellers-An Anthology of stories poems and illustrations-Edited by Raymond Wills-published by Francis Boutle publishers (2013)

English Gypsies and Their Language - Charles G. Leland [1874]

My friends the Gypsies   - Lawrence Bohme

The Forest Gypsies - H Leksa Manus's- The Roads of the Roma

As Gypsies Wander- An account of life with the Gypsies in England, Provence, Spain, Turkey & North Africa Faber and Faber Limited 24 Russell Square London W.C.I.   - Juliette De Bairacli Levy   Paris, 1953

The Traveller-Gypsies- Judith Okely- Cambridge University Press. UK

('The Lithuanian Gypsies and their Language,' - Mieczyslaw Dowojno-Sylwestrowicz, in Gypsy Lore Journal, I. 1889, p. 253.)

The Mysterious and Magical Gypsy/Roma Allie Theiss - paper for middle Eastern class 2009

Romany Life- Frank Cuttriss (1915)

The True Origin of Roma and Sinti -Sándor Avraham

When Dayton was the Home of the Gypsies By Howard Burba -Dayton Daily News, May 10, 1931

The Gypsy's Parson; His Experiences and Adventures (1915).The Rev. George Hall's

The New Forest: its History and its Scenery (1863)Konrad Wise-

Travelers and the built environment-Steve Staines of FFT

Charles Godfrey Leland's "professor" in teaching Leyland the Romany language -Journal of the Gypsy Lore Society-

The Gypsies in the Byzantine Empire and the Balkans in the Late Middle Ages George Soulis - -published by Archivarius

A History of the Gypsies^ Walter Simson

 Romany Nevi-Wesh An informal history of the New Forest-Len Smith

The New Forest its History and Scenery-The Gypsy and The West Saxon-John Richard De Capel Wise   (1863)

Report on New Forest Traditions Jo Ivey - Nfm_server\New Forest Museum Data\Trish folders\Website\Our New Forest.doc 2 -Report on New Forest traditions

Wanderers in the New Forest - Juliette de Baraicli Levy (1974). Juliette De Bairacli levy, Paris (1953

Dromengro Man of the Road Virgo in Exile Sven Berlin's

Genetic Studies -Studies from 2001 by Gresham, Morar and others

Memories of Hampshire -Sid Barker (subscriber to HAMPSHIRE LIFE)

        Dr. B. Bogisic on 'Die slavisirten Zigeuner in

Montenegro' (Das Ausland, 25th May 1874)

Le Folklore de Lesbos, by G. Georgeakis and Leon Pineau (Paris, 1891, pp. 273-8),

'Die Zigeuner in Elsass and in Deutschlothringen,' by Dr. G. Mühl, in Der Salon, (1874).

The Written Romani Language-Damian Le Bas

ROMBASE by Milena Alinčová May (2002) Prague, Czech Republic

 East Dorset Antiquarian Society   -EDAS Lecture – The Egyptians and other Travelling People in Early Modern Dorset - Judy Ford-Andrew Morgan

Queen Victoria's Sketchbook-M Warner-Macmillan, London (1979).

The Project Gutenberg E Book of The New Forest-Elizabeth Godfrey (1912)

Romany and Traveler Family History Society-rtfhs.org.uk

Hansard -Lord arthur Cecil

-An Artist's Life Sir Alfred Munnings (London 1950).

http://www.gypsyjib.com/page/GIPSY+LIFE+by+George+Smith

Romanies In Dorset and Hampshire- Sue Cole.

Genetic Studies -Studies from 2001 by Gresham, Morar and others

(Silverman 1995 -Helsinki Watch (1991).

Memories of Hampshire -Sid Barker (subscriber to HAMPSHIRE LIFE)

The World Their Homeland   by Francois de Vaux de Foletier

Le Folklore de Lesbos, by G. Georgeakis and Leon Pineau (Paris, 1891, pp. 273-8),

'Die Zigeuner in Elsass and in Deutschlothringen,' by Dr. G. Mühl, in Der Salon, (1874).

The Written Romani Language-Damian Le Bas

History and Politics - From India to Europe - Byzantium

ROMBASE by Milena Alinčová May (2002) Prague, Czech Republic

"Myths, Hypotheses and Facts Concerning the Origin of Peoples" -The True Origin of Roma and Sinti Avraham Sandor

"Comparison of Romany Law with Israelite Law and Indo-Aryan Traditions" Abraham Sándor- Hutchinson

An Artist's Life (London 1950)-Sir Alfred Munnings .